Destiny Calling

Your Beginning does not determine your End

Destiny Calling

Your Beginning does not determine your End

Dear Jessica
Allow the Lord to lead
you with greater Wisdom for
the greater challenges.

Naomi Dowdy

Blessings Naomi

Naomi Dowdy Ministries
Dallas, TX

Destiny Calling: Your Beginning does not determine your End

© 2015 by Naomi Dowdy Ministries

Naomi Dowdy Ministries
USA: P.O. Box 703686, Dallas, Texas 75370
Singapore: Tanglin P.O.Box 48, Singapore 912402
Email: info@naomidowdy.com
Website: www.naomidowdy.com

ISBN-13: 978-1-934201-11-4

Printed in Singapore
5 4 3 15 16 17 18 19

Cover Photography: Law Kian Yan
Book Design: [river] design, singapore
Editor: Huang Rui Lin
Editorial Advisor: Barbara (Liddle) Cavaness Parks

Contents

Acknowledgments 9

Foreword 11

Chapter 1: Growing Up with Granddad 15

Chapter 2: Turbulent Times 25

Chapter 3: Escape from Nashville 33

Chapter 4: Making the Choice 47

Chapter 5: The Stowaway Missionary 57

Chapter 6: Living Dangerously 69

Chapter 7: Island Hopping 79

Chapter 8: More Miracles 89

Chapter 9 : When God Speaks 103

Chapter 10: A Season of Growth 115

Chapter 11: Sufficient Grace 123

Chapter 12: A Nomadic Church 131

Chapter 13: Building by Faith 137

Chapter 14: The Greatest Battle 145

Chapter 15: Defining Our Call 153

Chapter 16: To the Nations 163

Chapter 17: Heaven's Gates Open 173

Chapter 18: Father Knows Best 183

Chapter 19: Success & Succession 195

Chapter 20: Letting Go 203

Chapter 21: An Attitude Problem 211

Chapter 22: The Journey Continues 221

Appendix: On Women in Ministry 229

Reflections *(by various contributors)* 239

Let The Lower Lights Be Burning

WORDS & MUSIC WRITTEN
BY PHILIP PAUL BLISS IN 1871

Brightly beams our Father's mercy from His lighthouse evermore
But to us He gives the keeping of the lights along the shore
Let the lower lights be burning, send a gleam across the wave
Some poor fainting struggling seaman, you may rescue, you may save

Dark the night of sin has settled, loud the angry billows roar
Eager eyes are watching, longing for the lights along the shore
Let the lower lights be burning, send a gleam across the wave
Some poor fainting struggling seaman, you may rescue, you may save

Trim your feeble lamp my brother, some poor sailor tempest tossed
Trying now to make the harbor, in the darkness may be lost
Let the lower lights be burning, send a gleam across the wave
Some poor fainting struggling seaman, you may rescue, you may save

On a dark, stormy, night, when the waves rolled like mountains, and not a star was to be seen, a boat, rocking and plunging, neared the Cleveland harbor.

"Are you sure this is Cleveland?" asked the captain, seeing only one light from the lighthouse.
"Quite sure, sir," replied the pilot.
"Where are the lower lights?"
"Gone out, sir."
"Can you make the harbor?"
"We *must*, or perish, sir!"

And with a strong hand and a brave heart, the old pilot turned the wheel. But alas, in the darkness he missed the channel, and with a crash upon the rocks the boat was shivered, and many a life lost in a watery grave.

Brethren, the Master will take care of the great lighthouse: let us keep the lower lights burning!

- D. L. Moody

Acknowledgements

I DO WANT TO THANK EVERYONE whom God has brought into my life through the years. *Destiny Calling* is just a way of saying that God shapes us and divinely connects us with people at different points of our journey, according to His good purpose. God has given me many such people on my journey, and I have been truly blessed.

As you are reading this, please know that you have played a significant part in my journey. God brought you into my life for a purpose. Your journey intersected with mine in different seasons – some through good times, some through hard times; some for a longer time, some for a shorter period – but all were important and divinely appointed.

Due to the limitations of covering the span of my life in a single book, it is impossible to include everything or everyone by name in this short volume. However, even if I may not mention you by name, God has a larger Book and your name is definitely in it.

Thank you for being on this journey with me. I am grateful for each of you.

Naomi Dowdy
22 March 2015
Singapore

Foreword

FOR CENTURIES there has been a debate in the church about the role of women in Christian leadership. Can they be worship leaders? Can they be pastors? Can they stand in the pulpit and preach, or are they relegated to second-class status? I put myself in the middle of this discussion more than fifteen years ago when I wrote my first book, *10 Lies the Church Tells Women*. My belief, based on Scripture, is that God does indeed call certain women to function in senior leadership roles – and to rely on the power of the Holy Spirit to move the church forward.

I see many examples of women leaders in the Bible: Deborah the prophetess who led Israel into a season of peace; Miriam, who served as an elder in ancient Israel with Moses and Aaron (see Micah 6:4); Esther, who delivered Israel from certain genocide; and the many women who served with the apostle Paul in the New Testament church, such as Phoebe, Junia, Euodia, Syntyche, Chloe, Nympha and others.

I also see that Scripture clearly states we should not only respect our fathers but our mothers. Proverbs 1:8 says: "Hear, my son, your father's instruction and do not forsake your mother's teaching; indeed they are a graceful wreath to your head and ornaments about your neck." Just as the family needs the spiritual leadership of both parents, we need spiritual mothers as well as fathers in the church. I do not believe the church can be healthy without both men and women in leadership.

It is one thing to recognize the role of women from reading the Bible; it is another thing to see healthy examples of women leaders

11

in the contemporary church. That's why I was so blessed when I first met Naomi Dowdy at a conference for apostolic leaders held in Dallas, Texas, in 2001. Her missionary courage inspired me; her willingness to defy cultural restrictions in Asia amazed me; her legacy of wise leadership gave me the encouragement I needed to continue my work in empowering women leaders around the globe.

In this book you will read more about Naomi Dowdy's unusual journey. As a missionary she was willing to go where few people would want to live – in the isolated Marshall Islands of the South Pacific. As a minister, she was willing to say yes to God when He asked her to pastor a struggling church in Singapore. (She has been honest about her wrestling match with God over that decision!) As a gifted leader among leaders, she has raised up one of the most amazing mega-churches in Asia, Trinity Christian Centre. I have had the pleasure of speaking at that church twice, and both times I came away invigorated by the spirit of excellence, generosity and spiritual maturity that is evident there.

I have cited Naomi Dowdy's example countless times when people ask me how God can use a woman in the church. When I visited Trinity Christian Centre for the first time, I was struck by the fact that almost every person I met in the church was a leader. Naomi has always believed that God calls every Christian to full maturity, and she developed a unique cell-based structure to facilitate discipleship and leadership development. While some people were arguing about whether God could even use women to pastor, Naomi was growing one of the most Kingdom-minded, Spirit-filled churches I've ever seen.

During my first visit to Trinity Christian Centre, I was asked to speak on a Sunday morning, and the leadership team told me I had total freedom to pick my sermon topic. Then I found out that on the Sunday I was preaching, the church would be taking up a special pledge offering to raise their annual missionary budget. I got nervous. I told Naomi:

"I did not plan to preach an offering sermon. Do you want me to change my plans?" "Oh, no, you don't need to preach about money at all," she said. "The people have been trained to give to missions, and they don't need any additional motivation. After you finish preaching, they will know what to do in the offering."

I was still a bit nervous about that arrangement, but I did as I was instructed. After my message, the ushers took up the offering – not only from the main auditorium, but also from a Chinese congregation that met in another room, and from a satellite church meeting in another location. Then we all waited as staff and volunteers calculated how much money had been promised. Before we were dismissed, we learned that members of Trinity had promised to give US$10.5 million to support missions work in several countries.

I have never encountered any church in the United States that gives that much to advance the gospel overseas. Yet this church, led by a humble woman (and pastored today by the man she trained to replace her, Dominic Yeo), is leading the way in demonstrating what a truly apostolic church looks like.

Naomi Dowdy is a modern pioneer. She blazed a trail for many others. She said yes to God, and her yes was both painful and costly. Her obedience opened the door for countless thousands to enter Christ's kingdom. I am happy to call Naomi Dowdy a mentor, a friend and a true spiritual mother. She has given me personal counsel in years past, and her example prods me to make sacrifices whenever I feel like giving up. I salute her legacy, and I pray that this book will inspire you to emulate her faith and courage.

J. Lee Grady
Former Editor, Charisma Magazine
Director, The Mordecai Project

CHAPTER 1

Growing Up with Granddad

When I was a child, Granddad and I were very close. He was my paternal grandfather, and I was his first grandchild. My family lived in the town, but I would ask to go out to his farm as often as I could. I usually stayed on the farm for several weeks at a time. From the time I was born in 1935, up until the time I started school, I enjoyed special times with Granddad on his farm. He was my hero, because my dad was never around.

My Granddad was very protective of his family, and always wanted the best for us. I still remember when he bought a real washing machine for my grandmother – it was a first for the community. He was so proud of it; he would position it out in the front yard, close to the road.

Everyone could hear it running because it had a gasoline motor. You had to pull and pull on the cord until it would finally catch and begin to spit out smoke. Finally would come a purring sound. Naturally, I had to be helping Grandma too, even though I did not know what I was doing. Sometimes while standing on a chair, pulling clothes out of the tub and sticking them into the wringer, I would get my hand caught. They would need to stop the machine, release the pressure, and pull both the clothes and my arm out of the wringer. I was just trying to help!

To have a washing machine was a big deal in those days. Before we had a washing machine, doing the laundry meant building a big fire and boiling water in a huge iron pot out in the back yard. When the water was hot, they would throw in the clothes with lye soap and 'boil' the dirt out. When the clothes were thought to be clean, they would take a long strong stick and probe through the kettle, stirring and lifting up the soapy laundry to go into the rinse water. Washing the laundry would take all day.

Of course that farm in rural Kentucky had horses, mules, chickens, pigs and cows. I discovered that cows have a temper. I'm serious! Granddad had one cow that was brown and cream in color. This cow and I did not have a good relationship. For some reason she did not like me. Every evening when the cows would come in from grazing in the pastures, Granddad and I would open the gate so they could come into the barn for the night. When that old cow saw me, she would give me the meanest look and even try to charge towards me. Naturally I would run.

Being a kid, I discovered a way to get back at the cow for not liking me. After Granddad would leave the barn and go to the house, I would climb up to the loft of the barn and crawl across until I was just above the stall of the brown cow. Through the cracks in the wooden floor, I would drop kernels of corn and bits of straw – anything to annoy that brown cow. Yes, she knew it was me! She would look up and give me that mean stare. Then I would quickly climb down the ladder and run back to the house. When morning came and Granddad opened the gate to release the cows back into the pasture, that brown cow would look for me. I wonder why?

I loved life on the farm. Often when my grandparents looked for me, they would find me sitting on a big tree limb, picking peaches or cherries from the tree and eating them. When all else failed, they just needed to look up to find me.

Granddad taught me how to shoot a rifle so when we wanted to eat meat other than pork, we would take our guns and go into the woods to hunt rabbits, squirrels or frogs. There was always a wide variety.

He also taught me how to plow the fields with a mule pulling the plow. He would hitch two mules to a 'pointed nosed' plow. He set the nose of that plow in the ground and told me to plow the rows in the field. Picture this: the handles of the plow were above my head, so I had to reach up to hold on. I also had to hold onto the reins to control the mules pulling the plow, keep the plow in the ground and keep it straight, all at the same time. Was it hard? You bet. But I was game to try anything, and I loved working with my Granddad.

When Sunday came, it was time to get dressed up for church. It was during one of those vacations on his farm that I first attended church. Granddad would leave the house early, go down to the barn to hitch two horses to the wagon, and bring it up to the house. Then Grandma and I would climb in. Now came the best part: Granddad would let me sit in the driver's seat beside him. He would pass the reins to me and let me 'drive' the wagon.

We were always the first ones to arrive at church, because Granddad was the church deacon and he had the keys to open the church. After the service, all the people would gather around long tables laden with food, which the womenfolk had cooked and brought with them. Church was a time to fellowship and catch up with all the neighbors. As the farms were not located near each other, Sunday was visiting day as well.

After everyone left, Granddad would lock up the church and we would hurry home before it got dark. There were no street lights so we needed to reach home before it got too dark to see properly. Compared to our modern conveniences today, that sounds like centuries ago! Those were the days when we had no running water, no electricity, and no indoor toilets. So much has changed over the years; new inventions have changed our homes and our lifestyles.

Once a week, Granddad would even let me drive the wagon into the little town (up to the edge of town, at least) where he would take the milk and butter from the farm to sell to the vendors there. With that money we could go to the store and buy some groceries; things that Grandma did not raise in her garden. Boy, did it feel good to drive the wagon and horses! It was an even better feeling than driving a car, which I did later.

All these things were key influences in my formative years. Granddad never said I could not do something because I was a girl. Because I did not grow up with any lids placed on me, I simply did not know that lids existed for girls. I did not try to be like a boy, but there was nothing I could not do. I was always ready to try new things, and I was given the opportunity to do so. Thus began God's shaping of my character and values. He gave me godly grandparents to nurture me. God says, "Before I formed you in the womb, I knew you, before you were born I set you apart" (Jeremiah 1:5). He knows each of us by name and has a good plan for us (Jeremiah 29:11-13).

Because I did not grow up with any lids placed on me, I simply did not know that lids existed for girls.

My happiest days were spent on that farm.

Childhood Misadventures

As a child, I was always doing unusual things. At the tender age of two, I staged my first escape. Mom was hanging her laundry on the clothesline in the back yard, when she suddenly realized that I was gone. She panicked, as any mother would, and began searching for me. She finally found me, hours later, many blocks away. I had climbed onto a big lion statue outside a funeral home. She found me just sitting there, enjoying myself and stroking the lion. (Maybe there was something prophetic in that, for I later ended up in the Lion City of Singapore.)

Another time, while Mom and Dad were in the apartment, I ran outside. Daddy's big truck was parked on the road. It was unlocked, so I climbed in and pretended to be a truck driver. I was so short, I could not sit in the seat and reach the brakes. So I would hold onto the steering wheel (to prop myself up) and stretch my legs until I could touch the brakes. These were air brakes, so each time I stepped on them, the brakes would give a big, 'sheee' sound. It was fun, so I just kept "driving," pushing the brakes just to hear the 'sheee' sound.

I am not sure how long I was doing this, but suddenly Dad came running down the street. He caught me and got me out of the truck quickly. I remember the shock even to my little mind when I realized that the truck was now down the street, a long way from home. Even at that age, I realized how dangerous it was, and was relieved that there were no cars or people on the street. I could have really smashed a car with the size of the truck I was 'driving'!

Growing Up Lonely

I was an only child. Due to difficulties at my birth, Mom could not have any more children. I was an introvert and somewhat of a loner. I was also terribly shy. Despite my shyness, certain situations would bring out the feisty side of me. When I was with people, taking on the role of a leader

I was an introvert and somewhat of a loner.

came naturally to me. When the children in the neighborhood played games like Cowboys and Indians, or as a sheriff hunting down the bad guys, I was always the one figuring out the strategies, and leading the attacks to capture the 'enemy.'

Once I had an encounter with some boys who attended the school just down the street. I was playing with all my dolls and doll house under a big tree in our front yard. Two boys came walking by on the sidewalk, on their way to school. They suddenly came into the yard, tore down my doll house and walked away laughing. I was younger and smaller than them, but I knew they were bullying me because I was a girl.

That was not right, so I took a stand. I vividly remember taking a broom and chasing them out of the yard and down the street, beating them with my broom as they fell into a ditch! From that day on, whenever they had to pass my house, they would cross the street and walk on the other side.

Starting School

When we moved further away to the town of Fulton, Kentucky, my trips to the farm became less and less frequent. It was in Fulton that I began first grade. The first few years of school were not good years for

20

me. I was so shy that I did not want to join in most of the classroom activities. The other kids would bully me and tell the teacher I had done things which I had not done, so I would get into trouble and be punished. School was not something I enjoyed. I was miserable.

Things were not good at home either. My parents did not go to church. Dad was a truck driver. His work meant that he was constantly driving on the interstate highways, and he was hardly ever home. Sometimes he would be home just one night in a whole week. I looked forward to his coming home, but whenever he was home, he and Mom would quarrel constantly.

The hostile environment at home and the bullying in school caused me to feel so inferior in everything. I was constantly picked on, and I felt lousy about myself. I did not like being me. I felt out of place, both at home and in school. It felt like I did not quite belong anywhere.

My years in Fulton were also the years of World War II. Naturally, events at school included activities that supported our American efforts in the war. Yes, even we as children had a part to play. One of our jobs was to collect the tin foil from our chewing gum wrappers and return it to the stores. Tin was a valuable commodity in wartime. I was very proud of our troops and I distinctly remember thinking, "When I grow up, I will join the Army and fight for freedom."

I had a penchant for driving trucks and cars – anything that involved navigation and which put me in the driver's seat. One day Dad came home in a car. He said, "Come on, I'll teach you how to drive a car." We hopped in and off we went. Then Dad asked me to climb over, sit on his lap and drive. Oh, I liked that. Without warning, he scooted from under me, and moved to the passenger seat, dumping me sideways. I held onto the steering wheel as we swerved off the street, onto the sidewalk, and back to the street. I was doing everything I could to find the brakes and steady the car. It was tough, because I was too short to reach any of the pedals. With some help from Dad, I did manage to get it straight, and we reached home safely. Thankfully, no one was hurt.

The Nashville Years

When I was nine, Mom told me that we were moving to Nashville, Tennessee. That meant a new school and new classmates for me, so I was happy to be moving.

We moved into an apartment in the middle of town. Ours was a one-room apartment; everything we had or did was in that one room. Living across the street from us were two girls who had a stay-home mom, and a dad who would spend time with them. They went to church as a family. Theirs seemed like a perfect home. I felt dejected when I compared my family to theirs, because my family couldn't be more different.

I would walk to school together with the girls across the street. One day, they invited me to go to church with them. I loved going with them as a family. However, since their church was farther away from where we lived, they soon introduced me to a big church just down the street from where we lived – the First Baptist Church, 7th and Broadway, Nashville, Tennessee.

I have wonderful memories of my times there. It was there that I received Christ and was baptized in water. It was only later that I realized that the church was like the 'headquarters church' for the Southern Baptist Convention.

I loved Sunday nights more than Sunday School in the mornings. In the evening, we would learn the books of the Bible. This was called Training Union. The teacher would line us up with our Bibles in our hands, ready for what was called 'sword drills.' We waited and listened carefully as the teacher would call out a book, chapter and verse, then repeat it again. The moment she said "GO!", we would all open our Bibles and search, to be the first to find the scripture and read it out loud. If you were the first, you got to move up toward the front of the line. Oh, I loved learning the Bible! After Training Union, we would all go to the evening service. It was in one of those evening services that I first heard God speak to me.

The best part came after the evening service, when we could stay for a fellowship time down in the basement of the church. It was special for two reasons. They served free punch and cookies, which was a treat for me, and the adults and kids would play games together, which I really enjoyed.

The best part, however, was that the Senior Pastor would also be there. Our pastor was so open, friendly and accepting. He was not officious or aloof; we could actually touch him and speak with him. This meant a lot to me as I had difficulty feeling accepted. Those were special times. Sunday nights became my favorite time of the week.

The Holy Spirit drew me into the warmth of a spiritual family.

Though I did not yet understand the concept of *koinonia* or the Body of Christ, the Holy Spirit drew me into the warmth of a spiritual family and formed a solid foundation for the future.

CHAPTER 2

Turbulent Times

WHEN I WAS ELEVEN, I was told the news: we were moving to another part of town. Dad had rented a whole house for us. This was exciting but it meant another change of schools. It also meant that I could not go to the same church anymore. There was a small church in our new neighborhood, but it was just not the same. I had no friends and a different pastor. Soon I stopped going altogether.

My parents continued to quarrel constantly. Whenever they quarreled, I would try to stay out of their way by cleaning Dad's shoes and polishing them to a 'high shine'.

Dad was never close to me but neither was he abusive. However, that year, he became abusive toward Mom and began to threaten her. One day, I was just walking into the room when I saw him raise his fist to hit her.

I could not take that. I knew that Mom was faithful and very hardworking. He had no reason to hit her or beat on her. In that instant, I grabbed a kitchen knife that lay on the table and jumped between them, shouting, "If you come one step closer to Mom, I will run this knife through you."

Naturally, as an eleven-year-old, I would have been no match for him, but my words stopped him in his tracks. He left the house that day and never came back. After the divorce, Mom and I moved to a smaller duplex in the same neighborhood, sharing the house with a widow and her son.

I never saw Dad again after that, until I was much older and already serving God as a missionary. When we had our first reunion, I shared with him about Jesus and prayed for him. Later when I was in Singapore, in my first few years as Senior Pastor of Trinity Christian Centre, his new wife called to say that Dad was in the hospital and not doing well. God gave me the privilege of praying with him on the phone to receive Christ. Thank God, I was able to pray with both my Mom and Dad, at different times, and lead them into a relationship with Jesus Christ.

Polio Comes Knocking

When I was thirteen, the doctors discovered that I had polio – a very deadly disease during those years. I was visiting with a classmate for the weekend. We went to the movies and then to her home for the night. During the night I had severe cramps in my legs that made me cry out in pain. My friend's mother was up all night trying to rub my legs and relieve the pain. As soon as it was morning, she told me to go home to see what was wrong.

I got on my bicycle and headed home. Our house was among many others located on the top of a big hill. My legs were so weak, it was like trying to walk on 'spaghetti' legs; I could not stand up. I got off my bike and lay my body across the seat, as I struggled to get both the bike and I up the hill. When I finally reached home, Mom panicked. I joked, "Don't worry Mom, it is probably only polio." That was the scary thing in those days. She shouted, "Don't even say that!"

When the doctor finally arrived, he examined me and immediately said, "Get her to the hospital quickly." The type of polio that I had required the doctors to do a spinal block in my lower back, to prevent the polio from traveling up my spine. If the spinal block did not work and the polio reached the base of my neck, I would have had to live in an 'iron lung' for the rest of my life. I would not have been able to breathe on my own, nor walk or feed myself for the rest of my life. I would have been paralyzed from the neck down. What a scary prognosis! The thought that kept going through my mind were, "Will I ever walk again? What will my life become? Can I still do something with my life?"

By this time, I had drifted away from God and was not serving Him. Although my heart was open, my life was not in alignment with His Word. Yet He was gracious and brought me through the adversity.

Sporting Glory

It took me quite a while to recover from polio. I was an avid basketball player, but after I had polio, my teacher would not allow me to play softball or basketball. She said it was too strenuous and that I should rest more. I tried to insist, but she refused and blocked me every time I tried to join in the game. This was a very frustrating time for me because I knew I could do it. Sitting and watching them play was no fun at all. Still, the answer was no. I said, "Okay, if you won't let me play in the games, I will be a cheerleader instead." Oddly enough, the teacher approved it. So that year, I became a cheerleader. At least I still got to go to the games! The following year, I got back into the game – and I could not have been happier.

Sports made up a big part of my life. I played on the basketball and softball teams as well as in track and field competitions. Being on the school debate team was also a highlight for me.

Basketball was my first love. In basketball I played both forward position and guard position. But I loved the 'point guard' position the best. To me it was more of a challenge to figure out how our opponents were planning to score and then quickly stop them, so our team would score instead.

Basketball was my first love.

Of all the sports, I loved basketball so much that during the regular season I would play on three different teams at the same time – in different leagues, of course. We were the champions in one league. Then during summer, I would play on a community softball team, which also won the championship.

Racing Downhill

When I was fourteen, I got injured while riding a bicycle. One of the boys in the neighborhood had a real good bicycle, and I borrowed it so I could go play softball. On my way home, I had to come down a bumpy hill. At the bottom of the hill was a cross street where cars would drive past. Beyond the street was the woods.

Riding down the slope, there was no need for me to pedal as it was a very steep forty-degree slope. But that day, for some reason, the brakes would not work! These were not hand brakes; you had to push your peddle backwards in order to slow down the bike. I was even standing up and jumping on the pedals to try to get the brakes to slow me down.

Try as I would, I simply could not slow down. Without any brakes, I sped down the hill uncontrollably. I just could not slow the baby down! I remember thinking to myself, "If a car comes by, I'll be completely wiped out." When I hit bottom, the impact shot me up over the road, over the fence, and into the woods. It was a good thing I did not hit a big tree. The bike went one way, and I went another. I lost consciousness, but later I managed to find my way out of the woods, albeit with some injuries. In contrast, the bike was all mangled and did not survive the fall.

These were only a few of the near-death experiences that I had. Time and again, God preserved my life. I did not know why, but He did for me as the Psalmist said, "He will command His angels concerning you to guard you in all your ways" (91:11).

Making Ends Meet

Since my mother had very little formal education, the only job she could get was working in a garment factory. Her wages were so low that what she earned was insufficient for our living expenses. We lived in a poor part of town, yet we still did not have enough to pay our rent and utilities, and sometimes we did not have enough food to eat.

At thirteen, in the summer between seventh and eighth grades, I started working part-time, and from then on, I would juggle school and work. I would go to school in the morning and head straight to work after school. I would work till the store closed and then walk home around 11pm every night. On weekends, I would be work all day into the evening. I didn't earn much, but it did help put food on the table. Because of this experience of poverty, one of my goals in life was to make as much money as I could and never be poor again.

All this while, I was eager to leave Nashville. I felt out of place and never felt like I belonged. I always knew that I would be leaving Nashville at some point. It did not feel like I was supposed to be there. It seemed as if there was something or somewhere else I was meant to be.

I could not imagine living the same life my mother did, where one woke up, went to work, came home, read the papers, went to bed – and started the cycle again the next day. It seemed to me like an awful way to spend your life, though my Mom loved it.

I believed there was more to life than spending your evenings reading the news, and occasionally going for a walk in the park. That kind of life was not for me. Yet I did not know what I wanted to do with my life. I had no idea or framework for what my life would become. There was simply a restlessness in my spirit. However, Mom was adamant that I could not leave home till I was eighteen, so I waited.

Just before I dropped out of school, I dated a man who was seven or eight years older than me. He was a nice guy and even let me drive his convertible to school, so for a while, I was the cool chick with the convertible! Yes, I got my first driver's license at the age of fifteen. Then he proposed marriage! I was agreeable to the idea, since I simply didn't know any better. However, when he took me home to meet his mother, she saw that I was just a kid. He then dropped the idea, though we remained good friends. I cannot imagine how my life would have turned out if I had really gotten married at fifteen!

Finding Me

When I was growing up, I got teased a lot. The other kids would call me 'Yankee'. I never figured out why, as I had grown up in the South. My impoverished family background, my introverted nature, and all this name calling contributed to my very low self-esteem. I was struggling in school and had been told that I could not succeed, that I could not do anything well. For example, I was told I did not have the social graces to handle a full setting of silverware at a formal dinner. These negative words were very hurtful to my spirit.

Because I felt inferior, I wanted to please people. I didn't know how to say 'no'. If someone asked me to eat something, I would eat it whether I liked it or not, and I was afraid to express an opinion. This continued until I did not know what kind of food I liked or didn't like, what my favorite colors were or what clothes I liked. I wanted to please people so that I would be accepted.

Because I felt inferior, I wanted to please people.

It would take me many years to finally discover 'me.' Who was I?

I had to discover how God made and wired me, and learn to be comfortable with myself. It was only much later that I learned to accept myself, and to be secure in my identity in God.

Getting Down to Work

At sixteen I dropped out of school altogether, so that I could work full-time. I changed jobs when a better opportunity arose. It was only years later that I went back to school to complete my education.

After I dropped out of school, my first full-time job was as a waitress in what would be called a coffee shop today. I did all kinds of things: serve tables, make sandwiches and ice cream sodas, and wash the dirty dishes. The shop was across the street from the courthouse, and so we had all these lawyers coming in for lunch. I remember there was this guy everyone wanted to wait on because he was a big tipper – he would tip fifty cents while everyone else only gave ten or twenty cents. Fifty cents was a big tip in those days.

Then I worked as a clerk or sales girl in a jewelry store for a while. That did not last too long, and here's why. Even though I was no longer in school, I was still playing basketball every season. One day, our team had to play a game out of town. We needed to meet at a certain time to get on the team bus that would take us to the other city. That day, I asked the owner of the store if I could leave work thirty minutes early to join the team. We were not busy and it was near closing time anyway. He refused to allow me to go off early. I tried to reason with him but he still refused.

Finally he said, "If you want to go, then you must quit."

It was the wrong thing to say to me. I retorted, "Okay then, I quit. Now give me my pay." That was how much basketball meant to me! I got to the game on time – but now I had no job.

Before long, a door opened for me. I was offered a job in the Federal Reserve Bank in our city – and it came with better pay. This job was very demanding, but I worked hard and was promoted to a team leader within a short time.

I continued to play basketball, even into the early years of my working career. In fact, I had just been selected and began to play on the semipro basketball team in our area, when my life took another turn.

From a later vantage point, I can see a life lesson from God in the events of this turbulent season. Though my motives were not God-centered, yet His merciful hand was guiding me, keeping me from evil, and "preserving my going out and my coming in" (Psalm 121:8).

CHAPTER 3

Escape from Nashville

WHEN I FINALLY TURNED EIGHTEEN, I decided to quit my job at the Federal Reserve Bank in Nashville. I applied for a job in Washington D.C., a full day's drive from Nashville. I felt comfortable leaving home as my Mom was now dating someone and would most likely be getting married soon.

In Washington I embarked on a new career, working for the Central Intelligence Agency. During this time I was introduced to computers, which were then in the very early stages of development.

My job was to operate a 'keypunch' machine. It functioned like a complicated typewriter, where the operator read information, typed a code into the machine, which would then punch holes into cards. The cards were fed into a reader that transferred the information into computer language, which was then conveyed to the big computers for processing.

I took one look at that keypunch machine and said, "I don't think I can do this." However, my boss insisted that I try it for three months. True enough, I ended up smoking three packs of cigarettes a day and drinking heavily at night, just trying to do the job. It was that stressful! When my three-month probation was up, I wanted to tender my resignation.

I said to my supervisor candidly, "I don't think I am doing too well."

He agreed, but what he said next took me by surprise. "Look around. Do you see anything here you can do?"

It was very gracious of him to give me such an opportunity. I walked around, and I saw that in another room they had control boards with holes in them. An employee had to wire them. These boards controlled many different kinds of machines, which were needed to process all the reports.

I told my boss, "That, I can do." He transferred me over to that department. I caught on quickly and soon became a leader in the department.

All this while, I continued to attend classes, working towards completing my education. However, while my career was going well, my spiritual life was heading steadily downhill. By this time, you could say that I had become a 'good' sinner. I lived life independent of God; God no longer had any place in my life.

I had become a 'good' sinner. I lived life independent of God.

Moving to San Diego

Two years later, I quit my job and decided to move to San Diego, California. I had heard about the city from my friends and was ready for a new experience. The problem was, I had no way to get out there. I had no car, and flying was not common in those days. Then I came across an advertisement: Someone wanted to drive across the country and was looking for another person to share the task of driving!

After meeting him, Mom felt it was safe to let me take off with him. He was a gentleman, and later we ended up working in the same company. Then he asked me to marry him! Although he was a nice man, I was not ready to think about marriage at that point.

In San Diego, because of my experience with computers, doors opened for me to work in an aerospace company. After a year or two, they transferred me to a new company that focused on building space rockets. My particular division worked around the clock producing engineering reports and payrolls related to the building of America's first space rockets.

They needed people to work the midnight shift. Being a beach bum, I was only too happy to work at night, so I could spend my days on the beach. I loved the white sand and crashing ocean waves in La Jolla, where I rented an apartment.

A Divine Setup

My work paid well and before long, I was able to make a down payment on my first house. I was so happy to finally have a place of my own. It felt like a big achievement for a 23-year-old!

However, just when I thought things were going well for me, God began to hunt me down. The company hired a new girl. While I ran the equipment, my new colleague would be in another room, running reports. As she was the only other person on the night shift, we had many opportunities to converse during our coffee breaks and meals. I found out she was a Christian; she was always talking about miracles, healing and the Holy Spirit. She could talk about Jesus all night!

It was a divine setup! There was no escape for me. Whenever I took a coffee break or had lunch (at three in the morning!), there she was, talking about Jesus. We had many conversations. Although I had gone to church in my very early years, God and church had not been on my mind since my early teens. I thought it was really wonderful for her, but I was just not interested and declined all but one of her invitations to church.

One Saturday, after I had just moved into my new house, I was mowing the lawn and had a chicken roasting on the barbecue. To my surprise, this girl showed up on my doorstep with a friend. I invited them in and made coffee. We were chatting at the dining table when suddenly, she stopped, looked me in the eye and asked, "Don't you want to receive Christ as your Savior?"

To my surprise, I found myself saying 'yes!' Before I even realized what was happening, we were in the living room. They had me on my knees and were laying hands on me, praying for me. As they did, I received a flashback of the personal encounter I had with God when I was nine or ten years old.

I saw myself seated in a Sunday evening service at the First Baptist Church in Nashville. There I was, singing an old hymn. The chorus of the song went like this: *"Let the lower lights be burning! Send a gleam across the wave! Some poor fainting struggling seaman you may rescue, you may save."*

When I sang those words as a child, I was crying. It felt as if hot burning lava was flowing down my cheeks, and I heard a voice say, *"And that's what I want you to do."* Turning around to see who was speaking to me, I saw no one. As I looked around, the

> *I heard a voice say, "And that's what I want you to do."*

church seemed like it stretched over a kilometer in width and length. No one was behind me, nor on my left or right. I was like a remote island, just a tiny little girl, far away from anyone else.

As we went on into the last verse of the song, the tears continued to stream down my cheeks. I knew I had heard a voice and I just knew it was God's voice. Not knowing what to do with this experience, or who to talk to about it, I decided to simply hide that word in my heart.

Now as my colleague and her friend prayed for me, these memories resurfaced. It all started coming back to me. Although I had been unclear about the significance of my encounter with God as a child, as my friends prayed, I now received a sudden revelation: God had called me to be a missionary!

Off to a Fast Start

This revelation powerfully redefined my outlook and my purpose in life. After this divine encounter, I was on fire for God. I was baptized at twenty-four years of age and became active in the First Assembly of God Church in San Diego. Pastor Emil Balliet was my first pastor. The head usher was very welcoming and helped me settle into the church.

I had only been saved for a few weeks when they had me preaching to the homeless and drunkards on skid row. Different churches worked together there to provide soup kitchens for the poor. I was out preaching, even without Bible school training. I was so excited about Jesus, and I just could not keep Him to myself.

At First Assembly, women were accepted in ministry. However, I did not see any of them preaching in the church service. Preaching on skid row, though, was acceptable.

My belief was: Whatever God said, He will do. I was crazy enough to believe that! Fearlessly, I would declare to alcoholics: "After we pray for you, you will not want any more alcohol." I just had the faith that God was going to do what the Bible said. I was sold out for Jesus, and everyone could see it.

Because of my passion to share Jesus, the girls (who had prayed for me) and I pooled our money to buy airtime and preached on the radio. The radio program was appropriately titled *The Missionary Call*. It was all about getting people saved and challenging them to get involved in missions.

Later God moved me from First Assembly over to a small Assemblies of God (AG) church in the Pacific Beach area to help the pastor with the new work there. My new pastor and church gave me many opportunities to serve, including leading worship and raising funds for the missions programs. They assigned me that task because missions was my passion.

Called to the Islands

In the meantime, my responsibilities at work increased, and my company sent me for further training. Once when I was on a business assignment to Los Angeles, the Lord gave me a night vision or a dream. I saw an island and a girl with long, flowing hair and with arms outstretched. There were no words spoken in the dream, but as I rolled out of bed and got on my knees to pray, it was like Paul's Macedonian call in Acts 16:9-10. I knew I was called to go to island people. After that vision, whenever I opened my Bible, every passage I read seemed to be about islands.

I was sure God was calling me to some islands somewhere, but I did not know exactly where or when. I became impatient with Him. "God, when?" became my heart's cry. I did not even know the name of any islands. Then suddenly, out of the blue, someone offered me a job in Hawaii. I considered it for a while. Yes, that would be an island... but it just did not feel like the islands God was speaking about.

As I prayed, I heard God say, *"In three years."* Now I had a time frame! I knew that there would come a shift and transition in my life in three years' time.

In 1962, God moved me to Los Angeles. I was not fond of LA, but God worked in an unusual way, through a series of events. I had been driving from LA up to Whittier, California to attend revival meetings in a Foursquare Church. These revival meetings were going on seven days a week, once every night and twice on Sunday. Miracles were happening, people were coming to Christ, teeth were filled with gold fillings, and we experienced just an awesome presence of God. After making that long drive back and forth for several months, I felt God wanted me to move to the area and be a part of this visitation of God. So I quit my job and moved in with a family living in the area.

Since God had led me there, I believed He would provide a job for me. Sure enough, after a few months, I found myself working as a computer analyst and programmer with Autonetics, an aerospace company in Anaheim. Once again, I was doing well financially. God gave me favor at work and before long I was assigned to be a troubleshooter for the four divisions of North American Aviation, our main company. All that meant was, if there was any problem that caused the computers to malfunction during the night, they would call me. Receiving multiple calls between 2am and 4am became routine.

A Tug of War

One thing I had been aware of, all my life, was God's protection. I knew He had a greater purpose for me than I had yet attained. I was also aware in my spirit that different things that had happened to me were efforts of the devil to cut short my life and abort God's plan. Now I was about to experience another of those attempts.

While living in Los Angeles, I thought I would take a short break and drive up to Oregon to visit a friend. As I was driving alone, singing and worshipping the Lord, I sensed an eerie presence in the car. Suddenly, I began to feel the chills down my spine, and felt like my hair was standing on end. I began to pray in tongues and worshipped as I drove on. Then I heard a voice which said, "I am going to kill you!" That got my attention for sure! I began to slow down and prayed harder. Again, I heard the same voice, saying the same thing. This time I pulled off the road.

As I sat there, I thought, "I cannot sit here beside this road forever. I need to keep driving." Before restarting the car, I prayed and said, "Lord, if something is going to happen, please do not let anyone else be involved." With that I continued my journey, worshipping and praying in tongues.

Soon the road began to wind up into the mountains of Northern California. The mountain pass was not only full of curves; there were rock boulders to one side of the road, and deep caverns on the other side. Still praying and worshipping, I began to notice that I was drifting off to the side of the road. At first it seemed like I was simply casually drifting as I drove. I quickly turned the steering wheel to the left to get the car back on the road. Then I began to notice there was a force resisting me.

I became aware that I was in warfare. The resistance became stronger and stronger, such that I needed to overcompensate to stay on track, thus causing the car to swerve back and forth. The wind was strong and the road shoulder was not wide.

I would easily plunge some two thousand feet down the cavern.

If I hit the gravel on the side, I would easily plunge some two thousand feet down the cavern.

As I crossed a small bridge over the cavern, the force started again. This time it was like a tug-of-war. It would push right, and I would struggle to break its hold by using both hands to turn the steering wheel to the left. We went back and forth like this, left and right, again and again. My car was now hitting the gravel on the side of the road. I remember thinking, "Oh God, this is too close. The next time I skid, I will go over into the cavern." Suddenly, just as I was using all my strength to steer the car to the left, the force released its hold on the steering wheel. Because I had been using all my strength, the sudden release caused me to slam into the rock boulder on the left side of the road.

I sat there stunned, in shock and feeling a little numb in places. As the glass and dust settled, I didn't move but began to use my eyes to look around and survey my situation. I saw some blood on my shirt so I adjusted my mirror to see my face. I could immediately see that the right side of my lip was cut wide open. My first words were, "God, that's sure going to look terrible as I preach Your Word." Thankfully, no one else was involved or hurt.

I slowly found a way to get out of the car. I was surveying the extent of the damage, when a car came around the curve in the opposite direction. It was a couple, and would you believe it, the wife 'just happened' to be a nurse. After she checked me over, they helped transfer my things from my wrecked car into their car and drove me to the nearest town. They seemed to know that there was a small hospital there.

When the doctor checked me, he smiled and said, "Well, today is your lucky day. A leading plastic surgeon in the state just happens to be visiting our hospital, and he can fix you up in no time." Well, I don't believe in luck, but I do believe in God's divine provision. While I was waiting for the surgery to begin, I called my insurance company to inform them about the accident. I called an automobile company in the town and arranged to buy a car, so I could pick it up once the surgeon was finished with me.

Within a few hours, my lip was stitched up and I had a car to continue on my journey. I was a little bruised and shaken, but nonetheless rejoicing in God's protection and provision.

Launching Off

Together with some friends within the company, I started a consultancy business as a second job outside my regular working hours. We served companies that needed computer services but could not afford to buy their own machines, or did not have space for them. We provided them a service by developing the programs they needed and renting the needed equipment from companies that only used their equipment during the day. We would rent these machines after normal working hours, churn out the necessary reports overnight and give our clients their reports by the next morning.

I was one busy 29-year-old! I was working almost ninety hours a week. My work was demanding and consumed most of my time, leaving me little time for the usual church activities.

Just as I was making even better money, God spoke to me again, reminding me about my call to missions. As I was passionate about preaching and doing ministry, I formed a singing trio. Two friends of mine joined me and we would go to different AG churches to minister. We would testify and sing as a trio, and then I would preach. It was thrilling to see people get saved and filled with the Holy Spirit.

Still, I longed to get to the islands God had shown me. As I prayed, I realized that the three-year time frame God had given me was up. I felt like a volcano about to erupt. So I became desperate in my prayers: "God, you said three years. The time is up. Which islands do You want me to go to?"

Again, God arranged a divine appointment. Whenever I was free on Saturday nights, I would drive people to Teen Challenge in L.A. for their Saturday night service. That Saturday night, a young man named Sam Sasser was speaking. He had been out preaching the Gospel in the Marshall Islands, and had just received his official appointment as a missionary with the Assemblies of God. He was now preparing to return to the islands, this time with his wife and young children.

As I listened to him speak, I felt that volcano rumbling inside me again. During the prayer time, I lay on the floor under the benches, crying out: "God, my three years are over. Which islands are for me?"

Within weeks, I met with Sam's wife Florence, and discussed my going to the Marshall Islands with them. She told me their intended departure date. After our meeting, months went by without any news from them. I thought, "They must have left for the islands by now. Okay, God, since I have not heard back from them, maybe the Marshall Islands are not the islands that You intended for me."

Several more months went by. One day, out of the blue, I received a call from Sam. They had not left yet. They were still in town, and he wanted me to meet him at a church where he would be preaching on Wednesday night.

After the service, a crowd surrounded Sam, wanting to speak with him. I lingered in the fellowship area, just waiting for him to finish talking. Sam eventually walked over to me and asked: "Are you ready to come to the Islands with us?"

"Yes!" I said.

He responded, "Then get ready and come as soon as you can."

That was the full length of our conversation! But sensing that God was in this, I tendered my resignation the next morning. I knew this was what God wanted me to do, because it aligned with what God had been speaking to me. I had peace; yet I had a question. Was God really asking me to quit my job, forfeit my income, and give up all I had worked so hard to achieve?

Was God really asking me to give up all I had worked so hard to achieve?

I was making good money, and I had been giving a good portion of my earnings to missions, far above what was considered the 'normal' level. I was giving far beyond my tithe. The devil can sometimes play mind games with us. I began to rationalize, "But if I stayed here, I could make money and give much more to the church, financially speaking."

As much as I tried, I knew God would not accept that argument. He did not want my money. He was looking at my heart, and He wanted me. I decided that He could have me. I surrendered my heart to Him.

The time had come for a transition in my life. I did not know what to expect. All I knew was, God had told me to go – and I was ready for God's next season. With excitement, I sold my car and proceeded to quit my job. However when I tried to resign, my boss would not let me. He offered me a year's leave of absence instead, and promised to keep my job for me.

I was then working in a team of three, doing advanced training to bring a whole new programming system into the company. I said to my boss, "You can't keep the job for me. The business is popping. It's expanding. You need somebody in that job right away. You can't keep it open for a year. You have to fill it!"

He insisted, "You go and do your thing in the islands. Get it out of your system, and then come back. Your job will be waiting for you."

I guess I never did get it out of my system!

CHAPTER 4

Making the Choice

AT THAT TIME I was dating one of my bosses at work. It was a steady relationship; we had progressed to a point where we were discussing the possibility of marriage. When I shared with him what God had been saying to me, he too said he would wait for me for a year. He wanted me to go to the islands for a year, and then come back and get married.

The more I prayed about this, the more pressure I felt. I did not know exactly what God had for me in my future, but I knew I had a missionary call on my life. Whatever He was calling me to do, I felt that it would be easier and better if I remained single. This was an inner conviction which grew stronger as I prayed.

I felt that it would be easier and better if I remained single.

God gave me a promise. He said, "I will be a Father and a husband to you. As you have given, so will I give to you, and you will never be without. I will take care of you." On top of that, He promised me many spiritual children: "More are the children of the desolate woman than of her who has a husband" (Isaiah 54:1). Because of my conviction and God's assurance to me, I broke off the relationship.

God never forbade me to marry; it was a choice I made. While it was a tough decision, I knew it was the right path for me. I have never regretted my decision not to get married. God has been faithful indeed and has given me much more than I have given up for Him.

A Divine Delay

At this time, I was helping a former AG missionary in his efforts to plant a new church in Arcadia, California. I shared with him what God was saying to me and about my plan to join Sam and Florence in the Marshall Islands. He advised me to contact the Southern California District Council of the AG and tell them how God was leading me.

Up to this point, I had been attending and serving in AG churches but I did not know much about the denominational structure or procedures. I did just what my pastor suggested. I looked up their phone number and called the office to ask for an appointment.

My appointment was with the Missions Director, Thomas Cunningham. (His son Loren Cunningham had founded Youth With A Mission in 1960, just a few years before this.) When I arrived, he was in a meeting with someone else, so I waited in the office area. In walked the Director of Women's Ministry for the District, Florence Beck. She said, "Why don't you come by my office when you are finished; let's talk."

"Sure," I replied. I had no idea what to talk to her about, but I was open to her invitation.

Tom Cunningham was wonderful. He did not know me, but he was so understanding and accepting. He understood that I did not have an official missions appointment, and he knew that I did not have any financial support. Still, he said, "If you feel God has called you, then go ahead." That was a big boost to my faith.

Feeling grateful, I left his office and walked down the hall to find Sister Beck. When I walked into her office, she invited me to sit down. She looked at me with a big smile and asked, "What can I do for you?"

I replied, "I don't know. What do you do?"

Now it was her turn to be shocked, because everyone in the AG knew who Sister Florence Beck was and what she did – everyone, except me! After getting over the shock, she told me what she did and how she helped missionaries get ready to go to the mission field. That day, God brought a mentor into my life. Although she would not have considered what she was doing to be mentoring, she helped me learn about procedures in the AG. But it did not stop there.

As part of my preparation for the islands, I had to undergo a medical examination. The doctors discovered that I had a ruptured hernia. This discovery was made just as I was in the process of resigning from my company. God used this, because my company insurance covered the cost of the surgery and paid me full salary for over four months while I recovered from the effects of the surgery. Those finances were a big help, because by then I had already sold my car and vacated my apartment. It was God's provision!

This medical condition delayed my departure to the Marshall Islands for almost a year. However, it turned out to be a divine arrangement. Upon each visit to the doctor, my medical leave would be extended again and again. During this time I was bunking at Sister Beck's house and sleeping on her couch. When I was well enough to move around, I would hop into her car and accompany her on her road trips. I helped out in whatever way I could. She would ask me to do the preaching when the other missionary did not show up. Soon I learned to be ready, in season and out of season. That year was a year of real growth and learning as I traveled with her. We developed a wonderful friendship that would lead her to come to the Marshall Islands several times, and later to join me in Singapore.

When it was finally time for me to leave for the Marshall Islands, Sister Beck flew from Los Angeles to Hawaii to be with me. There were no commercial flights into the Marshall Islands, so I had to make an official application for a seat on a military plane into Kwajalein, one of the main islands. As they needed time to process my papers and prepare thirty copies of all the necessary documents, this meant more waiting time.

Sister Beck knew some pastors in the islands around Hawaii, so we used that waiting time to travel to these islands and preach in different churches. This was a whole new experience for me. I was introduced not only to some wonderful pastors, but also to new bugs and giant spiders. It was a preview to what island living would be like, but Hawaii was still more modern than what I would soon be experiencing.

Before long the military papers were processed. I found myself waving to Sister Beck out of the small window of the military plane, as she stood beside the runway and the plane began its flight across the Pacific Ocean to the Marshall Islands. I was ready for my island adventure.

The Marshall Islands

The Marshall Islands are an archipelago, or a group of islands, located near the equator in the Pacific Ocean. Geographically, the islands are part of the larger island group of Micronesia. Countries and territories nearby include Guam, Hawaii, and the Philippines.

There were over 24 low-lying coral atolls in the Marshall Islands. An atoll is like the rim of a volcano. Around the rim, sand would accumulate over time and form little islets. There were as many as 1,156 individual islands and islets.

The Marshallese were of Micronesian origin and had migrated from Asia several thousand years ago. A minority had some recent Asian ancestry, mainly Japanese. They spoke Marshallese, which is one of the Malayo-Polynesian languages.

The population then was about 36,000 people, who were spread out over the islands. The most populated islands were Majuro, Ebeye and Kwajalein, which served as the administrative base of the governing authority.

Each atoll had its own king, a local traditional leader. Island life was simple and rustic. There was no formal employment or economic development, except a handful of jobs with the governing authority of the islands.

Militarily, the Marshall Islands were of strategic importance. They had been a German protectorate in the late 1800s, and were captured by Japan in World War I. In the late 1930s, Japan began building air bases on several atolls. The Marshall Islands were in an important geographical position, being the easternmost point in Japan's defensive ring at the beginning of the Second World War.

In World War II, the United States conquered the islands in the Gilbert and Marshall Islands campaign. The Marshall Islands were then consolidated into the Trust Territory of the Pacific Islands governed by the US, along with the other Pacific Islands.

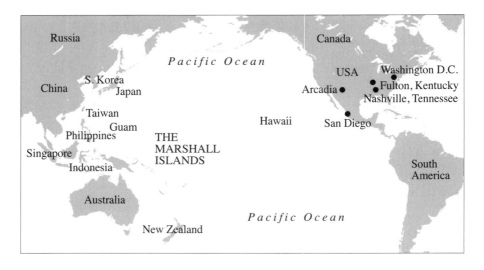

Robinson Crusoe

If I could describe life in the Marshall Islands then in two words, they would be 'Robinson Crusoe.' The year was 1965. The islands were beautiful, but remote and spread out over a vast expanse of ocean. It was a totally rural setting, worlds apart from my life in San Diego or Los Angeles. There were no shopping malls, no beauty parlors, no supermarkets, no electricity, no running water, no modern toilets, and no warm showers.

> *The islands were beautiful, but remote and spread out over a vast expanse of ocean.*

I lived with Sam and Florence Sasser on the island of Majuro. We lived in a village on one end of the island called Laura, some thirty miles from town. There were no proper roads. Going to town meant a two to four-hour trip over coral rocks. That coral track was one-vehicle-wide, and was so bumpy and spiky that our eight-ply jeep tires would wear out in six months.

The town had a little tiny post office that was about eight feet by ten feet. That's it – that was our post office! It only opened when a small propeller seaplane made its weekly trip to the islands, though it didn't always make it. The town had a little short runway that was left over from WW2, full of potholes but still usable. Everyone would hear the plane coming and run to the airfield. Someone would take the old WW2 Jeep and drive up and down the airfield to scare the chickens and pigs off the runway so the plane could land.

If the weather was bad and the plane could not land, the pilots would come back in and fly as low as it could and push the mail bags out of the plane onto the runway. That's when we prayed that no one had sent anything fragile or breakable to us! Then we would wait anxiously for them to sort out the letters. Everyone would be milling around and asking "Do I have mail?"

Another highlight was the supply ship that came, bearing precious cargo of sugar, salt, flour, and rice, and at times, some canned foods. The ship did not come often enough. If it came in twice a year, we were happy, and if it came three times a year, it was fantastic. Toilet paper was another luxury item which the ship delivered. When we did not have toilet paper, we would use leaves. That took some getting used to!

Island living was rustic, to say the least. It was back-to-nature, Survivor-style. God provided for our needs one meal at a time. The boys would go fishing for our meals. The fish they caught would be cooked and served with rice, which we brought from the supply ships.

If we were lucky, the guys would catch turtles. We would turn the turtle on its back to await its purpose, our dinner. If there was a wedding, the islanders would roast a pig. This was reserved for special occasions, as there were not many pigs on the islands!

Tropical fruits were a key feature of our island diet. Coconuts were our go-to source for 'clean water'. Opening coconuts was a tedious task, which the boys did for us. Sometimes the islanders would bless us with papayas or an entire stem of bananas. We would shred green papaya and make a salad out of it. Breadfruit was another common food, which we used as a substitute for potato. We made 'potato salad' with mayonnaise which we would bring back from our trips to Guam or Hawaii. We also cut the breadfruit into small pieces and fried them like chips. We didn't have these everyday; they were special treats.

Out in the islands, there was no such thing as an occupation. The people did not have jobs as we do today. When they needed to eat, they would go fishing. The closest thing to a trade or an export was copra, or the dried meat of the coconut. The locals would collect coconuts, husk them, break them open, take out the hard part of the coconut meat, dry the meat under the sun and pack them into big sacks. They would accumulate these big sacks until the ships came in. When the supply ship came in, they would trade the copra and get sugar, oil, and salt, and other supplies in exchange for it. Copra was valued because coconut oil could be extracted from it.

There was a little hospital on the island of Majuro which didn't have much in it except a few beds, a few nurses, and a doctor with limited training, but it was of some help to the local people. When we fell ill, we would self-medicate with medicines and pills we had brought with us from our rare trips back to the States or Hawaii.

There was another hospital on the island of Kwajalein, which was part of another atoll, but it was only for the Americans working on that island. The U.S. military used the Marshall Islands for missile testing. There were missile tracking stations on Kwajalein and other islands around the atoll. This was a secret operation, so Kwajalein was run like a military base. It was a secure site, and Marshallese or civilians were allowed to work there during the day but they could not stay there overnight.

While the islands were pristine, they were not entirely unspoiled. On some beaches we could see the remains of planes that had been shot down in WW2 – reminders of the military conflict that took place in the 1940s.

Precious Bread

Life in the Marshall Islands was simple, and yet complex, because there was none of the modern infrastructure or conveniences I was accustomed to. At least once a week, the Sassers and I would make the trip into town to get gasoline for our jeep and truck. Remember this was a two to four-hour trip over thirty miles of bumpy coral rocks.

Even in town, there were no bakeries like we know them today. When the supply ship came in with flour, the baker would make bread. He did this without a conventional oven. Instead, he used empty 55-gallon drums which had been cut in half. He buried one half in the ground, leaving *Bread was a real treat for us. It was very precious.* a space underneath to put wood for a fire. He would then cover the drum with the other half. This was how he baked bread!

Whenever we went to town, one of the first things we did was to see if the baker had any bread. If he did, we bought as many loaves as we could before they were all gone. Bread was a real treat for us. It was very precious. After getting everything we needed, my companions and I would jump into the back of the truck, with our bread wrapped in a banana leaf or whatever we could find, to make the journey back to our village. The back of the truck was unsheltered and totally open.

Now the Marshalls get about 365 inches of rain a year. It rained frequently, and heavy thunderstorms were a common occurrence. Often, when we were on the way back to our village with our precious bread, it would rain heavily. Since we had neither umbrellas nor raincoats, we would desperately try to cover the loaves with our bodies, our shirts or anything we could find, to protect the bread from getting wet and soggy. As the rain became heavier, I would begin to sing, "I surrender all, I surrender all... All to Jesus, I surrender, I surrender all."

I learnt then that our commitment to Jesus is never just a one-time commitment. There are situations where, again and again, we must stop and make a fresh commitment to surrender all to Jesus. Funny as it may seem now, surrendering my precious bread as the tropical rain came pelting down was a defining moment for me.

Despite the difficulties, knowing that I was in the will of God became my anchor. I knew that I knew that I knew, that I was right where God wanted me to be. He had promised me that – bread or no bread – "I will never leave you nor forsake you" (Joshua 1:5).

CHAPTER 5

The Stowaway Missionary

THE GOSPEL HAD FIRST COME to the Pacific Islands as a result of missionaries sailing across the Pacific from the Holiness Movement that came into Boston, Massachusetts, which in turn had come from the Keswick revival in Great Britain.

Missionaries set sail on ships called The Morning Star. They first sailed into Hawaii and then made their way across the Pacific into Micronesia. They came with Holiness teachings and the congregational form of meetings and worship. That happened some 100 years prior, but there had been no real ministry or follow-up after that.

When Sam first arrived in the islands, he found small white church buildings, hymnals and Marshallese Bibles which had been translated by the early missionaries, but no understanding of the truths in God's Word. There was form but no life.

Attending church was a cultural thing. Since there was no TV, and only local radio, there was no real entertainment. Church was the islanders' weekly get-together. The men would put on their white pants and the women would

Attending church was a cultural thing.

57

wear white dresses. They would sing hymns, someone would say something, then they would sing another hymn and go home. It was mostly the older people who attended church.

The Sassers and I set out to reach the younger generation and, through them, their parents. We wanted them to have a personal encounter with God. Our teaching was different; it was about a true dynamic encounter with God that would change our lives. That meant no more lying, cheating, or sleeping around. We wanted to raise up a generation of young people who would be transformed and go out and plant churches, as well as touch existing believers so they would want that life-changing power. We decided that we would do this through a Bible school, teaching young people the Word of God, and training them to reach the other islands.

Prior to my arrival, Sam had spent a couple of years in the islands, while Florence and the children had stayed in Hawaii. Now she was joining him for the first time, and the three of us became the team that would pioneer the work. It was an intentional effort to evangelize the islands, not just to bring them the Gospel but the full Gospel, with the infilling and power of the Holy Spirit.

Learning the Language

We had a vision to reach the islands, but it would remain a dream without the hard work of learning the language. In the beginning, we all needed to have interpreters for everything we did. But as more missionaries or volunteers came, it was impossible to have enough interpreters. This pushed us to learn the language, since most of the islanders did not speak English. There were no textbooks or schools for learning Marshallese, so I faced a steep learning curve. I had no training in linguistics, nor had I learned a foreign language from scratch before, so I devised my own system.

Holding up different objects, one at a time, I would ask the islanders to name them for me in their language. Then I would write the word down, and go on to the next object. After gathering a few words, I would then try to string the words together to make a sentence. That was when the fun began! My mispronunciation of the words and the way I put the words together would cause much laughter and merriment. Naturally, I received many corrections from the islanders, but I took it all in good humor. Missionaries have to learn to laugh at themselves.

Fresh Fire

Our students were young adults in their late teens and early twenties. After teaching them, we would take them out on field trips to plant churches on the other islands. My first field trip away from Majuro was special. The Sassers and I, along with a group of students from our school, had loaded ourselves and food into boats with outboard motors. Then we headed for the other islands.

On these islands, the churches where we met and the structures we slept under were all made from coconut palm branches. We depended on kerosene lanterns for light. We preached and then took a break to eat and fellowship with the people. Then we gathered again to study the Word of God and answer questions the people had about God and the Bible.

That night, there was a special presence of God. The study time went late into the night, until our lanterns began to run out of kerosene. The leaders sent one of the young men back to the area where the houses were located, to find some extra kerosene for our lamps. While he was gone, one lamp after another went out. Soon it was dark inside the church.

Until then, no one in the islands had been baptized in the Holy Spirit with speaking in other tongues. As we taught them God's Word and taught on the Holy Spirit, we did not raise our hands in worship nor speak aloud in tongues, because we did not want them to simply mimic us. We were praying for them to have a divine encounter that would cause them to have a spontaneous response to the Holy Spirit. It began that night.

In the darkness, as we kept teaching and praying, and then singing in worship, the Holy Spirit began to touch different ones and they began to speak in tongues. This was a new experience for them, but in the darkness, they became bold in releasing their new prayer language.

> *In the darkness, they became bold in releasing their new prayer language.*

As the young man was returning with the kerosene, he became afraid. He said, "I saw flashes of fire above where the church was located, and was frightened." He ran towards the church wanting to help put out the fire, only to discover that the only fire was in the people, not the building. That night, everyone on that island was filled with the Holy Spirit. This was the beginning of the revival. We rejoiced in God's breakthrough and were thankful that our kerosene ran out, because in the dark, their inhibitions and shyness were overcome.

On another occasion, on the island of Majuro, the worship was so powerful that people from some distance away came running to help put out the fire they saw above our location. They arrived only to discover that there was no physical fire – it was the fire of God. Those were awesome years. We witnessed God pouring out His Spirit on "all flesh," just as He did in Acts 2.

A New Generation

We named our school Calvary Bible Institute (CBI). Our students came from various islands and stayed with us for two to three years. We would teach them the Word and take them out on ministry trips to the other islands. In this way, we mentored them and equipped them with practical ministry skills. Our goal was that by the time they graduated, they would be ready to be placed on various islands to evangelize and pastor. Some would go back to their home islands to minister.

Besides teaching the Bible, we also included other subjects, so the students would have a well-rounded education. One of these subjects was music, because singing was a big thing in their culture. Oh, how the islanders loved to sing! They had dance movements to go along with their songs. It was not the Hawaiian hula, but similar in some ways.

Running a residential school was hard work. It was 24/7 work; we needed to teach, counsel students, and maintain some discipline and order. But through it all, God moved powerfully. Most of the students were touched by God and filled with a sense of purpose and power. This was very different from the islander mindset they had in the beginning, which tended to be laid-back, just drifting through life. Remember, prior to this there had been no jobs or economic opportunities. Whenever they wanted to eat, they went fishing. Whenever they felt like doing so, they would gather coconuts to make copra, but there was no hurry to do so, as they only needed to have something a few times a year, for when the ship would come.

There were already a couple of schools in the islands, but people came to view ours as a better option for education. Our school CBI was the only Christian school and the only school providing training for ministry. We teachers were all young, energized and doing something which no one else was doing, so this attracted the young people.

Because the Marshalls were a Trust Territory of the U.S., the government would give free rice to the schools, including ours. The rice came in 50-pound bags. Each school received its own allotment, which was delivered by the supply ship. These gifts of rice were critical for us to be able to feed the students. God was our real Source, but He used the government to deliver the rice we needed!

Building from Scratch

Most of the islanders lived in huts or shelters made from coconut leaves or pieces of driftwood. There were few concrete buildings like what we have in our urban areas. Our first house had been rented to us by the queen of the island. The house had a room for Sam and Florence, one for their children and a small room for me. We also had a small kitchen. The middle room, which was the entrance way into the house, became the sleeping area for the girls. They slept on the floor on mats. The first boys who joined our school slept in a small room just down the road.

Sam was able to create an extension at the back of the house. This served as our eating area and doubled up as our classroom at night. As the number of students increased, we faced great constraints in our space. We knew we needed a bigger and more permanent space, but there were no existing buildings which we could rent or move into. If we wanted a new space, we would have to build it from scratch.

If we wanted a new space, we would have to build it from scratch.

We wanted to preach the Gospel, teach the Bible, and train Spirit-filled leaders. Therefore we had to build physical structures where we could gather and instruct believers, away from the relentless sun and safe from the heavy tropical thunderstorms. The problem was, there were no building materials on the islands! There were no building blocks anywhere on the island. So when the supply ship arrived, we would buy cement, which we then used to make cinder or concrete blocks. These were hollow on the inside.

Sam bought several metal frames as moulds to shape the blocks. The boys would dig and bring in the sand from the beach. We would mix the sand with the cement and water, and push the mixture down into the metal mold. To hammer the cement mix inside the mould, we used the strong part of the coconut leaf (the part that attaches to the tree). We would pound the mixture and pellet it until it was densely packed, before removing it from the form and leaving it to dry under the sun. One by one, the blocks were made. It was painstaking work, all done by hand without any modern machines or appliances.

When there were enough blocks, we began to lay them together to build the walls. Our first priority was to build a dormitory for the boys. Even then, we only built the wall up to half the usual height. The top half would be a screen that kept out flies, with cloth used to provide some privacy. The roof was made of corrugated tin, which made a loud noise whenever it rained. We poured cement on the ground to form a concrete floor.

When we completed the girls' and boys' dormitories, we shipped in double-decker beds for the students. Up to this point, they had been sleeping on mats on the floor. Then we began work on the main buildings. Our next priority was to build some classrooms, to get the students off our back porch and into a better learning environment. This allowed us to ship in some blackboards, tables and chairs.

This experience served as a crash course in construction for me, for in a few years, I would have to build a house and a church on the island of Ebeye.

The Stowaway Missionary

I was on a journey of faith. I had left California without any formal support whatsoever, trusting God entirely to supply all my needs. I needed finances for my living expenses on the field, and for my travel to the Marshall Islands and back as needed. I was not sponsored or supported by a church back home. Only one pastor of a small pioneering church said that they would send me fifty dollars a month, if they could. (I guess in the end they couldn't, because I never did receive anything!)

After I had been in the Marshall Islands for almost a year, the AG national office in Springfield, Missouri, discovered that I was on the mission field serving God without an official missions appointment. This is how it happened. The regional director, Maynard Ketchem, came through the Marshalls to see how Sam and Florence were doing as new missionaries. That's when he discovered me. I was not on their radar. They had not known I was there!

I explained that I had met with the District Missions Director. I had taken the necessary test and was granted License Credentials with the Southern California District Council of the Assemblies of God.

After my explanation, he quickly concluded that I had not gone through the proper system, because missionaries going out had to be appointed by the Foreign Missions Division of the National Office. (For this reason, my friends would later call me a 'back door' missionary, because I had not gone through the traditional route.) He insisted that I make the journey to Springfield, go through the process and apply for official appointment.

So I dutifully made the journey to Springfield to begin the process. But before the process was completed, I received an urgent message from Sam. There was an emergency in the islands, and he needed me to return immediately.

I informed Springfield of this news. They responded, "But you cannot go now, because you do not have any money for your budget." They wanted me to complete the process and speak in different churches to raise funds, so I could return to the islands with a budget to support me and the work I was doing.

I insisted, "But Sam says there is an emergency."

Finally they said, "It is up to you. If you go, you will have no money."

Immediately I replied, "That's not a problem. God will take care of me."

I made arrangements and returned to the islands as soon as I could. Then in 1969, I returned to Springfield to complete the proper process. By then I had already been out in the islands for four years.

Blissfully Ignorant

I did not have a clue what the proper process entailed. No one had explained it to me, probably because they assumed I already knew. Hence I did not know what I didn't know! This resulted in a few amusing incidents which betrayed my complete lack of knowledge with regard to the AG's organizational procedures.

For instance, I knew all missionaries had prayer cards that were printed and given out in churches so people could pray for them. I had seen what those cards looked like, and what information was to be printed on them. I got my picture taken and quickly placed an order for my prayer cards, so I would be all ready when they called me for the official interview. I wanted to be prepared!

All aspiring missionaries were required to attend the School of Missions, so I attended the two-week course along with other missionary candidates. They then called each of us for an official interview, after which they would either approve or reject our appointment as missionaries.

Like everyone else, I sat outside the interview room waiting for my turn. When my name was called, I went in, not knowing what to expect. I looked around, and they were all men in black suits and ties. Feeling a little uneasy, I quickly pulled out my prayer cards and distributed them before sitting down. They all sat quietly, instead of asking me questions. Finally one of them spoke up, "So, how will you handle being single on the field?"

I responded, "Fine, but do you have someone in mind?"

They all laughed. That broke the ice, and before long, we shook hands and I left the room. Then I sat outside waiting for the 'verdict'. While waiting, I noticed that the other candidates were nervous as they waited for their turn. Trying to be friendly and wanting to help relieve their tension, I thought, "Oh, maybe I'll give them my prayer card."

As I was distributing it, suddenly one of the candidates blurted out, "But you can't do this!"

"Do what?" I asked.

She snapped, "You are not supposed to print your prayer card until *after* you have been approved – and you aren't approved yet!"

Just then, the door opened. I was motioned in and told that I was now an approved AG missionary. When I walked back into the waiting area, I announced, "I've just been approved!"

I left with a smile, yet well aware that I had just made another procedural boo-boo in the process.

CHAPTER 6

Living Dangerously

AFTER MY RETURN, we spent a lot more time traveling to the other islands. One time we were preparing to make a journey to the Arno Islands. Arno was just a couple of hours across the ocean from Majuro – if we took the short cut. This was known locally as 'shooting the pass.' If we did not take this shortcut, we would have to sail across the lagoon and around the atoll to get to our destination, taking an additional two hours.

Shooting the pass was a tricky maneuver. There was a narrow opening in the reef. During high tide, there would be tidal waters high enough to fill the opening, so that a boat could get through and move out into the open ocean, to make the journey across the waves to Arno. It was dangerous to attempt, but people would do it to save fuel and time.

We packed for the trip and boarded the truck which would transport all of us – Sam, Florence, their two children, a helper, some students and myself – to a section of the island called Rita, where the pass was located. We spent the night there waiting for the morning tide to be just right.

During the late evening, we heard a big commotion and learned that a man had died attempting to shoot the pass. He missed the wave and his boat crashed on the rocks. We also learned why he was hurrying to get back to Arno. He had made the journey from Arno to Majuro earlier that day to buy material for a wedding dress for his bride-to-be. Knowing that we were coming and that there would be an ordained minister to perform the wedding, he wanted her to have a new dress for the occasion. Tragically, he died trying to get back home the quick way.

This made me wonder, should we attempt to shoot the pass when we had two boats full of people and things? The next morning, the boats were loaded. There we were in the boats, watching and counting the waves to see when the big wave would come. I watched carefully because I wanted to learn how to tell if it was the right one.

Suddenly the man on the engine, gunned the motor full force, and we ran right into the incoming wave. We went up, over, and then we were out on the other side. We waited as the other boat made their attempt to shoot the pass. Again I watched carefully, because we would need to repeat this same process, in reverse, to get back home.

We had a busy week of ministry, which involved doing everything from marrying couples and dedicating babies, to raising offerings for their missions outreach. Offerings in this context were not money, by the way. The people would bring copra (dried coconut meat), pigs, chickens, fish and bananas. They gave whatever they had, because they had no money.

There were no modern toilets in Arno. We would dig a deep hole behind the house, and build a wooden seat over the hole. Panels of woven coconut leaves provided for privacy and modesty.

It was here in Arno that I was introduced to a new way of taking a bath and washing my hair. Simple daily cleaning rituals like brushing my teeth, washing my face, or taking a bath meant drawing water from a well. I learnt to take a complete bath out of one bucket of water. First, I started by brushing my teeth, and then washed my face. After that, I had to choose whether to wash my hair or my body first. Then I would pick up my bucket and pour any remaining water over myself, from head to toe.

All of this had to be done while I squatted down low behind a wall made from coconut leaves. There was no door! I had to try and cover the opening in some safe way, because if I stood up, I risked exposing myself to a passerby. Oh, how I missed having a proper hot shower!

A Close Call

The time came for us to return to our home island. The people blessed us with many things. Besides the things we had brought with us, there was now a pig, some chickens and many bunches of bananas on board! With songs and prayers, we bade farewell to the people and headed home. When we reached the opening, we idled our engines to watch and count the waves to see when we could shoot the pass to get into the lagoon, so we could transfer to our truck to get home.

Before long, the boat that Sam's family was in revved its engine. Off they went, trying to catch the wave to ride over the rocks. We watched in horror as they missed the wave. The boat flipped.

I shouted to our boatman, "Hit it, hit it! Get the engine going so we can go help them."

I grabbed onto the rope on the bow of our boat, still shouting, "Go, go!" We caught the wave and began rising above where their boat had flipped over. As our boat went pass theirs, I dove into the water and began swimming around, calling their names.

Thankfully, we found Sam, Florence and their daughter Renee, but we could not find their son Terry. We would dive in again and again, searching in the water. Then we found him right under the capsized boat! Their island helper had been holding him on her lap in the boat. When the boat flipped over, she had him in her arms. When she suddenly found herself in the water, she kicked around and her foot found a small high rock. She had balanced herself and held Terry up above her head, so he was in an air pocket under the upside-down boat.

It was a miracle that we found them before the air had run out. The pig and the chickens drowned, but all the people made it safely to shore.

This Is for That

The work of God in the Marshall Islands continued to grow, and there came another opportunity for me to return to the States to minister in churches and raise the money needed for the ministry. When I landed in Los Angeles, a friend met me at the airport to tell me that someone had given me an old car so I could travel from state to state, to preach among the churches.

I remember looking at the car and thinking, "This car will not get me across the street, much less across the whole USA, from the Pacific Ocean to the Atlantic Ocean!" The car burnt oil like water, the windows could not move up and down, the air-conditioning did not work – and these were just a few of its problems.

Instead of driving, I got on the plane and flew to Detroit and Flint, Michigan. Now God was about to teach me a lesson in faith and trusting Him. After my services in Michigan, one of the men in the church said he could get me a new car at a cheaper price because he was an employee at the factory.

I thought, "Wow, that is sure better than the old car waiting for me in California. Plus, I can get a car loan immediately from the AG Credit Union!" I called and made arrangements with the credit union. In just two days, I was ready to make the down payment on the car.

Then God dealt with me and said, "No."

Confused, I sent the check back to the Credit Union. I still had to pay them interest on the loan, even though I had not used it. Painful lesson.

I flew back to California and picked up the old car. "Well, God, you said to drive this thing across the whole USA, so here we go!" It was a miracle of miracles. That car did not burn oil on the trip. It made the trip wonderfully, across the desert and through the snow in the mountains. It looked horrible, but it drove great!

On the second night of missions meetings, while I was driving to the church service, I stopped at a red light. At that red light, the car bucked, sputtered, and went out with a big bang. I called the pastor I was preaching for, and he sent someone to bring me to the church. They also sent my old car to the workshop. The car mechanic told me, "You can forget about repairing this car, it is just impossible."

I could not understand what was happening, and began to argue with God. "Okay God, what is this? You got me all the way across the USA and now I have no way to travel to the other cities to preach. I could have bought a new car back in Michigan! Why did You tell me not to buy that car?" By now I was even more confused.

After that service, I stayed with the pastor and his wife. They knew I needed to go to a nearby city to speak at another church, so they loaned me their car for the trip. Their car was a big Lincoln Continental – a huge luxury car that had a stereo with speakers all round, and seats that could move back and forth. Most cars in those days had no fancy gadgets, so this was a big deal.

After the service in the nearby city, I was driving back to their home when I heard the Lord say, "*And this is your car.*"

> *I heard the Lord say, "And this is your car."*

This shocked me. I told God, "No, I don't need this big fancy car. I just need four wheels and a motor to get me safely where I need to go." I was also worried about what others would think if I, a missionary, drove up in this big car to a small church to preach and take a missions offering. They would probably think that I was well-to-do and not in need of an offering.

God said, "*This is because you were faithful then.*" I knew what He was referring to. He was talking about my tithing and my missions giving, which had all been above 'normal.' Now He was 'repaying' me. He was ensuring that I was taken care of, His way.

True enough, the next morning over breakfast, the pastor and his wife said, "My wife and I were talking last night, and we decided that we will give you the car."

"Oh no, no... I can't accept that," I protested.

"Well, we've been thinking about getting another car anyway," they said. Upon their insistence, I finally accepted God's miraculous provision with gratitude. That car drove wonderfully on those long trips on the interstate highways and did not give me any problems at all. It was truly God's provision.

My fears turned out to be unfounded. While driving that car, I received more in offerings than before. God taught me a lesson in faith and showed me that He could take care of people's mindsets. I need not have worried about what they would think.

After three months in the States, the time came for me to return to the islands. My cousin asked me, "What will you do with that car? I'll buy it from you." I sold the car to him for a whopping three thousand dollars, which was a big sum in those days. This provided some cash to support the work I did in the islands. Over and over I have observed the truth of Hudson Taylor's adage: "God's work, done in God's way, will never lack God's supply."

First Hot Shower

I began to pack for my journey back to the islands. Since there was no commercial airline serving the Marshall Islands, I booked a freighter ship out of San Francisco. It would be just me and a ship full of merchant sailors. When I arrived at the docks, I found out that the ship had been delayed because they needed more time to load the cargo. I asked how long the delay would be. With that information, I asked my friends who had come to see me off to drive me to the nearest hardware store. I was ready to solve my shower problem!

I decided I would build my own hot water system. When I went into the hardware store and told them that I needed materials for a shower, they peppered me with all sorts of questions: What size are your pipes? What is the distance from the water source to the shower? They had so many questions, and I had no answers.

With a basket in hand, we went up and down the aisles where there were open bins containing the various sizes of joints, corner joints and connectors. Reaching into each bin, I pulled out a handful of one size, and a handful of the next size. Since I needed pipes but did not know what the correct size would be, I bought 150 feet of three different sizes, as well as a handful of everything I thought I would need: a shower head, a tap, a soap tray, and the glue that would stick the pipes together.

While I was at it, I figured that if I could build a shower system, I could build a kitchen sink to wash dishes in too, so I picked out the necessary components for that as well. By the time we finished shopping, it was almost midnight. All these things were packed and loaded onto the freighter, with time to spare.

The journey by sea took a little over three weeks. During this trip I asked the radio officer to teach me Morse code in case I needed to use it sometime. We first off-loaded everything at Kwajalein and then loaded it onto a local-sized boat to ship it on down to Majuro. I now faced the task of putting all these things together. Could we pull it off? If so, it would be the first shower anywhere on the islands.

With help from the other missionaries, I assembled the pipes, shower and kitchen sink. We built a huge tower beside my little house, and mounted the big water tank on top of the tower. Then the students formed a bucket brigade. Someone would draw water from the well and pass the bucket to the next person, who would pass it on down the human chain. Each pail made the journey out from the well, across the yard, up the ladder, and into the water tank.

Now all we needed was for the sun to shine! The sun warmed the water, so at about three in the afternoon I was able to have a nice warm shower in my bathroom. Soon, every afternoon, the other missionaries would come knocking on my door, bath towels in hand, asking if they, too, could have a hot shower! It was a good thing I had a big tank.

By faith, I believed that it could be done. If Robinson Crusoe could do it, why couldn't I?

If Robinson Crusoe could do it, why couldn't I?

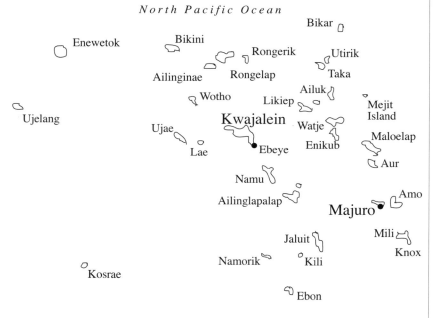

THE MARSHALL ISLANDS

North Pacific Ocean

Bikar

Enewetok

Bikini

Rongerik

Utirik

Ailinginae   Rongelap   Taka

Ujelang

Wotho   Ailuk

Likiep   Mejit Island

Kwajalein   Watje

Ujae   Maloelap

Lae   Ebeye   Enikub

Aur

Namu

Ailinglapalap   Amo

Majuro

Mili

Jaluit   Knox

Namorik   Kili

Kosrae

Ebon

The atolls of the Marshall Islands. Each atoll is a ring-shaped coral reef or coral rim that encircles a lagoon partially or completely.

CHAPTER 7

Island Hopping

As GOD MOVED, the revival grew. More people came to know the Lord and were filled with the Holy Spirit and with power. As the work grew, the number of students we had increased to 325 at one point.

Our school facilities were used on Sundays for church. Believing for expansion, we built a hall that could accommodate up to a thousand people. It was no fancy auditorium; people sat on benches that we made, and we would just cram everybody in. Unlike the house we built which had only half-height walls, this church hall had full-height walls, that came up to the roof, with frames inserted for windows.

Every two years, during the school break, we would plan for a conference. This was a time when we would invite the other islanders to join us at our missions base on the island of Majuro. These were powerful times of encountering God.

We could only plan for conferences once every two years because the schedule of the ship going from island to island was not regular. It was a challenge to travel from one island to another. The participants depended on the ship for transport. Because of the erratic schedule, some of them would arrive a month before the conference. Others needed to stay on for a few months after the conference before they could catch a passing ship to get back home to their own island. Can you imagine the major transport and logistical challenges we faced?

However, the conference was a major highlight for the islanders. They planned ahead, looked forward with anticipation, and came with great expectancy. To accommodate everyone, we would convert our classrooms into sleeping and living areas for the people. We also had to enlarge our cooking area so that we could cook enough food to feed everyone. Yes, that meant the guys needed to catch more fish each day.

Such gatherings were a very colorful and lively time. Besides the preaching and prayer times, there was lots of singing. Because singing was such a big part of their culture, to be able to write the best songs and outsing the others was a big deal. Each island had their own uniform. They would sew matching clothes – dresses for the women and shirts for the men – using the same material. They wrote their own songs and presented them during the conference. We had great fun! It was a friendly competition and a great way to celebrate their island culture.

More Hands on Deck

Whenever we had a conference, we would invite speakers from the States to be our speakers. It was a highlight for us to host these special guests. As female missionaries, we wore the islanders' muumuu dress everyday, but when we had these special occasions, we would put on Western dress and wear proper shoes instead of flip-flops.

Wayne and Judy Cagle visited us in 1968 when we had such a conference, along with Paul and Leta Bruton, leaders from the Southern California Assemblies of God Youth Department. Judy was the daughter of Pastor Emil Balliet, who had been my very first pastor in San Diego. When they saw hundreds of young people committing their lives to Christ and being filled with the Spirit, they felt led to join us in our work. They eventually arrived to live in the Marshalls in 1970.

Linfield Crowder, an evangelist from Idaho, would make trips in and out of the islands. He would come and preach for us, but he was also a handyman. Many times after his meetings, he would stay for several weeks to help in other ways. He was a great help to the work of God.

Others came but did not last very long in the islands. Some stayed for a year, some bailed out in less than a year. They could not take the rustic living! We would try to prepare incoming missionaries for the living conditions, but the reality hit them hard only after they arrived.

The reality hit them hard only after they arrived.

Loneliness is something everyone must deal with on the mission field. Even the missionaries who were there with their families felt homesick because they missed their loved ones back in the States. However, loneliness can be especially acute for the single missionary who is far from home, alone. It can get lonesome, especially when one sees other missionaries on the field enjoying their families. Therefore, singles must be prepared for loneliness and make a conscious effort to understand and manage it.

My strategy for managing loneliness was to stay focused and fully occupied on the assignment before me. My time was spent in planning, praying, preparing, and dreaming of how to overcome the spiritual challenges we faced. I immersed myself in the myriad of responsibilities. My schedule was more than filled with plenty of things to do. I was too busy to be caught up in any negative thoughts or emotions.

In this way, I did not feel excluded or depressed. I also developed good social relationships with the local people I worked with. This minimized the bouts of loneliness I experienced.

Some single missionaries were lonely because they desired to get married, and had their eyes on every single man who came along. This, however, was a settled issue for me. I also had the advantage of age and maturity, as I was older than most of the other single female missionaries.

There is an aspect of loneliness, however, that comes with the turf of being a leader. Later in life, as a senior pastor, I did experience the reality of the saying, "It is lonely at the top." I could not pour out my heart to just anyone, and there were very few people with whom I could share, who would understand the issues involved. I did what the old song says: "Take it to the Lord in prayer."

Special Guests

One year, our special speaker was Pastor Ron Prinzing and his wife from my home church back in the States, along with a couple of others.

All of our water on the island was brackish; it had a strong salty taste to it. Just before lunch, I prepared a big container filled with this water and wanted to help change the taste for them to something more pleasant. I poured in my precious packets of Kool-aid, which I had shipped out in my barrels along with other things and saved for a special occasion like this. This was a powder which dissolved in water to make flavored drinks.

I had also brought Purex, a brand of chlorine bleach. It was used to clean dirty clothes, but I had heard that if you put Purex into water, it would kill the germs and make the water safer to drink. Wanting to protect my pastor and guests from any germs, I poured a generous amount of Purex into the water and stirred it together with the flavored powder, so they would have a refreshing drink waiting for them when the conference session ended at lunch time.

When they arrived, I poured the drinks for everyone. Suddenly, all of them started to choke, cough and spit out their drinks. "What is this?", they sputtered. I learned that day that Purex was to be used sparingly. I had dumped in way too much bleach. It was an embarrassing experience. I had to throw out the special drink and start over.

Establishing National Leaders

After we had ministered together for about five years, Sam and Florence felt led to move to Hawaii to pastor and minister there. I was then working with the national leaders to officially establish the Assemblies of God of Micronesia. To begin, we needed a constitution not only in English but in Marshallese. We also needed to elect national leaders. We wanted to have only Marshallese as executives. We wanted this to be instituted from the very beginning, so that it would be owned and led by the locals themselves and not the missionaries.

They in turn elected me to be their advisor. I worked with them to help them learn what denominational leaders do to serve all the churches. This experience would prove to be invaluable as I would later be asked to help the General Councils of Singapore and Malaysia revise and update their constitutions.

Moving to Ebeye

Another transition in my ministry occurred when David and Sandra Duncan came to the islands to serve with us. Their coming allowed me to be released from my work at the school. I then moved to Ebeye, the second largest island in the Marshalls at that time. A growing group of believers was already meeting on Ebeye, and there was great potential for God to sweep the island with His power and glory.

The believers lacked a full-time pastor and an adequate meeting place. Their building was a small wooden structure that extended from solid ground on stilts, which stood in the waters of the lagoon.

My mandate was to build a missions base comprising a house for missionaries and a church building. At first, I rented a small hut while I approached the king with a request to give us some land for both a house and a church. It was a long-drawn process of discussions, meetings and negotiations about where these two structures could be built. Finally, he gave us his approval. We arranged for a grand ceremony to honor him as he came to sign the papers and present his gift to us. Naturally, it was a huge celebration.

Knowing that I needed help with this project, I contacted a retired engineer whom I knew in California and asked if he could come out to help with the construction of the house. He came to the islands and brought several teams of men.

Over a period of a few months, they constructed a house for me. The result was amazing: What they built actually looked like a real house! It was a two-story building with a living room, office, kitchen and a huge eating area downstairs, plus four bedrooms and two large bathrooms upstairs. There was even running water, showers and electric lights. Then the guys surprised me by doing the impossible. They brought out a garbage disposal system and installed it into the kitchen sink –

What they built actually looked like a real house!

84

the first and only one of its kind in the Marshall Islands. Boy, what a blessing that was!

They also built a large veranda that extended the dining area out over the water, such that we had the gentle waves from the lagoon washing up under the veranda 24/7, which created a very soothing sound.

While these men were building the house, they needed to eat. I ended up making endless trips to Kwajalein to buy food, load it onto the boat, and get it back to Ebeye. Then I had the challenge of what to cook for a team of hungry men – three times a day!

On one trip, a couple of their wives came along to help. I was thrilled because I needed a quick lesson on what to cook and how to cook for so many hungry men at a time. Those women were life savers! I learned quickly before they left me alone to do the job.

When I wasn't buying food or cooking, I learned to hang sheetrock. Even though the plasterboard sheets were very heavy, by God's grace I was able to get them up and nailed into place. I was learning a lot about construction and building, the hard hands-on way.

After the house was built, I had the task of moving things from Majuro to Ebeye and establishing our base there. I made a quick trip to California to buy some real furniture, but furniture that would fit in the islands. After these things arrived, we had a big dedication service and invited the king back to see the results of his gift. He was pleased.

It was around this time that Iris Brown from Panama City, Florida joined me as a co-laborer in the work. What a blessing she was! She was a powerful Bible teacher and prayer warrior. She came at just the right time and was a great joy to work and serve with.

All in Three Days

Among the different teams that came out to help us with the construction work, there was one man who felt called to return and continue helping us. Chris Bangert was a retired carpenter, and very experienced in many areas of construction. Soon his wife joined him, and both of them were such a blessing to the work.

One day Chris came to me with an idea. He said, "I think we can create a prefabricated church, load it on our 40-foot missions boat and transport it to one of the outer islands that needs a church building. This will enable us to erect a church anywhere we want, in just three days."

I studied over his proposal and decided it was a solid plan. I told him, "Get all the materials ready. I will arrange for the captain of our boat to prepare everything for sailing." I then consulted with our local leadership on which island we should go to, to build this first prefab church. We recruited some students to go with us. There was a young American guy then serving his internship with us, so he came along as well.

There was much excitement when we arrived on the island. While the others unloaded all the materials that we had brought, I met with the leaders of the island and explained the plan to them. I said, "We need all of your help. Where do we locate the church? We need permission from the owner of the land."

The plan was for an A-frame church, with the roofing coming low to the ground all round. That would allow air to circulate inside, while also preventing rain from pouring inside during heavy rainfall.

Our plan was to complete the building in three days. To achieve this, we needed to mobilize the women to bring sand to the site, so we could mix it with the cement in order to build the 'footings' for each of the beams. We would need some of the other women to cook our meals. The men would do the mixing and assist in building the frames for the footings.

After discussing our plans, we had a time of preaching the Word and prayer before resting for the night. We slept on mats, on the floor in the huts of the local people, who welcomed us graciously.

The next morning, everyone gathered at the location for the new church. We sang, worshipped, and prayed as we dedicated the project to the Lord. Work began. In the evening we stopped for dinner. After dinner we would have a service on the spot where the church was being built.

Every night we saw visible progress. On the first night, there were cement footings all around, so the people sat on mats as I stood to preach. The area was dotted with kerosene lanterns which provided the lighting. The second night, we had beams erected all around on the footings, and I preached from the small platform they had built. They even had a pulpit too. Best of all, they were able to connect a small generator, so we had one light bulb above the pulpit.

By the third night, the roof was set in place, the back of the church was closed in and the front door of the church was installed. Everyone rejoiced and we had a celebration service that night. We were scheduled to sail back to Majuro the next day.

Just One Problem

The next morning, the local leaders came to me. One thing was missing: they wanted to paint a cross over the front door of the new church. Oh boy, we had missed planning for that! The problem was,

I did not have any paint on hand. However, near the end of the island, there was an old shed where they would dump things left behind by the supply ships. I went down and began to rummage through the shed to see if I might be able to find some old paint.

As I worked my way through the pile of old discarded ropes, rusty chains and wooden panels, I suddenly felt something jump onto my arm. I looked down and saw that a scorpion had landed on my arm.

I gasped, thinking, "What should I do?" Then I remembered the Apostle Paul. When he was shipwrecked on the island of Malta, a scorpion had landed on his arm. He shook it off into the fire. However, I was inside an old shed, and there was no fire! Quickly, I began to shout "In the name of Jesus!" and I shook my arm. The scorpion went flying off somewhere. Praise the Lord, I was unharmed.

I still needed the paint. Again I asked God to show me, to help me find some paint, because to have that painted cross was so important to the islanders. Looking under another pile, I spotted a little paint can. It was old, and paint had spilled out over the edges and hardened. I grabbed the can of paint and quickly ran out of the shed. I found something to pry it open. There was a hardened layer on top but underneath, there was still a little paint – enough to get a cross painted over the door of the church.

God was with me and He kept me from harm, just as He had promised. He was also mindful of the desires of those islanders; they got their cross painted over the door. God is so good.

CHAPTER 8

More Miracles

EBEYE WAS A TWENTY-MINUTE BOAT RIDE away from the main island of
Kwajalein, where the American government personnel lived. Naturally,
Kwajalein had amenities which the other islands did not enjoy. As
missionaries, we were allowed to buy food at the supply store there –
a huge blessing for us. It was our only source for vegetables, meats,
and other groceries. Having this privilege, I regularly made trips to
Kwajalein to shop for food, load it on the boat and make the journey
back to Ebeye.

When all the other missionaries would come from Majuro to visit
me, I would cook some Western food for everyone. Naturally, my
house became everyone's favorite place for a few days of escape and
rest. It almost became a maternity ward for the birth of Wayne and
Judy Cagle's first baby, but that is another story for another time.

Living on Ebeye, my days now took on a different flavor: No more
teaching in the Bible school, and no more student problems to solve.
My focus shifted. I preached in the Ebeye church, conducted Bible
studies on Kwajalein, and recorded our radio broadcast for the Majuro
radio station. I also became the official photographer for the school

yearbook and other events. However, when it came to our ministry to the outer islands, I would return to Majuro, because all the boats left from there.

At first, we did not have our own boat. We had to book passage on the island boats, and work within their schedule. The boats did not have cabins as you would expect. We sat, ate, and slept on the open deck on mats under a million stars. Down each side of our space on the deck were drums filled with diesel fuel, so the smell was strong. These trips were not the easiest.

Later, we were able to have our own 40-foot boat built in Hong Kong. We then hired a Christian captain in Hong Kong to undertake the whole journey in Majuro to deliver the boat to us. His island hopping across the Pacific was a real adventure.

David Thompson and his wife Vivian came from Hawaii to serve as the captain of our new boat. Sam, David and I undertook trips to the islands in the other atolls. Having our own boat gave us greater freedom and flexibility. We could travel further, bring more students with us to evangelize other islands, and set our own schedule. Later Brother Thompson would also take students out on his own, without us, thus expanding our outreach.

I remember one trip I made with Brother Thompson. Although he knew navigation, the islanders had insisted that we take an old Marshallese seaman along with us as a navigator. The seaman's method of navigating was to sit with his eyes closed on top of the cabin of the boat. He would just 'feel' the waves and ocean current, and based on this intuitive method, he would tell us which direction to go. That is the method the islanders used for smaller canoes that moved much slower. Now that we had a bigger and faster boat, I did not feel comfortable relying on this traditional method alone. Since it was not a canoe, if we strayed off-course and ran out of fuel, we would be adrift in the middle of the ocean, with no way to get back to shore.

So I asked Brother Thompson to teach me how to navigate. I wanted to ensure that we would arrive at our intended destination and not end up thousands of miles out in the open ocean. I knew he was intimidated by the 'authority' they had put on board, but I wasn't. If, between us, we felt that we should alter the commands from our local navigator, I would make necessary adjustments without offending the man on top of the cabin.

Flight Frenzy

One of the longest trips that Brother Thompson and the students ever made with our boat was to sail from Majuro all the way to the Gilbert Islands for an evangelistic outreach. As leader of the team, I needed to get there ahead of the team to make sure all the arrangements were made before they arrived. By this time the airline had started a new flight path that would island hop, connecting several island groups together for the first time. So I flew on a small plane down to the Gilbert Islands via the island of Nauru.

Nauru was a very small island that hosted hundreds of workers from Hong Kong who came there by the boatloads to work in the phosphate mines. There were also Britons and Australians there who ran these mines. As our plane approached Nauru, a storm also arrived, and the winds were so strong that we could not land. So we circled around the area, waiting for a letup in the wind conditions. Our small plane could not be diverted to another location; there were none nearby. We did not have enough fuel to turn back either. We needed a miracle.

Then the pilot said, "Buckle up tight, we are going in." We attempted to land but the crosswinds were swirling around so strongly that he had to abort the attempt. We tried again. The same thing happened. Finally, the pilot brought us around for another try. As he started to descend, I could tell that he was not going to abort the attempt this time. The lower we got to the ground, the more the plane shifted from side to side, at times almost 30 degrees off center. He held the plane and with another drop in altitude, the plane straightened itself just seconds before the wheels touched the runway. What a flight!

With this weather, it also meant that I could not fly out to the Gilbert Islands and would need to stay overnight on Nauru. With all the excitement of our landing, naturally the whole island was abuzz with anticipation. Remember, the arrival of planes was a time for celebration. I was treated to a grand reception upon arrival, and they arranged for me to stay in a small hotel. Then they discovered that I was a woman 'Reverend'. This they had never seen before. So they asked me to wash up and come back down to the lobby because they wanted to call all the pastors on the island and the government leaders to a wine and cheese reception in my honor. What an evening! I felt like an exhibit on display. I was glad when I was finally able to excuse myself to get some rest because we would try to fly off the next morning.

The next day the weather was good, but we did not fly. The leaders drove me around their beautiful island. After a while, we stopped at a roadside market to get something to drink. It was there at that stall, that I saw the most beautiful, amazing Indian sari I had ever laid eyes on. Well, actually, it was my first time seeing a sari; before this I had only seen one in pictures. I bought that sari, because it was just so beautiful. I had never worn a sari, nor had an occasion to wear one, but I simply knew it was for me. Years later it would be one of the first saris that I would wear when I went to India. When I look back, I see again God's divine arrangements and preparation for things I did not yet know about.

Nocturnal Warfare

The following day, the weather was beautiful and with a rested pilot and a tank of fuel, we took off and continued our journey to the Gilbert Islands. The leaders there met me and drove me around to show me the location they had prepared for our outdoor meetings. Then we headed back to town for a meal, Bible study and prayer. The next day our boat from Majuro was due to arrive with the rest of the team.

After they arrived, we transported everything out to our revival site. The islanders had built some special shelters for us, one for the boys and one for the girls. Then, just for me, they had built from fresh coconut leaves the most elaborate toilet I had ever seen. I wish I had a picture of it to show you, but let me describe it.

They had chosen a lovely spot on the beach, a raised sandy area. They had dug the hole and built the enclosure. It had a very stable door that could open and close. On the inside they had built a shelf to hold a tub of water for bathing. They had fixed a wall inside to separate the toilet area from the bathing area. They had even woven a triangular tray across the corner that could hold the soap, with a place for the towel. I was so honored and surprised by their efforts.

Then they showed me the space for the meetings. Oh boy, what a challenge! They had chosen to erect the structure for our meeting right beside the strongest witchcraft tree on the island. They knew there were evil spirits around, and they wanted us to deal with these spirits. At night, all of us girls rolled out our mats on the ground, and crammed into this one shelter. For our 'protection', they assigned an older lady to sleep with her body across the doorway, so no spirit could come in to bother us. I distinctly remember lying there and thinking, "Spirits will not disturb you by stepping on you; they would just 'float' in!"

As I lay there with my eyes closed, thinking about our protection, I began to feel something brushing across my face in the dark. It would come and go several times, trying to disturb me. I chose to just pray and rebuke it quietly, as it would have caused a panic if I stood up to do the rebuking. As I prayed, it moved off to the side of our sleeping area.

The meetings were filled with warfare but God still did a great work. I will never forget that place and that tree. We spent one week there in meetings before making our journey back home. The team sailed home, while I flew back and transited in Nauru to Majuro. From there I took the boat home to Kwajalein and Ebeye.

Cultural Lessons

Going out to the islands meant we had to become familiar with the customs and protocol of the islanders. Now that Sam had left, I was the only missionary who spoke the Marshallese language. Knowing that the others needed to learn the local language and customs, I invited them to Ebeye to stay with me so I could conduct some training classes.

Our training times were always fun while achieving the goal of learning. I brought along some recording equipment and earphones, so they could listen to a word repeatedly until they could pronounce it correctly.

I had a Marshallese girl to assist me. I thought it would be helpful for us as missionaries to hear from a local person, so we would know why islanders did things differently. For example, I wanted the missionaries to learn not to be shocked if they saw boys walking around holding hands, or girls holding hands. That was normal for their culture; a boy holding a girl's hand would be forbidden. Where clothes were concerned, women wore only long dresses or muumuus. These were worn at all times, even when we went swimming – no swimsuits allowed! Of course, the men could wear walking shorts, without shirts, when they went fishing or did other types of work.

We also learned the protocol for relating to the kings of the atolls. If we entered the room where the king was, we had to stoop down or crawl across the room – whatever was required to always keep our head lower than the king's head. This rule had to be observed whether the king was sitting on a chair or on the floor.

If we happened to be riding at the back of the king's truck, no one was allowed to sit in the front seat beside him. Even in the pouring rain, that seat remained empty. Only his wife or children could sit beside him. However, he could invite us as missionaries to sit beside him if his family was not there. This showed the high regard they had for missionaries.

Reclaiming Land

My mandate in Ebeye was to build a missions base comprising a house for missionaries and a church building. After we built the house that I would live in and use as our base, there remained the task of building a church where we could have services. The piece of land that the King had given us was located between the road that circled the island and the lagoon. The distance between the road and the water's edge was all of ten feet. How were we going to build a church on such a narrow strip of land?

As I looked at the piece of land and prayed, I felt the Lord impress upon me to "build into the water."

I wondered, could it really be done? I wrote to an engineer friend in Inglewood, California again and asked him, "Can I build a wall in water?" He responded in the affirmative. I jumped for joy on the inside because now we could enlarge the land. We could create a larger piece of land on which to build the church. Thank you Jesus!

Then I asked the engineer, "Will you come again and oversee the building of this 'seawall' that I want to build?" He agreed. Praise the Lord for retired men and women who volunteer to serve God with their skills in the mission field.

Before he and his team arrived, we had several challenges to overcome. One was the need for rebar or steel rods with ridges, to reinforce the concrete walls. I would make trips over to Kwajalein, a twenty-minute boat ride away, and walk around the construction sites they had. If I saw any steel rods lying around, I would ask the foreman in charge, "What are you going to do with those? Do you still need them?" If they had no need of it, I would ask if I could have it. I kept collecting these steel bars and transporting them back to Ebeye. The same was true for pieces of plywood or lengths of wood. I became a real scavenger, collecting anything that I thought we might need.

At the same time, I began to study the tidal charts to see which months had the lowest tides and which days had the lowest tides of the month, when the corals and rocks would be exposed. I estimated just how far out into the lagoon we could build. These studies were done before our building crew arrived. I wanted to have the information ready so I could show the engineer the lines I had calculated. Before long, the engineer landed with a group of men to start building. Oh boy, that meant more cooking for me!

Making cement blocks was a big challenge. We could buy cement from Kwajalein, but we did not have sand or the aggregate (small stones) needed to make the blocks. God miraculously provided an old block machine that was powered by a motor. It could shake the cement down into frames to shape the building blocks. This was one step up from the way we had made blocks in Majuro.

While the men operated the machine, I would gather the women and at low tide, we would climb onto the outboard motor boats and cross over to the rim of the lagoon. At low tide, there was a small spot of sand that would appear for a short time near a lone tree. The sand in that area was coarse, which was perfect for the aggregate we needed. Upon reaching that spot, we would climb out of our boats. Standing in the water, we would begin to dig with our hands, lifting the small stones and putting them into large rice bags. We would fill as many bags as we could. Then the men and boys would come out and load the heavy bags into the boats and take us back to Ebeye.

We would work at this for at least two hours each day, before the waters became too deep and we had to return to land. We did this day after day, making the precious blocks needed for the church building.

While this was going on, the guys were busy building a wall in the sea. Now, no one had ever seen such a thing! It caught the attention of everyone on the island. When the big boat, which took the local workers from Ebeye to Kwajalein each morning, passed by our stretch of island, the boat would actually tilt in the water as everyone would rush to one side to take a look. They must have wondered, "What is that crazy missionary doing?" Again in the evening, they would do the same thing on their way back.

The Miracle Sandbar

It was exciting to see the steel rods being tied together and the forms built around them. The men worked quickly to finish the length of the wall before the tides shifted back to a higher level. Then they began to turn the wall inward on each end in order to enclose the area. They came to me and asked, "Where will we get the sand to fill this huge hole we have created?"

This was the biggest challenge of all. There was just no more sand or small rock to be had. The island was only about five-sixth of a mile long and two football fields wide – and that included the Coast Guard station at one end of the island where we found the aggregate! "God, what do we do now?" The people on the boat each morning were also wondering what would happen next. Everyone knew there was no extra sand on Ebeye.

Days passed as I prayed for an answer to our situation. "God, You told me to build this wall. We have come this far. Now what?"

One night a big storm came up. The winds howled and rain poured, as the trade winds seemed to be shifting their direction. In the morning I was awakened by a banging on my door. I rushed down to open it, and was greeted by some excited workers. "Come and see," they shouted in rapid fire. "A large sand bar has appeared overnight at the opposite end of the island. We don't know who it belongs too. Does it belong to the king? There has never been a sandbar there before. Whose is it?"

I had not yet seen it, but I began to claim it. I shouted, "It is mine! God has sent us the answer to our sand problem!"

I got dressed and drove down to that end of the island to see the miracle. As I thanked God for providing the sand, it suddenly struck me: How would we get the sand from that sandbar down to the church site?

God works in mysterious ways. It so happened that the governing authority on Kwajalein had chosen that exact time to move heavy equipment over to Ebeye to build a medical clinic. So, for the first time, we had some heavy equipment on Ebeye! Some of their workers were members of our church. So I walked over to their building site and spoke to the supervisor. "Sir, the men in my church drive this equipment for you everyday. So they know how to operate it. I want to present you an opportunity to help us. You only use the equipment during the day. Our men return to Ebeye at night. Since you only use the equipment during the day, would you let us use the equipment during the night?" He agreed!

That night, I asked the men to use the backhoe, begin to load the sand from the sandbar into the truck, and bring it down to our church site to fill the big hole we had created. We would haul sand each night until we had taken all we could from the sandbar. Then we would clean the equipment and retire for the night. While we slept, the trade winds would blow and create another sandbar in the exact same location. The next night, we would again haul the sand to our church site. Lo and behold, the winds would create a new sandbar again by morning. This same cycle continued night after night.

Finally, our hole was full. The crew asked, "Shall we stop now?"

99

"No," I replied. "We still need sand to pour floors inside the building, and sand to mix mortar to lay the blocks, so keep hauling it in. Pile it up real high on each side of the church site."

After many weeks, I told them, "Now we have enough. Let's return their trucks and equipment, and I will thank them for all their valuable help." That night after having thanked the supervisor for his kindness, I returned to the house and went to bed.

That very night a big storm came up again. This time, the winds blew and began to shift their direction back to their normal pattern. By the next morning, the sandbar had disappeared, and it never returned during the time I was serving in the islands. God had done another miracle! He had shifted the trade winds, like the parting of the Red Sea, and manifested Himself in signs and wonders to provide for His people. With God's miraculous provision, we were able to more than double the size of our land in Ebeye. Now the believers had the space they needed to build an adequate church building with classrooms, a worship hall, and even a balcony.

Across the (Air)waves

By this time, we had been going out to the other islands in the atolls by boat. Knowing the vastness of the ocean and the thousands of islands scattered across this huge area, I understood the challenge of reaching them and ministering to them on a regular basis. We had seen many islanders receive Christ. However, because the islands were spread so far apart, weeks or even months would pass before we could visit the same island again. How could we follow up and continue ministering to the islanders who had responded to the gospel? Beyond our island groups, there were many more islands in the South Pacific, such as Vanuatu and Nauru. How could we reach across the vast distance?

I decided that one key strategy was to build a radio station and reach them via radio. Our plan was to build a radio tower, and to give out pre-tuned radios that would be tuned to the station we would build. In this way we could minister to the islanders regularly.

Along with a radio engineer from the States, I undertook a research project, which involved going to the different Micronesian island groups to search for an ideal spot for this radio tower. We would make our way through swamps, up hills and into remote areas to try and find these places, and figure out how many island groups could be reached from each particular location. In the process, I drew many maps and plotted the different angles and distances that could be covered. Having figured that out, we then strategized how to get the local kings to give us or sell us the land to build the radio tower. However, the plan was never completed.

Nine Years in the Islands

The time had come for me to return to the States for my furlough. When I began to prepare for the trip, I packed all my maps and sealed them in barrels because I felt that I would not be coming back. However, if I did, the research would be there. Although I did not know what I was going to do next, I sensed deep down that my assignment in the Marshalls was over. I did not share this with anyone.

One day as I was packing, Iris came into the garage and said, "You are packing as if you are not coming back, aren't you?" I did not know what to say. I felt really bad inside, because I knew she had come to the Marshalls to work and serve with me, and now, I had no answers for her. I had no answer for myself either – only a feeling that my season in the Marshalls was coming to an end.

By this time, I had spent about nine years in the islands. As I looked back, I could see what I had learned in these back-to-nature, rustic conditions. Because of the lack of electricity and modern amenities, I had learned to do whatever was needed to get the job done:

- How to trim a wick on a kerosene refrigerator. If the wick burned cleanly, it would be able to make the water cold, and I would even be able to make ice.
- How to mix cement, aggregate and sand to make concrete blocks.
- How to build houses, schools and church buildings.
- How to dress appropriately for the culture and how to relate to, honor and work with the traditional kings of the islands.
- How to cut and prepare the materials for a prefab church, before loading them onto our 40-feet missions boat and sailing to an island that needed a church building. We were the first to pioneer this methodology in the islands.
- How to navigate the seas to ensure that we arrived at our intended destination.
- How to speak, read and write Marshallese. I was able to tutor new missionaries in the basics of the Marshallese language, teach Bible School classes, and do radio broadcasts in their language. These weekly radio sermons were broadcast from Majuro, but could be heard by several islands. I was not perfect, but God used me anyway.

CHAPTER 9

When God Speaks

THE YEAR WAS 1974. Many things had changed in the nine years I had been away from the States. I was shocked each time I walked into a grocery store; there were many new things I had not seen before. I had such a wide range to choose from, and so many variations of each product! After years of simple, rustic living in the islands, where even plain bread had been a prized commodity, it was overwhelming to suddenly have access to so much.

Being back in the States was a blessing for several reasons. Firstly, the doctors discovered that I was anemic, and had numerous other health issues, as a result of not having proper food to eat during my early years in the Marshalls. I began to take vitamins and iron regularly, and it took almost a year for my body to recover and rebuild itself. During this one year while I recovered physically, I traveled to different churches to preach and raise funds for my missions budget. I still had to raise funds for a budget, even though I did not know where I was going.

The second reason was, I was required to attend the School of Missions in Springfield during this furlough, plus seven weeks of classes at the newly established Assemblies of God Graduate School.

The School of Missions was held annually for all AG missionaries who were back in the States for their furlough. It was here that I made two new friends, Debbie Menken and Barbara Liddle. We had lots of fun and powerful times of prayer together.

Debbie would later spend one year with me and the church in Singapore, while also teaching in our Far East Advanced School of Theology (FEAST) in the Philippines, before pursuing her doctoral studies at Fuller Theological Seminary. Besides Debbie's wonderful outgoing spirit and energetic teaching in the classroom, she was remembered for playing on a small ukulele just before she preached.

Our friendship has continued for many years. She taught at North Central Bible College, after which she pioneered and pastored her own church. She would later serve at AG Headquarters for a season before joining the Assemblies of God Theological Seminary in Springfield. I am so proud of her life. She is such a scholar and so dynamic in the classroom that she continues to impact future leaders with a passion to transform nations.

Barbara was assigned as a missionary to Indonesia. She learned the language, worked at the AG publishing house, and taught at the Bible school in East Java. In her second term she worked with the Cagles and others to establish a Bible school in Jakarta. She was remembered for the chalk drawings she would make to illustrate her sermons. She would later join me from time to time in Singapore to teach and preach in Trinity. I would also be invited to minister at the Bible School in Malang and the churches in the area, and she always graciously hosted me during those trips.

God provided a wonderful friend in Barbara in 1974, just before He shifted me into my next season. Little did I know that she would become a lifeline and an encouragement during those years when, as senior pastor, I needed someone to talk to about all the things I was experiencing. Our friendship has continued through her eight years of teaching at the Asia Pacific

Little did I know that she would become a lifeline and an encouragement.

Theological Seminary in the Philippines, her marriage to R.B. Cavaness, their three years in Singapore, and beyond.

A New Role

During my itineration, the Division of Foreign Missions gave me a new assignment as a missionary evangelist. Instead of being based in one country, I was asked to travel and preach wherever I was invited in the Far East.

In 1975, as Barbara and I returned to Asia, we attended a conference in Taiwan, a gathering of all the AG missionaries and national leaders serving in the Far East. At that meeting, the national leadership from Singapore met with me, asking me to return to their country and minister in their churches.

I had been to Singapore once before in 1972, when I had been invited to minister at their monthly AG youth rallies. Missionaries Howard and Rosella Ridings were the organizers of those meetings, and they were friends of Iris Brown, my coworker in the Marshall Islands. Iris and I spent a month ministering in Singapore and Malaysia. We were invited to come back, but I had not been able to return to Singapore due to ministry commitments in the Marshall Islands.

Now Singapore reappeared on my radar. There was one problem though; my schedule was fully booked for the coming year because I had agreed to spend a few months each in the Philippines and Indonesia. However, I did have a window of a few weeks before these engagements started. The leaders asked if I would fly to Singapore and spend those few weeks ministering in the churches and meet with them to plan for the following year.

From Taiwan I flew directly into Singapore. Among the churches that I ministered in was Trinity Christian Centre (TCC), a small church that I found to be 'dead.' In my opinion, the worship and prayer at that time were lifeless.

After the service, the leaders asked me out for dinner, but I politely declined. As I walked out of the church, I muttered under my breath, "Thank You Jesus, I don't ever have to come back to this church again!" I had never said those words before in my life – and I have not said them since, but at that moment, those were my honest feelings!

But, as I was going to soon discover, God had totally different plans – and a great sense of humor. That week, I had lunch with the Assistant General Superintendent of the Assemblies of God in Singapore, Rev Andrew Yeo Boon Hin, discussing when I should return. After lunch, he said, "I need to run an errand. Why don't you ride along with me?"

I went along for the ride, and it turned out that he was on his way to the Department of Immigration. As we were walking up the wooden steps of the old immigration building, I asked, "Why are we here?"

He replied, "Because the missionary pastor of Trinity has a visa problem. He has been given seven days to get out of the country. I am coming down to see if there is anything I can do to work it out."

The very moment he said those words, the Holy Spirit said to me, "And you are going to take the church."

It was an audible voice, like the time God spoke to me as a child. I was stunned. My first thought was, "Oh no, not me!"

Becoming a pastor was not my calling. "I am an evangelist, and I am happy being an evangelist. So, God – I don't think so!" was my instinctive retort. I continued to argue with God that I could train pastors, I could write constitutions, but not pastor. Pastoring was not my desire, nor did I feel it was my anointing. I must admit, my attitude was not the best.

True enough, the problem with the missionary's visa was not resolved. Now there was a vacancy urgently needing to be filled. I returned to my hotel and argued some more with God. I was even prepared to change hotels, because I figured, if they could not find me, they would not be able to ask me! As it turned out, they cornered me before I could get away.

One morning, the hotel desk called my room and informed me that I had a guest waiting in the lobby. I knew in my heart that they had found me. The visitor turned out to be Pang Yan Leng, one of the board members, who had come to share their desire for me to become their pastor.

My reply to her was, "I will have to pray about it." It sounded like the right, religious thing to say. In reality I already knew what God had said, but inside I was still wrestling with Him.

An Inspiration

Part of the real issue for my aversion to becoming a woman pastor was because of the negative examples I had witnessed in my early years. All the women pastors I had met were domineering and manly, and this had made a negative impression on me. In those years, at least, some women seemed to feel they had to compete with men to be a leader. They try to steel their emotions and, as a result, appear demanding and domineering.

I had come across only one positive role model so far, and she was an AG missionary named Eva Bloom, whom I had gotten to know on my way out to the Marshall Islands. Her church was one of the churches in Hawaii where Sister Beck and I had ministered in, while waiting on the documents to be completed, so I could fly on the military plane into Kwajalein. Eva and her sisters had been missionaries in China but had to leave because of the war. When their ship stopped in Hawaii, they felt called to stay there to minister.

One thing that struck me about Eva was the way she carried herself with such dignity. She dressed nicely, yet she was not flamboyant. She was strong, yet not masculine. She was fun, yet gentle. She would cook and preach for all the service men – and these were tough Marines! The men respected her. When I visited her home, I left thinking to myself, "Now, that's the way a woman pastor should be!" Her shining example had a deep influence on me. She provided a positive picture of what a woman pastor could be in God. A woman can be a strong, effective leader without becoming masculine. This would become an inspiration and encouragement to me now in Singapore.

A woman can be a strong, effective leader without becoming masculine.

Humble Beginnings

Although God had already spoken to me, I still tried to wiggle my way out of the situation. I called everyone who was a spiritual authority over me, and tried to get them to agree that it was a bad idea. To my dismay, every one of them encouraged me to accept the invitation to pastor. So I did the next best thing to 'satisfy' God: I agreed to pastor the church for six months while they looked for a permanent pastor.

There was another missionary couple living in Singapore at the time, who had been approached to pastor the church, but they had refused. To put it mildly, it was a church no one wanted. I would soon find out why.

Although I was supposed to take the church in late 1975, it was delayed by four months. The day finally came for me to be installed as the senior pastor of the church. On February 1, 1976, I walked into the little house where the church met and looked around. No one was there to introduce me to the congregation. I simply greeted everyone, "Well, good morning! Let's all open our hymnals... and worship the Lord." That was my beginning at Trinity Christian Centre: No welcome, no official introduction, just rolling up my sleeves and getting down to work.

Chopstick Lessons

Not only was I new to the church, I was also new to the culture and environment in Singapore. The majority of the population was Chinese, along with Malays, Indians and Eurasians. The only Chinese skill I knew was how to use chopsticks!

Many years earlier, while working in San Diego, I had this strange feeling that I needed to learn to use chopsticks. So I would go alone to a Chinese restaurant, order some food and read the instructions on the paper sleeve about how to hold chopsticks. I would take the chopsticks out of the sleeve and try to place them in my hand the way the pictures showed.

I would start eating, trying to hold the chopsticks properly and lift the food to my mouth. I continued doing this until my hand would begin to cramp. Then I would finish my food with a fork. For many months, I kept doing this until I could pick up food, move it, and eat a complete meal using chopsticks.

Many years had passed, and now here I was, in Singapore, eating with chopsticks! People would ask me, "Where did you learn to hold your chopsticks? You hold them the proper way, even better than we do!"

Again, it was God's divine preparation for things I did not yet know about. It was just a prompting, that I should master holding chopsticks, and I did it without even understanding why. Who would have thought that it would mean anything?

A Word of Knowledge

Trinity was a small church, five years old, with forty-two members and as I jokingly say, seventy-five problems. They had been meeting since 1970 and had three different missionary pastors during those five years. The leaders were very welcoming and gracious to me, and offered to help me get started.

The missionary pastor who had preceded me had previously promised a local young man on staff that the church would be handed over to him when the missionary left. However, because the missionary had to leave in such a hurry, things were not turning out the way the young man expected. He wanted to be the pastor and naturally resented my being there. At a church board meeting, he accused me, "You will be like all the other three missionary pastors we have had in the last five years. You will leave and desert us!"

Earlier that day, I had written down some notes at the prompting of the Holy Spirit. As I listened to this young man's outburst, I glanced at the notes I had been prompted to write. When he finished speaking, I began to share from the notes that I had written on my pad earlier in the day. They were words of knowledge from the Holy Spirit, which exposed the root of the problems in the church. Evidently all the major problems could be traced back to the misconduct of this young man. When confronted with the truth, he turned pale and decided to leave the church. The moment he left, the problems ended, and the church soon began growing.

The young believers in the church were very committed and willing workers. Those on the Trinity church board were all very supportive. Pang Yan Hoong was a tremendous help in getting the accounts of the church in proper order. Brother David Lum was the oldest board member then. I would drop by his office for coffee and seek his views on the different challenges we were facing. Our working together formed a strong bond that endures even till today.

When God Speaks

Later in 1976, not too long after the issue with the young man had been resolved, we were in a Wednesday night prayer meeting. There was a grand total of three of us: Brother David Lum, one other person, and myself. We were on our knees, in front of our chairs, praying.

Suddenly the Lord spoke to me and said, *"Three thousand."*

It jolted me. I knew He was saying that we would reach three thousand people in the church. I looked up and looked to my left and to my right – there were only three of us. I began to question God, "There are only three of us! We are so small, we have no musicians, and we don't even have a regular place to meet. How can we hit three thousand?"

As usual, when God speaks, He only says it one time. I thought to myself, "I cannot tell the people we are going to hit three thousand – even I am struggling with that number."

Finally, I said, "Okay God, I will tell them that You have spoken, but I will only tell them a little at a time, so they can believe."

Sunday came. Our service was still in that house deep inside the housing estate. Because of what God had spoken to me during the prayer meeting, I told the church, "God knows where we are, and He is saying we will hit 150 by the end of this year. Let's trust God and invite our friends, because God is going to move in this church." God did move, and we did hit 150 by the end of that year.

Overcoming Lack

When I had initially preached at Trinity as a guest speaker, they were holding their services at Equatorial Hotel. But in the two months before I became pastor, they had moved deep into a private housing estate. No buses came into the estate, and the house was a long walk from the main road.

I learned that this was a result of their worries about their church finances. They had retreated and taken a step backwards. Their faith was shaken and there was no vision.

As soon as I learned about this situation, I said there were two things we had to do. First, we had to move our Sunday services back into the hotel, and trust God to provide for our needs. We could not grow the church in a house located deep within a residential area. So I went back to the Equatorial Hotel and spoke to the manager, asking to make a new contract so we could use the hotel ballroom for our Sunday services. Finally, he agreed.

Secondly, I said, if we have a money problem, then we had to give our way out of lack, and give to the thing that is closest to God's heart – missions. We needed to have a Missions Convention and raise money to 'give away.' When we align ourselves as a church with the heart of God, He will take care of our financial needs.

> *If we have a money problem, then we had to give our way out of lack.*

So we planned for our Missions Convention, the first that the church had ever had. I began to teach them about the principle of faith promises, not pledges. It was not about pledging a sum of money they knew they had, but about hearing from God and believing He would provide whatever amount He spoke to them about. The faith promises were between them and God. As an expression of faith, they would indicate the amount on a faith promise card, but we would never chase them for the amount. It was a faith endeavor.

I asked Barbara Liddle to come over from Indonesia and help us. She worked to prepare a choir for the occasion. We invited missionary Jim Anderson to be our speaker. We were making our plans and praying for God to do a miracle.

The decorations were simple: We had a monkey climbing up a coconut tree. The objective was to have the monkey reach the coconut at the top of the tree! Each time a faith amount was read out, the monkey would move higher up the tree. It was exciting to watch that monkey climb and the numbers grow. That first missions convention

113

in March 1977 saw a grand total of S$35,300 committed in missions faith promises.

This set the tone and culture for Trinity. Missions giving became one of the foundations upon which the church was built. Since then, Trinity Christian Centre has never suffered lack. God has always provided for the vision He has given us. When I handed the church over in 2005, the missions faith promises for that year had grown to S$5.1 million. There is no way we can out-give God.

CHAPTER 10

A Season of Growth

THE CHURCH GREW QUICKLY, and I found myself trying to keep up with the increase God was bringing. Trinity did not own a building, and in no time we outgrew the original venue and had to move to a larger one. Things were happening at such a rapid pace that I had forgotten about my commitment to be there for only six months. God had changed my attitude. I discovered – to my surprise – that I loved pastoring!

Once I grasped my new assignment, I embraced it with gusto. The change to pastoring demanded major adjustments on my part. There were many changes I had to make to adapt to my new ministry. I had to move from preaching evangelistic messages to more pastoral or teaching messages. I had to move from outline preaching to manuscript preaching, because of multiple services and wanting to be sure they all got pretty much the same message.

However, officially speaking, I was still an appointed missionary of the AG. This meant that I was required to return to America every two years for four months to raise money for support, or return every four years and stay for a year. I was aware of their requirements and procedure but after they agreed that I should become the pastor of this church, I told them, "I will not be returning to raise money because I do not believe that a senior pastor should be gone for extended periods of time. My strong belief is that you need to be committed to the church and the people." When I realized that this would be the place for me to dig in my stakes and build deep, I did just that.

By 1977 and 1978, there had been a shift in the spiritual atmosphere of the church. God showed up each week and people were filled with the Spirit. Lives were being touched, and miracles were happening.

However, there was one major problem. The majority of our congregation were young people. When adults would come into the services, they would look around and see mostly young people. Feeling out of place, they would not return. This made it difficult for us to grow beyond a certain point. We needed more adults, so I prayed, "God send us mature men and women, whom these young people can see as steady believers."

A Gift to the Church

The young people who were getting saved were mostly first generation Christians and did not have a Christian family model. God's answer came in the persons of Ang Beng Siong and his wife, Bertha. They were both very enthusiastic about Jesus. They actively invited their friends and family to church. They believed that if they had a problem, God would heal, restore, and forgive. Whatever the problem, big or small, God would answer prayer. Their addition to our church opened the door for many new adults to become part of the church.

One of our first cell groups in the church met in my apartment on Tomlinson Road. The Angs brought a friend and distant relative of theirs, Ng Buck Chua and his wife, Kim. They would come to my apartment every Friday night for the cell meeting.

One Friday, after the meeting, Brother Buck Chua asked if he and his wife could stay back to speak with me. "Sure," I said.

You have to understand Brother Buck Chua. He was a serious person, a man of few words. He was then the managing director of the insurance company, Lloyd's of London. When everyone left, he began to pull three chairs into a circle, and we all sat down. Then he factually stated, "Well, we are ready. My wife and I want to receive Jesus. Will you pray for us?" What a joy to see the transformation in their lives!

Shortly after that, the Lloyd's of London office in Singapore was closed, and he retired. Before long, he came to me and offered to help me teach the new converts class. Then he offered to teach a class for the older folks who did not speak good English. He would go with me to the hospitals to pray with people. Before long, the younger church members began calling him to talk to their parents about Jesus – because he was older and their elderly parents would be more inclined to listen to him.

I truly believe Pastor Ng Buck Chua (we later commissioned him as a bi-vocational pastor) has individually won more people to Christ than anyone I know. He is loved by everyone and has served God and the church without salary, for more than forty years. He is now in his 90s and still available to God, sitting on the front row every Sunday.

Within three years, we were reaching people in the business community. God brought them in, and we ministered to them. People experienced healing, financial provision, relationship restoration, and other types of miracles. Some couples who had been divorced were now reconciling and getting remarried. The church was doubling each year and continually relocating to a larger auditorium. The spirit in the church was being completely transformed. The congregation grew and became focused on changing lives and impacting the nation.

Tackling the Drug Menace

As I embraced my assignment to make disciples, God brought me to another level – that of impacting the nation. One of the first responsibilities I undertook after becoming pastor was to start Teen Challenge Singapore. This was in the 1970s, when the drug problem was a menace in Singapore and the government needed help to grapple with this issue.

Singapore Anti-Narcotics Association, or SANA for short, was in its early stages of development, so I joined them and became part of their training team. I had frequent opportunities to visit schools and speak to students during their weekly assemblies about the dangers of drug use, how to spot if their classmates were taking drugs, and what they should do. I would always end my talks with the emphatic declaration: that the Jesus Factor is what makes the difference. This was the trademark claim of Teen Challenge.

The Jesus Factor is what makes the difference.

During those days, the police would put the addicts in jail and 'dry' them out but once they were released, they would return to their drug use. Only Christian leaders or ex-drug addicts who had become Christians and started rehabilitation centers were having any success with keeping people off drugs.

The government took note of the success of these Christian organizations and asked SANA and those of us involved to help develop counseling and rehabilitation groups within each religious organization in Singapore. We developed training materials and conducted workshops for the Buddhist, Catholic, Hindu and Muslim leaders, training and preparing them to work with drug addicts within their various faith-based groups.

118

I also had the privilege of working with the head of Central Narcotics Bureau, learning about Interpol and other agencies that worked together to curb the drug problem during the mid-70s.

It was during all of these activities that Teen Challenge Singapore was birthed. I was pastoring and knew that I could not pastor and also 'live in' with the addicts to help them. Having some knowledge of the Teen Challenge ministry and its effectiveness elsewhere, I felt this was a ministry the nation needed. So I prayed and asked God for a couple to work with me in this project. God spoke to Philip and Monica Lee and they joined me. We rented an apartment in the Serangoon / MacPherson area. Philip and Monica lived there and we began to take in people who wanted to kick the habit. It was hard work with long hours.

I remember Philip calling me in the middle of the night, "Hurry over, one of the guys going through cold turkey is trying to climb out the bathroom window and jump." So I dressed and drove as quickly as possible to be with them and try to talk the guy down. Finally, with God's help, he settled down. He was in physical pain, going through 'cold turkey'. 'Cold turkey' is when the body is experiencing withdrawal symptoms from narcotics – and only God can help during this time. Once all the drugs are out of the system (the painful process), the body is free, but there is still the battle for the mind. Their minds will still tell them that they need the drugs, when in reality the body does not need them any longer. The mind becomes the battlefield for their soul.

Once there was a medical doctor who was hooked on prescription drugs. To help her, I took her into my home. She was with me for weeks and experienced extreme difficulty. I asked Pang Yan Leng to come over to my apartment to help me through the nights. Being a doctor herself, she still had access to any drugs she wanted at any time. She became unwilling to change and finally left, choosing to return to her old ways. I was really sad, but even God cannot work in us if we reject Him and refuse to change.

I was really sad, but even God cannot work in us if we reject Him and refuse to change.

Teen Challenge further developed under the leadership of missionary Irvin Rutherford and later executive director Sam Kuna. It was formally recognized by the government and we were able to rent some government land and buildings to continue the work. The subsequent success of Teen Challenge Singapore and my involvement with SANA gave me many open doors into schools and other institutions in the community.

Challenging Stereotypes

When some of my friends back in the States heard about my appointment as a pastor in Singapore, they tried to dissuade me. They said, "Women leaders are not accepted in Asia. Women are put down. They have to walk twenty paces behind the men. They will never accept you, and your ministry will die." They said this out of good intentions, but because I knew what God had spoken, I did not let such remarks hinder me. (Asia was changing and female leaders were even becoming heads of state, such as Indira Gandhi, elected as Prime Minister of India in 1966.)

As it turned out, God had me in the right place at the right time. When I began pastoring in Singapore in 1976, the larger churches were mainly from the traditional or mainline denominations. All the Pentecostal churches were small and mostly went unnoticed by the larger Christian community. Over the next two years, the Holy

120

Spirit moved powerfully in Singapore and beyond. The Charismatic Renewal saw waves of revival meetings. Believers from the mainline churches were baptized in the Holy Spirit. People became increasingly open to the Gospel. The population of believers in the nation increased. All these spiritual developments within the Body of Christ formed the larger spiritual context in which my ministry took place.

This move of God opened more doors for women to lead and serve – as has been true during other times in history. When there is a mighty move of God, gender becomes less of an issue. It was true again in the 1970s. More women became visible in ministry, especially in the areas of intercession and deliverance. Along with this was a brand new phenomenon: A Pentecostal woman leading the fastest growing church in the nation. This was unheard of. God had brought me here at the right time by maneuvering my life's course.

Initially, saying yes to God had been a real struggle because I had never walked this way before. Eventually, I surrendered my will to His. Evidently God knew something that I did not: that this was to be my destiny. God had more confidence in me than I had in myself. As I surrendered my will to His, God brought out something in me and moved me to another level. I might have had success before, but my significance would now come as I found my place of destiny.

It was only later on that I realized that Singapore... was an island!

CHAPTER 11

Sufficient Grace

THESE RAPID, GROUNDBREAKING DEVELOPMENTS did not escape the notice of the local pastoral association, which was male-dominated and traditional in its thinking. The pastors debated amongst themselves about whether it was biblical for a woman senior pastor to be leading a church. One of the male faculty members at the Singapore Bible College responded with these remarkable words of wisdom: "We see the evidence of an anointing and a ministry that is producing results. If the same miracles and growth were taking place under a male leader, we would be cheering and praising the Lord. However because it is a woman, you are murmuring among yourselves. If we have problems with that simply because it is a woman, then perhaps we should be examining our theology."

If we have problems with that simply because it is a woman, then perhaps we should be examining our theology."

That was a significant leap for someone from a traditional theological background to make, and to this day, I respect him for taking that courageous stance. It was a timely word of divine wisdom, much like the word of wisdom Gamaliel gave to the Sanhedrin in

Acts 5:34-39. God was at work to defend my ministry, even though I was unaware of it. I did not know what had transpired until almost a decade later.

Expressions of Affirmation

I was also blessed to have the affirmation of other leaders. One of those whom God used to affirm me was my first pastor, Emil Balliet from the First Assembly of God church in San Diego. Upon my invitation, he came to preach in Trinity in 1977. As it happened to be a Communion Sunday, I asked if he would facilitate serving of the Lord's Supper during the service.

He refused and said, "I want you to remember that this is the senior pastor's job. You don't give that over." He was intentional in affirming that I was the spiritual leader God had appointed over the church. This deep affirmation has stayed with me all this time. God used him to affirm me at a time when women senior pastors were rare.

After his services with us, Pastor Balliet and his wife were going to Bali, Indonesia to preach for a missionary retreat. He asked me to join them. I thanked him, saying I could not go because I did not have money for the trip. Immediately, he said, "You are going and I am praying for the expenses." Pastor Balliet was a blessing to me in so many ways.

Whether the people in the church had problems with a woman being a pastor, I really do not know, but I assume that if they did, they would not have stayed in Trinity Christian Centre. Conversely, those who felt it was an issue would have stayed away. I believe the anointing opened the way. By God's grace, when I preached, God showed up. People were filled with the Spirit, healed, and delivered. The ministry made the way.

God's grace flowing through a weak vessel was always foremost in my thoughts. I would wonder, "Why me, God? There are so many others more worthy than me." While I struggled internally with the magnitude of God's blessing, I never doubted God's call. I could say with Paul, "We have this treasure in jars of clay to show that this all-surpassing power is from God and not from us" (2 Corinthians 4:7).

I realized that if God wanted me in the ministry, He would have to open the way and make it happen. Therefore I was determined not to fight my way into it. I felt the ministry should speak for itself. This was a deliberate strategy. My philosophy was that the ministry should bear fruit, and the fruit would be the evidence of whatever gift God had given a person. It is evident that God created us different for a reason and He gave us different gifts for a reason, so we should never try to function in a way we were not created to function. Skills can be learned to a certain extent, but it is the Holy Spirit who distributes gifts, "and He gives them to each one, just as He determines" (1 Corinthians 12:11).

Some people thought that with a woman pastor at the helm, the church would attract more women. They were surprised to discover there were, among our members, proportionately more men than women, especially in the early days – and these were strong, powerful men. I never allowed gender to be an issue in ministry. I looked for God's gifts and anointing on a person and then tried to train them to function at a higher level of effectiveness according to their gifts.

Although Singapore was still mostly conservative in its religious practices, it never was a major problem for me as a woman pastor. I was too busy preaching, teaching, developing, and building people to be bothered with what someone might be thinking. God was blessing, lives were being changed, and there was no time to waste on such issues.

A Visible Identity

There was one issue, though, that required some creative adaptation. As a pastor of a growing church, I was often invited to participate in the dedication ceremonies of new buildings. At such ceremonies, representatives from different religions would be present and take part in the blessing ceremony. I was invited to represent Christianity at some of these ceremonies. As I looked around me, I could see that every representative donned a religious garment – the Buddhists, Hindus, Muslims, Sikhs. The Christians from the mainline denominations had clerical collars. I was clearly the odd one out among all these men in religious garb: I was a Westerner, a woman, in modern clothing, and I wore heels!

Although I was an ordained clergy, I certainly did not look the part. Now I had never worn a collar or been around people who wore collars, but I recognized that there was an issue here. It was not just about crossing cultures from West to East, but crossing gender barriers in a mixed-religion setting. I was crossing every barrier there was: cultural, religious, denominational, and gender barriers.

I encountered a similar issue at weddings. When I presided over weddings, I would wear a suit, but so would everyone else. People would ask, "Who is the religious leader here?" I needed to provide some visual cues that I was an ordained clergy. Remember, this was at a time when people were coming to the Lord quickly. These were first-generation Christians who needed a visible representation and a visual way to identify the spiritual leader who represented the presence of God.

So I prayed and asked God to help me with this visual identity issue. I went to the Catholic clergy tailor and asked them to make me a white gown with a cummerbund, collar, and a stole with a big cross on it, because these were what the Catholic priests wore. I wore it for official settings and for special occasions in the church. I also stopped wearing short skirts. I wore long dresses or skirts, and to give it a more formal look, I would wear a feminine top, much like Kathryn Kuhlman.

Many people were coming to Christ, and these were first generation believers. Some thought that to be Christians, they had to become more Western. I spent a good part of those early years learning about the Chinese culture and its customs, and teaching them to distinguish between culture and religion.

Building Bridges

Mainline denominations in Singapore did not have a good impression of Pentecostals. The reputation of the Pentecostals was that of 'holy rollers' – loud, boisterous, and not theologically sound. When local Pentecostal preachers preached or prayed at a meeting, they had a tendency to be loud, to the point of yelling. They seemed to think that the louder you preached, the greater the anointing. God instructed me to build a bridge between the Pentecostal and mainline churches. Somehow the mainline churches saw that I was balanced in my teaching and sensitive to their doctrinal beliefs and expressions. This put me in a strategic position to build a bridge of relationship between the two groups.

The Charismatic Renewal provided opportunities to break down denominational barriers. The Methodist churches invited me to teach on the Holy Spirit. At this time, they had not yet ordained women in ministry, and so I was surprised by their invitation and asked them why. They said they felt they could trust me.

I persisted in asking, "Are you sure you want me to come and teach on the Holy Spirit? If I do, something might happen..." I was referring to the move of the Spirit.

Their reply was, "If something does happen, it's fine."

As much as I wanted a breakthrough to happen, I did not lay hands on anyone. I just trusted God to move, and He did. The Holy Spirit came, touched people, and filled them. By providing biblical teachings and by showing respect for their doctrinal distinctives, such as their beliefs regarding water baptism (sprinkling vs immersion), speaking in tongues and so on, we saw breakthroughs and gradually a greater acceptance of the Pentecostals.

On my part, I honored the trust of the Methodists by never overstepping my authority and teaching in their churches something contrary to their doctrines. I did teach on these issues, of course, but never in their settings. Later on, the Methodist churches did recognize baptism by immersion and now offer it as an alternative to baptism by sprinkling. Today, almost every Methodist church in Singapore has two kinds of services: the usual liturgical service as well as a more Charismatic renewal service with prayer for Holy Spirit baptism and healing.

Sufficient Grace

I was a woman minister, and a single one at that. I had chosen not to get married, but that does not mean I did not have physical desires. God gives all of us physical desires and He intends that we learn to manage them. My practical advice for dealing with physical desires comes from personal experience: Exercise faith; pray and fast, asking for God's help; go jogging or expend physical energy; spend time in the Word; and if possible, find an accountability partner to pray with and for you.

Whether single or married, we all must learn to guard against times and places of vulnerability. Often these are times when we are relaxed, and we let our guard down. Remember King David, who did not go out to battle with his army but instead remained behind in his palace. This resulted in his affair with Bathsheba. Some find that the battle intensifies during times of stress. Mood music, too, can make us vulnerable by playing with our thoughts and emotions. Also, physiological urges for women are strongest between the ages of (age) thirty-five to forty-five. Understanding all this will help us identify areas of vulnerability and take counter measures to manage our God-given desires, impulses, and emotions, with His help.

Paul's prayer was that he would "learn to be content whatever the circumstances... whether living in plenty or in want" (Philippians 4:11-13). This was often my prayer: "God, help me to find contentment in every situation." Sometimes this was easier said than done. I had to wrestle for contentment. I experienced again and again my own Garden of Gethsemane, where I had to say, "If it is possible, let this pass from me..." (Luke 22:42, NKJV). I had to come to that place of laying my life on the altar and saying, "God, I need your grace and mercy. Know my heart, hear my cry and be with me."

Just because you love God does not mean you do not have human emotions. When hormones were raging, I struggled, like everyone else; it was a journey. When situations arose and temptation came knocking, I remembered who I was in God and what God had called me to become. I also knew that if I caved in to temptation, God would be with me and forgive me but, like David, I would reap the consequences. God's plans for me would be aborted or derailed.

I am not perfect; I have had to repent and ask forgiveness for times of weakness. When I stumbled, I came before God and found His grace. Like Paul, I would pray and declare, "I must forget those things that are behind me, and press on toward the mark of His high calling" (Philippians 3:13-14), remembering that I am what I am, only by His grace.

If you have stumbled, don't allow Satan to replay any footage from your past. Some things we have to leave in God's hands and trust that "As far as the east is from the west, so far has He removed our transgressions from us" (Psalm 103:12). God's grace was sufficient for me (2 Corinthians 12:9), and it will be for you too. Cry out to God for help, and bring these struggles into the light of His call on your life.

Defining your identity by faith is crucial to winning this battle. When you know who you are in God, you will not sell your soul and your birthright for a bowl of porridge as Esau did (see Genesis 25); neither will you sell your future and your destiny for a one-night stand, so to speak. It will be a journey, but you can overcome the struggle, maintain your honor and integrity, and press on toward the mark of His high calling.

What I have shared here might come as a surprise to you. But I am human, like everyone else! Another fact that often surprises people is that I am an introvert. Just for the record, I *really* am an introvert – and I do what I do only by God's grace!

CHAPTER 12

A Nomadic Church

As TRINITY DID NOT HAVE its own building, we remained a nomadic church for a long time. It would be twenty years before we would have our own building to hold classes and services. Not having our own building also meant that we had no space for our office, classes, Sunday school, or Bible study. Then we were able to rent one of the old pre-war houses on Ewe Boon Road. It was a typical house built up on blocks with a row of rooms built separately across the back. These rooms were used for servants, storage, and cooking during the old days.

The house was a wonderful blessing because it gave us a place for other activities besides the worship service. However, there was a problem – none of the rooms would work as a small office for me and a secretary. Seeing the challenge, I called an American couple who was attending our church. I wasn't sure what work he did but I knew that many American men would have some tools on hand. I needed a wood saw, nails and wood. Sure enough, when I called him, he said he had a hammer and a wood saw. I quickly rushed out to buy some 2x4 lumber and some plywood. I decided that I would build my own office.

After I had borrowed the tools and bought the supplies, I began to measure the lumber that I needed as a frame to build a wall between my new secretary and me, while creating a window so that we could pass work back and forth without needing to walk around. I worked on it all day and made good progress.

As evening approached, the American man got off work and made his way over to Ewe Boon Road to check on how I was doing. When he saw the task, he quickly jumped in to help. Soon he took over the job with a few guys that had arrived, and before long they finished the project. Wow – now I had a real office!

Singing for Special Events

There were also other areas of the church that needed to develop. Music was a key area needed. Slowly interest began to grow. One of our university students, Choo Lai Ying, accepted the challenge to lead our choir. So our music ministry began, but they only sang on special occasions.

A special occasion would be when Equatorial Hotel would tell us, "In two weeks' time, you cannot use our ballroom. You will need to find another location."

The leaders would come to me, worried. "What are we going to do?"

I told them, "We can never be negative. Let's make it a special event. Let's rent the Shangri-La Hotel and have something special." The Shangri-La was then the most prestigious hotel in the nation.

I would announce to the congregation, "We are moving to the Shangri-La for a special meeting on Sunday, in two weeks' time. Bring your friends." I never told them that we were being kicked out of the ballroom. That would have been negative. I prayed, "God, work it for good."

So everyone would invite their friends, we would all dress up and have a special meeting. Now Lai Ying would have her choir ready and they would sing special music for the meeting. This happened several times, until one day when I bumped into Lai Ying outside the ladies room after one of our special meetings. I challenged her, "It is time to stop having special music only on special occasions. It is time to have a choir every Sunday!" Reluctantly, she accepted the challenge, and our music ministry leaped to a new level.

Pioneering New Ways

We began to pioneer new avenues for ministry that had not yet been seen in Singapore. Trinity developed a powerful music and drama ministry, which staged many performances that had a lasting impact on lives across denominational lines. We staged a Singing Cross in Toa Payoh one Easter, and then staged the first Singing Christmas Tree on Orchard Road in 1982.

We were able to receive the favor of business leaders who owned a large vacant piece of land right on Orchard Road, the main tourist and shopping belt in the nation, which became a national attraction every Christmas.

Our tree was about seven stories high, constructed on the hill along Orchard Road where the big Takashimaya Shopping Complex is located now. We constructed row upon row of wooden platforms, to create the different levels of the Christmas tree, with railings to prevent choir members from falling over. Lai Ying led the music ministry. We had a live orchestra and a live choir standing on each rows of the 'tree'.

I wanted dancing lights that would move in sync with the music while the choir sang. No one really understood what I had in mind, until Barbara connected us with a Baptist missionary living in Malang. He was a handyman, and came to Singapore to help us. He built for us an entire board of light switches. As the choir sang, he and our lighting guys would operate these switches manually, keeping up with the music! When Low Lum Soon, our lighting volunteer in the church, saw this, he understood what was needed. The next year, he created a pre-programmed light display that automatically changed in sync with the music. It was outstanding.

The message of the songs carried a long distance. Each night, about five thousand to seven thousand people stood to watch and listen to the singing, often under umbrellas because of the evening drizzle. While the police accused us of creating a traffic jam, the Singapore Tourist Promotion Board would call us each year to find out our planned dates because they wanted to include the Singing Christmas Tree on the slate of Christmas events for tourists. It was a highlight for several years from 1982 to 1987, with a break in 1984.

God was present. Our church members would dress as shepherds to mingle with the crowds and share the gospel. I was also dressed as a shepherd on stage, telling the Christmas story of the birth of Jesus on stage. Hundreds of people received Jesus Christ. Many of them became leaders in the church and still are serving today.

Many of them became leaders in the church and still are serving today.

134

Music and drama proved to be a powerful combination to reach the different ages groups in the nation. In 1985 and 1986, while we had our services at the old World Trade Centre, we staged a three-hour stage production called The Master's Plan, in partnership with a church from America. The queue stretched from the ground floor all the way up the stairs to the eleventh floor, with people standing and waiting to get into the auditorium.

These dramas were powerfully used by God. They also presented an opportunity to upgrade our local members with new techniques in presenting dramas. These productions were also a valuable time of learning for Beatrice Kang, who was active in the music ministry while also serving as our office manager. We were the first church in Singapore to stage such large-scale productions.

Looking for a Home

As the church grew, it was not easy finding a venue that could house our services, with separate rooms for our children and Mandarin services, and our equipping classes. Moving in and out of a meeting venue, storing our big organ (that was the main instrument back in those days – and boy, was it heavy!) and carrying our other musical equipment was no joke. Praise the Lord for dedicated men and women who faithfully came early and stayed late in order to transport and then to set up and store all of the equipment. What a blessing they were! I am glad to report that many of these same people are still serving in the church today.

Without our own building, the church was still very much at the mercy of landlords and external events. Whenever the auditorium where we were meeting had an event, we would have to make way for the event. This would throw us into a tailspin as we had to find alternative venues for our worship services, often at very short notice. We had to use any place we could find that was big enough. We moved often and used almost every available venue through those growing years. We met in concert halls, hotels, conference halls, the American School hall, theaters, and the World Trade Center auditorium. It was clear that we needed a permanent home of our own, so I was on the lookout to find a property we could buy.

CHAPTER 13

Building by Faith

TOMMY CHUA, A NEW CONVERT in the church, knew we were looking for property. Many times after our squash games, he and I would spend time talking about the need and praying for God to supply. At the time he was interested in property as well. Soon he found two houses along Adam Road and asked if the church would be interested in one or both of them.

We drove by Adam Road where I could see the old houses. They were located along a main thoroughfare. Immediately I said, "Yes!" So he began negotiations with the owners, while I called a board meeting to share with them the possibilities. The church board was equally excited about purchasing the land.

Finally, an agreement was reached – S$2.6 million for both pieces of land. Now the challenge: After making a down payment of about S$30,000, we had a deadline of four months to completely pay off the land. If we did not raise the full amount in four months, we would lose the down payment, which happened to be the sum total of our building fund.

This was in 1981, when Trinity had less than five hundred people in the congregation. Immediately, I arranged to have a Faith Promise Sunday and rented the Victoria Concert Hall for the meeting. This purchase was going to be a stretch of faith for us as a church. How much came in faith promises and how much in cash, I do not remember. But we still did not have enough for the full amount.

So we talked to the church members about giving the church a loan from their savings. We would pay them the same interest as the bank, and also repay them their money any time they needed it. Many people responded with both small and large amounts. Some had been saving up for their children's university studies, but loaned their funds to us until the time they really needed them. Others went to the bank and pledged their condominiums as a guarantee so the bank would release that amount to the church.

Amazingly the miracle of provision took place. We were able to raise the full amount and complete the sale. In the following years we also repaid everyone who had loaned us their money, with interest. This miracle was the foundation for many more miracles to come.

This miracle was the foundation for many more miracles to come.

more miracles to come. The miracle of finances and the bond of trust between the leadership and the congregation continues in Trinity Christian Centre today.

Place of Beginnings

It was during this time that God used Lim Kay Kok, who was then the President of the Metropolitan YMCA on Stevens Road. He and his wife Alice brought a strong presence of the Lord into the different areas of ministry we had. They opened their home for cell meetings, and Alice was a powerful leader in our deliverance ministry. As Kay Kok was on our church board, they joined us after our Easter service at the old World Trade Center, when our board members with a few of our pastors and leaders drove over to Adam Road to have a prayer of dedication of the land.

I remember there was only one small tree in front of the old house on #21. It was maybe about two meters high, with a few small branches – definitely not enough to shade our group from the hot sun. We stood there together, with our perspiration pouring down, holding onto that little tree and thanking God for His provision. Brother Lim looked toward heaven and said, "It is fitting that we are here. Adam was the first of God's creation in the place of beginnings. In the same way, this land on Adam Road is our place of beginning." With that prophetic declaration, I led us in prayer of thanksgiving as we dedicated Adam Road, our place of beginnings, to God.

As I began the planning and development of Adam Road, the Lord raised up Danny Yeo, one of our board members who dealt with properties, to help me work with the architects and builders. What a blessing he was then, and has continued to be through the years! He worked with me on every one of our building projects from the purchase of Adam Road, to River Valley, to Lavender Street, right through to Paya Lebar. He has been God's gift to me and the church.

In those early days, Danny and I trekked all over Singapore looking at buildings and theaters to see what might be available for church use. During that time, the government began to allow churches to buy abandoned theaters. We looked at many theaters of different sizes, but we chose not to buy them. Why? Because they did not fit my philosophy of ministry. There would be only an auditorium, with no rooms for training, children's ministry, and so on.

When considering a particular space, we must consider whether the space will accommodate our philosophy of ministry. If we don't, the space will limit our vision and our ministry, instead of facilitating that which God has called us to do. Not all spaces will fit your vision and ministry. You need to consider the size of property, the rooms, and whether it gives you the ability and flexibility to convert from one size to a larger size.

In reality, a church must look for more than just space. It has to build for the future. A building should not be just enough for the present. However, most leaders do not plan for growth. They are just excited to get a new place to accommodate their current congregation. They factor in growth for maybe another fifty people. They don't think, "If we grow to a thousand, what will I do?"

Most leaders do not cast vision that way, so people are content with a space that is comfortable. There is no vision for expansion. There is no vision to give or sow into. Because leaders under-build, their churches remain small.

The faith of the leader is critical. Faith is the substance of things hoped for; God gives us the ability to believe Him for that which is unseen (Hebrews 11:1-3). God also gives us the ability to have godly foresight. He says, "Watch out... You will hear of wars and rumors of wars..." (Matthew 24:4-6) and He mentions, "When you see Jerusalem being surrounded by armies..." (Luke 21:20). These scriptures indicate to us that God expects us to discern the times and prepare for the future. He expects us to be discerning, to be able to perceive the direction in which things are moving – not just relating to the end times but also for the shifts and changes in society.

Seeing the Future

Another area God led us into was building a Bible school. In the late 1970s, the Assemblies of God in Singapore wanted to start a Bible school. Rev Patrick Lau, who was General Superintendent at the time, asked Pastor Winnie Wong and I to help him find a location to start the school.

During those conversations, I urged Pastor Lau to start at least a four-year Bible school that would lead to a theological degree. My reason was that Singapore was a growing nation. We were a young population, and great emphasis was being placed upon higher education. That meant more people would become university graduates. This would in turn mean that pastors needed to be equipped at a higher level of biblical training to lead a changing community. If the pastors had only a basic education, their training would not prepare them adequately to pastor and teach a highly educated congregation.

After the AG leadership chose to establish a Bible institute that would award qualifications up to the diploma level, I felt that I needed to start a Bible school to train future pastors beyond the institute level.

From its humble beginnings in 1979, Trinity School of the Bible and Ministry (TSBM) was a training school for those who desired biblical training beyond what was offered by the Assemblies of God in both Singapore and Malaysia. We needed to conduct proper classes with qualified teachers so that students who desired to pursue further education would be able to have credits recognized by other schools.

Although we were unknown and small, qualified teachers whom I knew from the United States answered my call to come and teach one subject at a time. Wonderful examples include Dr Raymond Brock (who had taught at Oral Roberts University and the Assemblies of God Graduate School in Springfield), Barbara Liddle, and many others.

We had to develop a library from scratch. Grace Chin, one of our church members, devoted her time and energy to develop our library, ordering books from overseas and getting all of the books numbered properly and organized on shelves. Our first library was housed in two containers stacked on top of each other at the back of our first property on Adam Road.

One of our church members, Dr Y.S. Lau, was a renowned engineer in Singapore. He helped me ensure the floors of the containers were strong enough to hold the weight of the books and the students who were studying in the library. God is so good; I marveled at His provision.

With this progress and growth, by 1983 we felt the need to change our name from Trinity School of the Bible to Theological Centre for Asia (TCA). We wanted students to know that we were not just a school for our Trinity church members, but a school open to anyone desiring to increase in their knowledge of God's Word and ministry. We began to see encouraging growth in the number of students from other churches.

Line upon Line

Line upon line, class upon class, we began to have graduates. They were accepted in colleges overseas to further their Bible training. Slowly, the school began to be accepted and received accreditation from Asia Pacific Theological Association (APTA) and Asia Theological Association (ATA). We began to have international students from the region, including Thailand, Philippines, Myanmar, and Indonesia, with some coming from nations as far away as Ghana and Romania.

Over the years, God sent others to join our TCA faculty. One of those who served with us was Dr Bill Robertson, my former District Superintendent in the AG Southern California District. He and his wife Jeanette had been serving in Malaysia for several years and felt that God was moving them into another season of ministry. When I heard about this, I contacted them to ask if they would consider joining me in Trinity to teach in our Bible school and also to join our preaching team. He and Jeanette were a wonderful addition to our team.

Pastor Robertson was a great father figure, like a grandfather to some. He would continually share his preaching outlines and was a great encourager and mentor to our younger staff. He also worked with the Singapore AG Council, preparing a process for discipline and restoration of ministers who had fallen. The Robertsons were greatly missed when they later decided to return to California to be near their children and grandchildren.

Through the years TCA continued to grow under the leadership of Derek and May Ling Tan. Derek led the development of TCA for many years, until it grew into a college with full accreditation. May Ling was an outstanding theologian who studied at Regent College and Cambridge University, and could hold her own with the best of them.

In 1992, we introduced our first Master's program. In 1997, we began to offer biblical training in Mandarin, which required Mandarin-speaking faculty. Again God supplied. When I was in Taiwan doing some training at the AG Bible school, Joy Tsai was my interpreter. We shared many conversations about ministry, her life, and her calling. As an answer to prayer, Joy felt led to leave Taiwan and move to Singapore to join our faculty. While she was teaching with us, she also completed her doctoral studies and now serves as our Dean of the School of Theology (Chinese).

After Pastor Derek went to be with the Lord in 2006, Dr Wilson Teo became TCA President and further developed the school such that it began to offer training in the areas of counseling, creative arts, and leadership, up to a Master's degree. Desiring to have some continuity and semblance to the original name, we chose to rename the school TCA College.

Today TCA College is the largest Pentecostal-Charismatic college in the nation. It has come a long way from its humble beginnings, but it all started because God helped me to see a need and fill it – a need which no one was addressing at the time. As a leader, you must perceive the direction in which your city or nation is going, observe the demographics, and anticipate its trajectory of growth, so that you are prepared to meet both present and future needs.

It all started because God helped me to see a need and fill it.

CHAPTER 14

The Greatest Battle

WHEN I HAD LEFT NASHVILLE, I knew that my mom would probably remarry. She did marry a wonderful man and they enjoyed many years of marriage. When my stepfather died in the early 1980s, his death caused Mom to become depressed. She was not prepared for life alone, because he had always taken care of her and had done everything for her. He had not allowed her to learn to drive, because he drove her anywhere she wanted to go. While he meant well by doing everything, it left her unprepared to handle her own affairs. She did not even know how to write a check on their joint account.

Her emotions were in turmoil and I needed to make numerous trips back to the States. I brought her out to Singapore for a visit, hoping that she would become familiar with my home and with the church here. However, after a few weeks she wanted to return to Nashville. She did so, but within a short time, she would fall into depression again. Then family members would call me back to Nashville.

Mom wanted me to leave Singapore and come back and live with her. She wanted me to drive her around the States in the beautiful new sport utility vehicle or SUV that James had bought shortly before he died. I had to be firm. "Sorry, Mom, but there is no way I am leaving Singapore. God called me here and I am not returning to Nashville."

With the help of some friends, I tried to resettle her into a retirement home where there were people to keep her company and activities to keep her busy. That did not work out either. Finally I said, "Mom, there is no choice. You must come to Singapore and live with me. I cannot keep flying back and forth like this."

Reluctantly, around 1983, she finally agreed to move to Singapore. This meant I needed to pack her things, sell some and give some away, and prepare her for a big change in her life. At first she struggled, but before long she adapted and was comfortable here. Many of our pastors and church members would drop by to visit her, and she enjoyed their visits. But when Pastor Steven Tay dropped by, he would sit down beside her and tell her joke after joke. She loved Pastor Steven; he always made her day.

Pastor Robertson and Jeanette were also a great support and encourager to my mother. They would invite Mom over to their home to eat, or to dine with them at restaurants. She liked that.

When Mom came over to live with me, Sister Beck was also living in my home. When I had first met Sister Beck, she had been serving as the Director of Women's Ministries for the Southern California District of the AG. Now she had retired, and as the church in Singapore grew, I had asked her to join me in Singapore. She was a great help as she handled most of the premarital and marriage counseling load, which freed up my time to lead the church and spearhead new areas of ministry.

Now I had two people living in my house: my mom and Sister Beck. As both of them were about the same age, I needed to hire a helper to do the cleaning and cooking, and help take care of things in the house. This ensured that Mom and Sister Beck had their meals, even when I was not home to eat with them.

After Sister Beck returned to the States because of her declining health, I needed to adjust my schedule to ensure that Mom was not alone too much. Thankfully we had a reliable helper, and folks like Pastor Robertson, his wife Jeanette, and Pastor Steven, who would drop by to see her. Because of this, taking care of her did not hinder my ability to fulfill my responsibilities at the church. I was still able to go on mission trips, though I could not be away for too long.

Expanding the Base

In the 1980s, God began prompting me to begin training a preaching team to increase the number of preachers in the church. He was directing me not to be the only preacher every Sunday, nor to have someone else preach only when I was not around. He said, "*It is not good that the church is growing on your pulpit ministry alone. It is time for change.*"

He said, "It is not good that the church is growing on your pulpit ministry alone. It is time for change."

This strategy launched us into a whole new phase of development within the church. I worked simultaneously with several emerging pastors and leaders. To help each of them discover and develop their spiritual gifts, I would give each one different platforms where they could grow and expand in the use of their gifts. It was also a way for me to become aware of areas of weakness that needed to be improved or overcome before they could move on and move up in their calling and destiny.

Lord of the Valley

In 1986, I was doing my doctoral studies at Bethel Theological Seminary in the States where module classes were held at different time intervals, for two to three weeks at a time. In the months between each class, there were readings, report writing and research that had to be done. I did the reading, research and report writing in Singapore, and flew into the States for classes as required.

As the time drew close for me to leave for my next study trip, I felt a deep troubling in my spirit that I should not go. I really needed to go in order to continue my studies, but there was just a deep unease that I could not shake off. Reluctantly, I canceled my trip and later realized the truth of the passage, that a person may plan his course, "but the Lord determines his steps" (Proverbs 16:9).

I had known God as Lord of the mountain tops, but I was about to learn to know Him as Lord of the valleys too. I would soon discover that one of my spiritual sons was attempting to split the church while I would be away. Needless to say, it was a time of change, adjustments, and pain. I felt like I knew what Jesus went through when He was despised, suffered grief, rejection, and betrayal by one of those closest to Him (Isaiah 53:3). I tried my best to follow Christ's example and not open my mouth. I chose not to explain nor defend myself. I shared with the congregation that a group was leaving, that they were starting a new church, and I took an offering for them. I wanted to let God handle the matter.

The Aftermath

Deep down, I was shaken and deeply hurt. This was not someone on the outside; these were my closest spiritual 'children' whom I loved and whose lives I had poured into. Now to have them leave in this way really shook me. It was like being punched in the stomach and having the wind knocked out of you. I could not preach for many weeks. I was in a daze for a few months. Yes, I would be in church, and I would lead the worship and prayer times, but I scheduled someone else to preach.

I had preached that nothing ever comes to a believer without God's knowledge, so I knew He was not surprised by what was happening. God was not only present, He was guiding us all through this valley of the soul. In prayer I experienced what Paul described in Romans 8, when "the Spirit himself intercedes for us with groans that words cannot express" yet "in accordance with God's will" (vv. 26-27).

I searched my heart and honestly asked God to work "for the good of those who love him, who have been called according to his purpose" (Romans 8:28). Years earlier I had heard a powerful message on Psalm 84:5-7; now was the time for living it: "Blessed are those whose strength is in you, who have set their hearts on pilgrimage. As they pass through the Valley of Baca [weeping], they make it a place of springs... they go from strength to strength, till each appears before God."

Holding Together

Some of our other leaders were overseas at this time. Pastors Yat Wan and Angelina Eu were completing their Masters program in Springfield. I called to tell them what was happening.

When I spoke with Yat Wan, I said, "I don't know how you feel and where you stand in this whole thing, whether or not you would want to come back."

He said, "We are with you, Pastor."

They came back and provided continuity. This spoke a lot to the church, because he was a long-time pastor, and the only other pastor preaching at that time. Beatrice Kang, who was our office manager; Choo Lai Ying, and Patsy Wong, who was my secretary, and others, gave strong support. They were firmly committed to Trinity and to the people.

Shortly before all of this happened, we had really just gotten the cells going in the church. Later many said that the stability of relationships in the cells had helped to hold the church together. Because of the cells and the training, people were more stable in the Word and more firmly rooted in the church.

The Real Battle

I had some initial thoughts that maybe I should just resign from the church, rather than to face the pain. As I prayed, the Spirit of the Lord said, "No, you don't desert the church, you don't leave the church."

So I rose up on the inside and declared, "I am not leaving. I'm staying and I'm going to walk with the church through this." I determined in my heart to come out in victory. If I had given in to that momentary thought to leave, I don't know where I would be today – or what would have happened to the church.

One thing I focused on was keeping my spirit right, and not letting bitterness and mistrust gain a foothold in my spirit, in accordance with

150

Hebrews 12:15: "See to it that no one misses the grace of God and that no bitter root grows up to cause trouble and defile many." It was a battle. Winning this battle has been very important in my life. Getting through such a battle in the valley takes time and a lot of prayer.

You must have the determination to put it down. If you feel anything, deal with it, and don't let it build up. If you feel it, put it down. Not doing so would isolate you. It will cause you to trust people only so far but not trust them further. I could not let it be a barrier between myself and the present staff or those who would join us in the future.

I did not want to develop a blind spot. I did not want what one person or group had done to cause me to hinder the growth of others. So I asked those who were working with me to help me. I said, "You guys watch me very carefully. Don't let me project on you or limit you in any way because of what has happened. If you feel I am holding you back, not trusting you, not releasing you, let me know. I don't want the hurt I have experienced to cause me to withdraw and not mentor leaders."

I knew I could not let my deep valley experience hold me back from trusting people. If leaders don't trust people, we won't release authority, we won't give them responsibility, we will keep them in the background, just so the congregation won't get attached to them. Despite any great disappointment, we must keep believing in people. If we have a fear of releasing ministry to others, it will quench the multiplication of ministers and disciples.

I knew I could not let my deep valley experience hold me back from trusting people.

In the months following this valley experience, the church needed time for healing to take place. It was not a time to be casting vision or moving forward with new plans. We could not advance and move forward aggressively because some key leaders and members had left. This would impact everyone in different ways. There were emotions that had to be dealt with at all levels. This took one to two years for healing and refocus to take place. Over time, the church recovered emotionally. By the late 1980s, we had raised new leaders. Once again, we were growing and thriving.

Over the years, almost all of those leaders who left have since renewed and restored their relationship with me. Some years later, God brought about a beautiful reconciliation. We jointly called a combined service for both churches, where we each spoke and then had communion together. Later, they invited me to preach at their church, and to speak with their church board on their vision and church direction, which I did.

God has restored what had been lost for all of us. What the devil intended for harm, God has turned it around for good (Genesis 50:20). This is all to the glory of God.

CHAPTER 15

Defining Our Call

WHEN I FIRST BECAME PASTOR of Trinity Christian Centre in Singapore, I stopped all of my travels and focused totally on the church. There was so much to do – ministering, training, planning, building relationships, developing training programs, and mentoring staff – that I did almost no travel for several years. A pastor cannot travel and be gone all the time and still expect the church to grow. I slowly resumed overseas travel, however, when I began developing our missions program.

Shortly after we stabilized the church and it was growing in strength, I began to take small teams of leaders from the church with me on quick weekend trips into Malaysia for ministry. I wanted people not just to give to missions; I wanted them to *experience* missions. I wanted them to get missions and winning the lost into their spirits and for it to become their lifestyle.

I would get our music team together so we could bring a shift in music and worship, to attract people to come to the churches where we ministered. I started with churches that were within driving distance into Malaysia. The roads then were not the wide expressways of today, but just two-lane roads filled with speeding cars and heavy trucks jammed one behind the other. Those of us who did the driving really had to stay alert.

Again, there were no nice hotels like we have today. We would stop at the old British-style rest houses and sleep on mats on the floor at night, before having a simple breakfast and continuing our journey the next morning. But those were good days. People were hungry for God. We helped new churches that were being planted. Miracles were happening. Our team members gained a real heart for missions.

After a while, I decided it was time for them to go further from home, so I arranged for us to conduct evangelistic rallies in Indonesia. The objective would be to channel all converts into existing churches, or if there was no church in the area, to start a new church with the new converts as the first members.

For a number of years we planted churches or helped plant churches in both Malaysia and different parts of Indonesia. We helped pay for the repairs of churches which were damaged because of persecution. In some cases we helped support pastors so they would be able to plant new churches.

This experience built in our members a greater sense of confidence that comes from knowing 'God can use me, God can use our church, and we can do more than has been done before.' I knew that their experience in missions would change them personally and enhance their burden for missions. It was all part of their training and implanting a vision for winning the lost.

On one such trip, Pastor Beatrice Kang accompanied me to Seremban, Malaysia. It was a particularly memorable trip because that evening, while the Spirit of God was moving in the service, there were thieves moving outside the building. I was driving an old Volvo and had parked it beside the church. For some reason they liked the front grille of my car, so they took it out and stole it.

This created what I considered a potentially dangerous situation. With the grille gone, the radiator was totally exposed. I knew that on the journey back to Singapore there would be pebbles or other debris that could fly up off the road and puncture my radiator. If that happened, the radiator would lose water and the engine would overheat.

So we went looking for something to cover the opening where the grille had been. Unable to find a replacement, we went to a hardware shop to buy wire mesh (the kind you would use to build a chicken coop). We bent the mesh into shape and wired it firmly to the car, so it would not loosen and drop off on our way home. Well, our innovative solution worked, and we made it back to Singapore without any problems.

Making Disciples

People were getting saved, but my goal was to make disciples, not just win converts. I knew we needed to develop a process that would nurture new believers and help them grow into disciples who would then win and disciple others. However, discovering exactly how God wanted me to make disciples would become a journey in itself.

Before I had left the Marshall Islands, I had made a quick trip to Guam, where a group of leaders prayed over me. They asked me to sit on a chair as they gathered around me to pray and prophesy. Even though I was not flowing in the prophetic in those years, I did not think it was strange. I felt that God was speaking. They prophesied about me making disciples, building a strong church, and many other powerful things. All I heard was *"You will make disciples."*

155

I then considered myself an evangelist, so I struggled with how to include disciple-making into my calling as an evangelist. But now, in the context of Trinity, what God said about making disciples made perfect sense. I began to understand why God wanted me to become a pastor. God wanted me to lead a local church and create a new model for churches in several areas. You cannot create God's new model unless you are actually doing the new things He is saying. The church became a laboratory for God's new assignment. Suddenly, I knew it was time to integrate the things God had been speaking to me about – what the church should be and how the church should function.

While I knew God wanted me to make disciples, I was not sure exactly how I was to go about it. I would teach, train and conduct classes. Then God would say, *"But I told you to make disciples."*

> *Then God would say, "But I told you to make disciples."*

Then I would call people back and teach them another course on discipleship. God kept on saying, *"I told you to make disciples."*

I became frustrated. "God, I am trying. I just don't know what else to do!" I was hearing but not understanding. I was struggling to know how He wanted me to make disciples. I was doing all I knew to do and it was obviously not producing the results that He wanted. I tried to figure all this out in my head, but to no avail.

During those years I made several trips to Seoul, Korea, to sit under the teachings of Dr David Yonggi Cho. I studied his model of cells but did not feel that his model was exactly what God wanted us to do.

After one of the sessions in Korea, Cho gave us a blank chart with the years all marked out. He challenged us to draw, by faith, a line across and up at any angle that would reflect the growth we believed God would give our church. I took the chart back to my room, sat down, and stared at it. I prayed, "God, what do You want? Show me!"

After a long while, I picked up my pencil and I drew a line at a 45-degree angle from the lower left corner to the upper right corner. "God, I believe for this kind of growth." I brought the chart home and kept it for years. One day, as I was going through some old files I saw that chart. I looked at it and then checked those past years of growth. Praise the Lord, we have broken through the barriers. God has given us that kind of increase, even though we had been nomadic with no real home for our worship services.

India Calling

Dr David Grant has been a dear friend for many years, and is greatly committed to the nation of India. I had first met him when he visited the Marshall Islands. Every time we would talk or when he would speak for our Missions Convention, he would keep urging me to go to India. He especially wanted me to minister with Rev David Mohan in Madras (now called Chennai).

In 1991, I invited both Mohan and David to Singapore to minister at our Missions Convention. In between the missions services, I was sharing with Mohan about our Carecell model and about making disciples who would become Kingdom-minded leaders. At the urging of David Grant, Pastor Mohan reluctantly invited me to Madras to teach them about our Carecell model. Before long, I arrived in Madras for the training sessions.

About ninety people had signed up for the training. However, Pastor Mohan cautioned me, "Many will come the first night, fewer will come the second night, and on the third and final night, very few will come." He wanted me to be prepared, and to manage my expectations.

I said, "Okay, I understand."

They translated our materials and we began our first night of training. The second night, the same people returned. In fact, more showed up and wanted to join the sessions. Pastor Mohan was shocked by the response.

I told him, "Pastor Mohan, new people cannot come in now. Because they have missed the first night, they don't have the foundation. They will be lost and will not understand what we teach tonight." Each night, people kept coming to glean whatever they could, as they were eager to learn. The teaching, and the response to the teaching, turned Pastor Mohan from a skeptic to a believer.

This turned out to be the first of many trips to India. Mohan's church shifted onto a new growth trajectory. New Life Assembly of God (NLAG) was 2,500-strong then. In the twenty-five years since, it has grown to 40,000. They have become a model church for our Carecell system for all of India and an inspiration to many leaders in other nations. Mohan is a powerful preacher and a great leader. Yet, he also is a very humble man – a rare combination indeed. He attributes his growth to the leadership training he received, coupled with the effectiveness of the Carecell model from Trinity. It has been an honor to work alongside him as his church grew to become the largest church in India.

Pastor Mohan and his wife Getziel became very dear friends of mine. Getziel, who was already a powerful leader, had limited herself to doing only women's ministry. I encouraged her, and affirmed God's calling and plan to use His gifts that He had deposited in her. They joked that I had a kicking anointing, because I kicked her out of the kitchen!

After I challenged her to get out of the kitchen, I turned to Pastor Mohan and asked, "Is this okay with you?"

He quipped, "Yes, yes, out of the kitchen – but first, finish cooking tonight's dinner!"

Getziel proved to be an effective leader and a powerful woman of faith. She became a regional pastor overseeing hundreds of carecells. This was a breakthrough of great significance and symbolism in a country like India where gender discrimination is deeply entrenched. NLAG continues to release women into their Kingdom destiny. Since then there have been thousands of women released to serve God, and Pastor Mohan says his best carecell leaders are women!

Defining Our Call

As we continued to work with pastors like Mohan, God began to shift my understanding of our calling as a church. We had always believed in church planting, but there were already thousands of churches planted all over the world, and many pastors were struggling to survive. They did not have tools or resources to work with. They did not have a plan or strategy to reach their village or their city. They were struggling and discouraged, but were trying to carry on their work and be faithful to Jesus.

Most churches were sending out church planters, but no one was sending out experienced leaders to help these who were struggling without any help. I knew that God had given us an effective cell model that could change these pastors and their churches – if only they had the training and the tools. Around this time, we received a defining word of prophecy, that we would go into areas where the harvest had been broken, and "reap the broken harvest."

I had witnessed this broken harvest many times in many places. Whenever I conducted training in various countries, it was not unusual for pastors to come up to me after the training to say: "I came to this training with the intention of resigning from my church after I return. I was so discouraged, I had no answers, I wanted to throw in the towel. In fact I have my letter of resignation all ready, to be submitted upon my return. But now, after this training, I know what to do. I have the answers and the skills learned in this training. I can go back and fulfill my calling to pastor the church." Many a ministry was saved through the training and tools provided.

The more I prayed, the more I felt a shift in our calling. I had planted churches. I knew what it was like to learn a new language, and to work in a new culture. I knew what this demanded of a family, the implications on their children's education and many other issues.

I also observed the caliber of people God was bringing into Trinity. They tended to be university graduates, capable and highly educated. I asked God, "These are the people you have given to us. How do You want to use their gifts?" As I looked at the people we had, and the needs that were waiting to be met in the nations, things came together. As I prayed, God impressed upon me, *"You are not an Antioch Church; you are to be an Ephesus Church."*

"You are not an Antioch Church; you are to be an Ephesus Church."

What is an Ephesus Church? I had to look it up. An Ephesus church is modeled for us by the Apostle Paul in Acts 19:1-7. Paul visited the church in Ephesus where Apollos had been preaching. Apollos was away in ministry in Corinth when Paul arrived. Immediately Paul began to ask, "Did you receive the Holy Spirit when you believed?" They responded, "No, we have not even heard that there is a Holy Spirit."

When Paul heard their reply, he began to give them what I call a spiritual upgrade. He upgraded their theology. He helped the church move to another level in their relationship with God. He brought an upgrade to the teachings that they had access to in the past, which had been limited. Paul could take the church to a new level of revelation in God. I felt that was the way God wanted to use me and all of our pastors.

We were not to plant churches, but to train and help pastors grow and build their churches and then to encourage those churches to send out church planters into their own regions. Yes, new churches needed to be planted, but we were not to do so directly. We were to come alongside pastors who were doing everything they could with whatever they had, and like Paul, come along to train them and lead them to another level.

An Ephesus Church

When I understood this clearly, we made a major shift in our missions program to flow with this strategy. We made the shift from planting to equipping. We started to come alongside pastors and churches in over thirty nations through training and church consultation. Where churches have committed themselves to the change process, we have gone back repeatedly over a number of years, to literally co-labor with them and strengthen them so they can move to another level.

In 1999, Pastors Steven and Margaret Tay spearheaded our training and consultation work with the churches in India. For nine years, they did an excellent job of organizing pastors' conferences in five different states, conducting follow-up training for the churches, and coordinating teams of Trinitarians going in to work with these churches.

Today, churches all over India are growing, developing leaders, and planting effective churches. Now they no longer need us to do these things! All the training is done in India by the leaders in that nation. We just keep praying and encouraging them to do the work of the ministry. They have the training, they have the tools, and they are extremely effective.

According to a report by David Grant, this strategy has resulted in some two thousand churches being planted in India in one year, by churches we helped. NLAG itself has planted over 200 churches. As a single church, Trinity would never have been able to plant that many churches. But as we came alongside pastors who were already out there doing the work, trained them, and made resources available to them, they have become an army of pastors and leaders strong enough to take new territory at an accelerated pace. It was accelerated because when they went out to plant new churches, they could send out workers who already spoke the language and who were familiar with the local customs. It was faster and more effective.

As a single church, Trinity would never have been able to plant that many churches.

Once again, God's direction and wisdom proved to be right. His ways are higher than our ways (Isaiah 55:8-9).

CHAPTER 16

To the Nations

MANY HAVE ASKED ME why Pastor Mohan has been so successful while others have not succeeded. The answer is simple: Pastor Mohan followed our Trinity Carecell model without trying to change it. He is a strong and committed leader. Even though he was already a successful pastor, he was humble enough to learn. He did not try to pick and choose which parts of the model to use, and which parts to discard; he faithfully followed the model and ensured that his leaders did the same.

The pastor is always the key to change. If he/she does not or will not change, then the church can never grow beyond their present level. This means the pastor must be willing to pay the price of change. There is always a price to pay:

- You must change your leadership style.
- You must change your sermons.
- You must not fear some church members becoming upset with you.
- You must discard some of the old programs in the church in order to make room for and embrace new, more effective ones.

Yes, there is a price to pay for change. Frankly, some pastors are too comfortable or too set in their ways; they do not want to go through the perceived pains of change. If the pastor is willing to pay the price for change, so must the people of God. There are some Christians who love to be pampered by the pastor. They let the pastor do all the work while they remain spiritual babies, just wanting to be fed the Word and prayed for all the time, at every service. Now suddenly, they are required to grow up spiritually and begin to take responsibility in the Kingdom of God.

Change is something that must be continually in our planning. Change is a constant for us and the church; there is no way to avoid it. Our biggest issue then is how to *manage* change – that is the most delicate part. Because we mismanage change, we have bad experiences and end up retreating back into our old patterns, afraid to attempt new things for God.

The Rubber Factory

In my ongoing efforts to both communicate and reinforce the key elements of our cell training, I am always looking for ways to communicate like Jesus, by creating a modern day parable. I try to use something in everyday life that people know about and give it a spiritual application. One such example is the rubber factory illustration, which I use in my training of pastors.

In a factory, you need to produce the same effective product year after year. It would not do for a factory to produce a rubber tire one day, and an eraser the next. Therefore, the equipment you use, the processes you have in place, and the activities you undertake are intentionally designed and repeated to achieve the same desired results – day after day, year after year. The processes are kept consistent so that the product or outcome will always be the same.

However, in most churches, there is no consistent, repeatable process. Someone joins a church service and hears one thing, but when he brings along a friend, the sermon has progressed to another topic. When someone is invited to a Bible study or cell group, rarely is the Bible study material repeated, so a newcomer who joins today goes through a different process from someone who joins a year later. We have no consistent process – so why does it come as a surprise when we do not get consistent results?

We have no consistent process – so why does it come as a surprise when we do not get consistent results?

We must understand that what we do in church (our activities and programs) will shape the lives of those who attend. The internal processes of a church determine the product or outcome – the results reflected in the lives of those who belong to that church. Every church needs to have a reproducible model of making disciples.

The process we have developed is called Spiritual Parenting. A new believer is nurtured by a spiritual parent, using a basic nurturing tool that covers the basics of the Christian life. The spiritual parent is responsible to nurture the new believer by relating with him, modeling the Christian life, answering his questions, and providing the care and prayer support that every new believer needs. As the new believer grows in his faith and is baptized, he receives training to be a spiritual parent, and in turn makes the commitment to pray for, win, and nurture two people in a year.

All this takes place in the context of an open carecell. Our open carecells are not to be a mini church or a Bible study group. They are open relational networks where people reach out and where others find their place easily. Our open carecells are always open to new members, and never closed.

While the open carecells cater to everyone, the leadership carecells provide an environment where leaders can relate to one another and be discipled. Intentional leadership development takes place through our open and leadership carecells. The result is a culture of leadership development, where potential spiritual parents and leaders are identified early on, nurtured, and groomed to become leaders.

Without this leadership base fueling and supporting its growth, Trinity would not have grown to where it is today. By the time I handed over the church in 2005, I had multiplied myself, expanding the pastoral team from one (me) to forty-five pastors. More than ninety-eight percent of our pastors were homegrown, and they were all anointed and gifted. The church had effectively multiplied its leadership base, from a handful of leaders to approximately a thousand lay leaders and spiritual parents.

Creating New Tools

When we first began this process, however, we did not have the right tools for nurturing new believers. I searched for possible materials from what was available, because I did not want to create materials from scratch. At that time, we did not have church staff who could write materials.

We tried several kinds of materials before finally connecting with Don Hill, the founder of Lay Leadership Institute (LLI). I developed a working relationship with LLI and he allowed us to adopt and further develop his materials for nurturing, while developing our own track for training.

Things were going much better but again God said, "*I want you to make disciples and leaders. Don't just put them into groups for teaching. They are growing spiritually but the church is not growing in numbers. You must reach new people."*

The LLI materials were great materials, but because they focused on teaching, the needed element of evangelism was lost. They had materials and a teaching model, but we wanted an evangelism-oriented, disciple-making model that would develop leaders. I explained this to Don and we agreed that I would not continue using his material.

By now we had grown as a church and had staff that could help us develop our own materials. One day, I called all the pastors into the conference room: I spread out all the current materials we were using and challenged them. I said, "You know we need to change. We need to develop our own material that will accomplish the full scope of disciple-making, from nurturing a new believer right through to discipling them to become Kingdom-minded leaders. The material must be simple to understand, presented in bite-sized segments, so people (even new believers) can feel they are progressing in their spiritual walk."

With the old materials spread out and the challenge of the task laid out for the pastors, I said, "Now my contribution to this process is to leave this room, while you rewrite our materials. You know our vision, you know our purpose, and you are not from my generation. I would only be a hindrance to this process. If I were directly involved, I would keep saying, 'but put this in' or 'oh wait, but here is something else, put it in.' My old training and thinking would hinder your forward thinking. You develop our new materials to take us forward."

Our pastors did a fantastic job. There materials have been translated into different languages and are being used all over the world to bring people from being a new believer to becoming a godly leader. Huang

Rui Lin, who had been trained in communications and journalism, was given the task of editing and overseeing the publication of these new cell materials. Her intense study and research helped us ensure that our English was up to international standards, without any local colloquialisms, as we knew God wanted to use them in many different nations. She still works with me on all the books I am now writing.

Colombia's Time

While traveling as an evangelist, I ministered in many nations. By God's grace I have had the privilege of preaching on nearly every continent. However, there have been some nations where God has sent me, not just to preach, but to establish something over several years. You could say these were divine assignments to specific nations. For a few years I was in the Philippines, Malaysia, Hong Kong, Japan and Indonesia, before the focus shifted to India for about ten years.

There have been some nations where God has sent me, not just to preach, but to establish something over several years.

Then another shift began to happen in the 2000s. Actually it had its beginnings in 1991, when I was first invited to Colombia, South America. The first invitation came from Dr Hernando Avila and his wife Claudia, and Ruth Cortés, who were the leaders of the Haggai Institute in Colombia. The three of them were among my students when I taught a class on evangelism at the Haggai Institute in Singapore.

After inviting me, they looked for an interpreter who, as the job description went, "could keep up with me." They selected a young woman by the name of Esther Victoria Milian. From those first sessions, Esther and I became great friends. Later her pastor released her to come to Singapore for theological training.

After three years in our Bible school, Esther returned to Colombia and later became our bridge to the Spanish-speaking world. In 2001, she established our Global Leadership Network (GLN) office in Colombia, to serve Latin America. This facilitated our training and consultation efforts not only in Colombia, but also in nations such as Ecuador and Mexico, and for Spanish-speaking churches in the States. Esther has been a real trailblazer and has grown to be a recognized prophet in her nation.

Some of the early supporters and adopters of our cell model were Randy and Marcy MacMillian, founders of the Community of Faith Church network. Marcy was greatly involved in editing some of my books into Spanish and interpreting for us for many years. Isai Avendaño and his wife Natalia in Medellín have not only implemented the cell model, but are actively training many other churches to transform their community through carecells.

After several years of cell-related training, another expression of ministry developed in Colombia. There was much abuse and confusion regarding the apostolic and the prophetic ministries. There were large churches but there was little training and understanding of the restoration of the fivefold ministry gifts (Ephesians 4:11-13). This became a critical need. To address the issue I called for a meeting among the key leaders across the nation, challenging them to rise up and protect their pastors and nation from abuse of the spiritual gifts. This meeting in 2003 concluded with their asking me to lead a team to help them accomplish this task. I agreed to do this for three years, by the end of which they should assume the responsibility.

A Strong Team

Knowing that I needed mature, balanced, and experienced pastors to join me in this thrust, I called upon Pastor Ong Sek Leang, the

General Superintendent of the Assemblies of God of Malaysia, and Pastor Gerald Tan, who was on staff in Trinity then (now the senior pastor of Calvary Assembly of God), to join me as anchor members of the team. Although Pastor Dominic had traveled with me on earlier trips to Colombia and he loved the people there, I could not select him because I needed him in the church. Together, the three of them are prophets who speak into my life, and they make a great team.

Working with the two anchor members and Esther, we developed three block sessions to be used for teaching on the fivefold ministries but especially on the offices of the Apostle and the Prophet, and how all the gifts must work together. We called this the Apostolic and Prophetic Leadership Institute. This is where the wisdom and experience of Sek Leang – both as a powerful leader and as an accurate prophet – became a great blessing to the leaders in the nation. He would join me in some of my times of consultation with the executive officers of the Assemblies of God in Colombia. His commitment and partnership touched the nation.

We returned to Colombia at least once or twice a year for several years. It was not a physical institute; rather, each time we went, we would conduct the same sessions in various cities. We developed different levels of training. Every time we went back, we would build upon the understanding the leaders had gained the previous time, and bring them to a new level. Whenever he was available, Les Bowling from Eagle Rock Ministries in Columbus, Ohio, would join us in the training. Les is a great Bible teacher and preacher of the Word.

Naturally, with multiple trainers, all the interpretation could not be done by one person. God spoke to Cynthia Figueroa and her husband Harold Beltran to join us as we did training across the nation. She travelled with us, faithfully interpreting for us and helping in the translation of my books and our training materials. Another faithful member of our team was Edgardo Peña who not only went through the training, but became one of our Colombian trainers. Thank God for raising up powerful men and women in that nation with a passion to mentor others.

More than twenty years have passed since we became involved in Colombia. I have developed a relationship with so many different individuals, it would be impossible for me to name them all and list all the ways in which they have blessed me and their nation. Each of them are special and remain deep in my heart and prayers.

Shifting a Nation

The Apostolic and Prophetic Leadership Institute training created a greater unity among the pastors and churches as it strengthened them in their biblical understanding of what God is doing and how He is working in the world today. It also enabled them to be more discerning of teachings that different people brought into their nation. This brought everyone to a new level in God. Our sessions were open to all pastors in the nation, regardless of their affiliation. All of our training was coordinated with the ministerial associations in each city or region.

At the first meeting we convened, there were about eighty-eight apostles and prophets present. At the end of our training, I had the participants pair up – an apostle with a prophet. They each had to find a partner before they could pray. In unity, they made powerful declarations over their nation. A few months later, the news emerged that the drug cartel had released some hostages whom they had kidnapped.

We believe something shifted in the spiritual realm that day because of the united prayer of the nation's spiritual leaders.

171

Kidnapping was a persistent problem in the nation, and no hostage had been released before, but now they were releasing them! We believe something shifted in the spiritual realm that day because of the united prayer of the nation's spiritual leaders.

During this time, one of the pastors in our training was working among the people serving in the military. Through him, we were given an open door to minister to the Colombian Military and Police Force. Over a period of three years, we were invited to preach and teach at their conference.

At one particular conference, high-ranking officers from most of the South American nations were present. That night as I spoke, there was a powerful anointing on the Word. When I gave the altar call, all these generals and officers in uniform were standing at the altar praying, with their hands lifted. I began to release a prophetic word over them and suddenly, they fell backward onto the floor, still worshipping the Lord.

After the Lord had done a powerful work in them, I released another prophetic word, saying, "The Lord is showing me that the enemy is in your camp; he is in your midst. Do not be deceived, but be watchful and God will reveal them to you." One of the generals just looked up at me, winked, and smiled. I knew that the message had been meant for him, and that he now knew what to do.

I still have the honor of maintaining a relationship with one of the leading generals in Colombia, General Reinaldo Castellanos and his wife. He is retired now. When he was leading the military forces in the nation, he earned the nickname 'the Jesus General' – because of his life of prayer and his practice of seeking the Lord for strategy.

CHAPTER 17

Heaven's Gates Open

IN 1981, TRINITY HAD BOUGHT two plots of land at 21 and 23 Adam Road. However, we only developed 21 Adam Road, because we were hoping to first purchase a third plot of land at 25 Adam Road and then develop the whole stretch.

We had been in negotiations with the owners of #25, but it had taken much longer than expected. Sensing that we should not be held up any further in our building plans, we began to develop 21 Adam Road into a four-story building with an auditorium that could sit six hundred people, along with offices, classrooms, and a childcare center.

As we were nearing completion of the first phase of the building project, the owners of #25 got back to us and said they had decided to keep their property. This meant that we would need to continue building to fully maximize the land we had. The plan was to demolish the old house that stood at 23 Adam Road, construct a new four-story building, and then join it, floor by floor, with the first building at 21 Adam Road.

It was a daring plan that required great precision. Dr Y.S. Lau, an accomplished architect, worked with me. He was a dream to work with on this bold project; he never said it could not be done. The ideas were never too crazy for him! Whenever I bounced my ideas off of him, his reply was always "Anything is possible – it is only a matter of cost." He made it his goal to engineer the solutions needed to fulfill the vision God had placed in my heart. It required him to have one of the beams we needed built in Japan and shipped down to Singapore.

The result was an expanded auditorium that could easily seat 1,600 people. There were a couple of times that we packed in 2,000 people for special events. In 1995, we finally moved into the expanded building and auditorium, in time for our church's 25th Anniversary.

Heaven's Gates Open

In 1996, after our enlarged auditorium was ready, we had another powerful evangelistic drama called 'Heaven's Gates, Hell's Flames.' This was conceived and conceptualized by a ministry in the States. Someone recommended them to me, because the reports of the conversions in the States had been overwhelming. However, when I saw the script, I felt it was too simple. In fact, everything about it was so simple and straightforward – the script, the props, the presentation. I questioned God, "God, is this really going to be blessed and effective?"

As we were preparing for the presentation, I was overseas in ministry and our pastors called me. They had been praying and asking God how many salvations they should trust Him for. They said, "Pastor, God is saying to believe for five thousand decisions. What do you think?" Memories of major citywide meetings quickly flashed through my mind. Billy Graham's meeting in our National Stadium – they did not have five thousand. Meetings with Dr Yonggi Cho from Korea – they did not see five thousand. These were all meetings with many churches coming together in a big stadium. Who were we? We were only one church with a small auditorium. *"God, are you sure?"*

Finally, I responded to the pastors, "Look, I trust you to be hearing from God, and if you are hearing five thousand, then let's prepare for five thousand – by faith."

On the first night, less that fifty people came to the altars. My faith was being challenged. We had prepared five thousand packets of materials to be given to people who came forward to make a decision. To record the large number of decision cards we were expecting we had scheduled young people to be on duty to key the information into our database after service, and into the night as needed. We even had a special row of computers that we had prepared for this purpose. We also had a few hundred spiritual parents interceding during the presentation, and positioned at the altars to pray with those who came forward to receive Christ. Yet now – only fifty decisions!

The second night came, and again, only a small number came forward. Our faith was really being tested. We kept praying and we kept scheduling the young people to come and key in the information. Our spiritual parents continued to pray.

Then the third night, God broke through. Our prayers were answered. People began responding by the hundreds every night. But would we reach five thousand? We prayed and counted every night.

Through all this, God again taught me a great lesson. Things do not have to be long and elaborate. We just need to hear His voice and obey. When He is lifted up, anything can happen. We had originally planned to only have a few nights of this drama. But the people kept coming, and they were accepting Christ by the hundreds. It was unbelievable! We extended the nights of this presentation again. God was still touching lives. We

We just need to hear His voice and obey. When He is lifted up, anything can happen.

extended again, for a total of four weeks before we finally allowed the meetings to finish.

When it was all over, a total of 17,000 people had seen the evangelistic drama, which presented the Gospel in a clear and uncompromising manner. We had almost 5,000 decisions for Christ recorded. We contacted the churches that had supported us and distributed the decision cards to them for follow-up. We shared the harvest. We contacted those who had made a decision and directed them to attend one of the churches nearest their home.

To my knowledge, the Singapore Church has never experienced anything like that since. But there is no reason why God cannot move like this again. Faith, even "faith as small as a mustard seed," can move a mighty mountain (Matthew 17:20).

Serving the Community

As the church grew, I realized that it was not enough for us to be a typical local church, where ministry took place only within the four walls of the church. There were many needs in the community, and some of these needs could not be met in a traditional church setting, or even through our carecells.

Because of our call to impact the community and the nation in practical ways, I felt we needed to begin a social arm that would minister to the poor, families of prison inmates, the elderly, and disadvantaged children from low-income or dysfunctional families, who were having learning difficulties in school.

With the help of Pastor Eu Yat Wan, Care Community Services Society (CCSS) was birthed in 1996. Then it was entrusted into the hands of Pastor Patsy Chan who diligently worked to expand this outreach. Under her leadership, CCSS was so successful that it was able to receive tax deductible status in 1998. To receive that recognition in two years was a miracle.

Today, under the leadership of Pastor Beatrice Kang, CCSS is an established charity with a solid track record of helping lower-income families, children, the elderly, and the families of incarcerated persons. They also run after-school care services in government schools, working with students from lower-income families. Many of these students are struggling with their studies, or are not motivated to learn and do their homework properly. It is wonderful to see these students completely turn around after a few months. They begin not only to learn but also to excel in their attitude and confidence.

Releasing Leaders

During the 1990s I would take several key pastors with me on exposure trips to the States. I wanted them to attend conferences and see what others were doing. Through this I wanted them to appreciate how God was blessing Trinity, but also be inspired to a greater vision of possibilities, if they would dare to believe. These were wonderful times of bonding and learning. Each evening, after the sessions, we would return to the house where we were staying. We would meet in one room, sit on the floor and review what they had seen, what they needed to clarify, and how they thought changes could impact Trinity and Singapore. Those were wonderful times of sharing and growing.

One of these pastors was Christina Onn, who was heading our childcare center and our children's ministry. The prevailing approach among churches towards children's ministry was that of babysitting, rather than ministering to the children and helping them experience God. But Christina had a different vision.

So I took her on these trips overseas to further develop her in her calling. She did an excellent job with our children's ministry for many years. Then I challenged her, "Christina, I want to transfer you from children's ministry to working with adults. I want you to become a district pastor over one of our cell districts." She shuddered. She did not feel comfortable to make the big switch. However, I continued to talk and pray with her. I could see that she was very good at developing leaders around her. She was good at training and motivating them to accomplish more for God. I knew there was more in her than she realized.

Finally she agreed to the move. She did a great job. After a few years, I challenged her to make another move, this time to become the pastor of our Chinese ministry. Again, she shuddered. "I am schooled in English, I am very poor in Chinese." I told her, "But you can improve!" Soon, she made the shift. She rose to the challenge and with God's help, she did well.

Through the years, Christina has been an example of what God can do in a person's life and ministry, if the senior pastor or leaders will recognize God's gifts in individuals, and then commit to help that person discover the greater potential that God has for their life. Through the many transitions Christina has continued to grow, and has become an apostolic trainer and equipper of churches all over the nation of Taiwan, especially among the Presbyterian churches.

LoveSingapore

In 1995, a group of pastors in the city, led by Rev Lawrence Khong, came together and launched a movement that become known as LoveSingapore. God began to bring the churches in Singapore together in a new level of unity, beginning with prayer for the nation.

In 1997 I joined with them as I saw God moving in new ways and many people coming to Christ, but especially because of the unity.

The group matured in relationship, and their levels of cooperation expanded into many joint efforts to both equip believers and to bless the nation. Lai-Kheng Pousson served as the coordinator for the group and led in training thousands of intercessors both in Singapore and beyond. She was God's gift to the nation.

In just a few short years, before I resigned in early 2002, we saw the spiritual atmosphere in Singapore shift. Attitudes changed at every level of society and government because of the unity and coming together of God's people to bless the nation, at a level never experienced before. Those were some of the most intentional, coordinated efforts of churches ever experienced in the nation.

Marketplace Ministry

Having been in business and having worked in the marketplace in my early years, I understood that God can call you and use you for His purposes, both in the church and outside the church. However, as I interacted with Christian business people, especially those from other churches, I realized that this was not a common understanding. Hearing the cry of their hearts, I began to pray and seek for answers.

God can call you and use you for His purposes, both in the church and outside the church.

I quickly remembered unspoken impressions given to people whenever they felt called to serve God. Often without actually intending to, pastors and leaders communicated a message from the Dark Ages: that some things are sacred and others are secular. Since serving God was sacred, that would mean you needed to resign from your job (in the 'secular' world) and go to Bible school and then work in a church (the 'sacred' place). This mindset was communicated to people in sermons and through counsel given to individuals who felt called to serve God. Over many years this has caused business people to feel like they were second-class citizens in the Kingdom; that being in the marketplace was second best.

One of the young men in the church, who was serving on staff as a bi-vocational pastor, understood this challenge because he was serving in the church while also working in the marketplace. As I shared the need to minister directly to business people, Chee Kang Seng immediately became involved in this new venture in God.

Before long a new outreach called Global Business Network (GBN) was birthed. Kang Seng was passionate to shift mindsets and to empower business people to be successful in both areas of their life. He traveled with me to several nations reaching out in missions, cell training, and in efforts to empower business people. He was one who was always open to new challenges in the Kingdom of God.

After he left, God sent Victor Leong to pick up the mantle of GBN. Victor traveled with me in matters related to the business community. As we worked with the business community, we felt God leading us to make some shifts in our approach and clarify our mission from the Lord. A new leadership team was formed, comprising experienced business people and professionals: Boyd Au, Gan Choon Beng, Jacob Tay, Raymond Choudhury, and Seow Kiat Wang.

These pioneers have taken the ministry to a new level. They have through the years mentored and raised up new leaders for the marketplace ministry. Today, I only serve as a spiritual advisor to the team. GBN and those associated with them are touching nations in a positive way to break systemic poverty. They have a successful model for micro-financing that is working.

Again, all these various initiatives – from community service to marketplace ministry – were started because there was a need, and because we felt God leading us to meet that need.

CHAPTER 18

Father Knows Best

IN OUR JOURNEY AS A CHURCH, God always worked in a certain pattern regarding property. We would buy a piece of land, develop it and then quickly pay off all of our debts ahead of time. Just as we completed our construction of 21 Adam Road, the Lord led us to buy a property on River Valley Road, which we used for different purposes for several years before we sold it.

Then in 1996, the opportunity opened up for us to buy a freehold property on Lavender Street. It was on a main road and within walking distance of a train station, but it was not a popular location. This was an area known for funeral services. It was a place that people associated with death, rather than life.

Comprising three shophouses, the property was zoned as a conservation building. This meant we had to retain the exact features and the original design of the building facade. The price was S$10.5 million, just for the three shophouses totaling 5,000 square feet. In addition, we would need to tear them down and rebuild, while retaining the old façade for conservation purposes. I thought, "This seems really expensive, but we do need another location closer to the east side of the island."

Then God spoke, *"I want you to buy the property and bring light and life into this area."*

So I sent in prayer teams to prayer walk the area. We did events to build relationships with those living in the area. We wanted to obey God by bringing both light and life in a seemingly dead area of town. We proceeded to buy the shophouses and to develop them, keeping the old design. We started having worship services there, and again, we soon paid off that building. But even with this new location at Lavender Street, I knew we still needed at least one more site, and it would have to be bigger than this one.

Around this time, the government began to earmark land parcels in new neighborhoods for religious use. Churches could bid for the land, which would come with a 30-year lease. When the government released these land plots for tender, churches would bid for the land to see who would be able to buy or lease it. (Today those bids must be over S$15 million to lease some 30,000 square feet of land for just thirty years.)

After getting the land, whoever won the bid was required to complete their building within two years. It would cost another S$20-30 million to construct the building, depending on how they would build. The total bill easily exceeded the financial ability of most churches. I thought this was too much to pay for rent (which is essentially what it is), because, in thirty years, the government could take it all back! While it was not likely that they would actually repossess the land, the possibility that you might have to pay to extend the lease was high.

I said, "God, I know I am asking a lot but I want freehold land." However, there was none on the market. The Psalmist says, "Delight yourself in the Lord and he will give you the desires of your heart"

(Psalm 37:4). It does not mean God will give us whatever you desire; rather, as we delight in Him, God puts *His* desires in our hearts. I believe freehold land was a desire placed in my heart by God.

I believe freehold land was a desire placed in my heart by God.

Chaos and Crisis

In July 1997, the Asian Financial Crisis hit. What began as a currency and financial crisis in Thailand soon spread to Malaysia, Indonesia, and the Philippines. One by one, the region's currencies came under speculative attacks and were sharply devalued. Countries spent billions of dollars trying to defend their currencies, only to seek emergency bailouts from the International Monetary Fund and the World Bank. Investors started to flee Asia, and the crisis spread rapidly to South Korea, Hong Kong, and China. On 27 October 1997, rattled by Asia's currency crisis, trading on US stock markets was suspended. That was how bad things were.

While the decline of the Singapore dollar was more gradual, as an open economy we were not spared the economic impact of the crisis. Market sentiment was jittery. Investor confidence was shaken. In early 1998, food shortages and mass unemployment led to panic buying and racial riots in Indonesia. Student protests rocked Indonesia and led to the end of the Suharto government. All these were unprecedented and historic events.

Before all this happened, I had shared with the church the vision of having another regional center by the year 2000. Seeing all this, I asked God, "God, how is it going to happen? It is already 1998. That means that we only have about thirty-six months to see this vision become a reality."

The Lord told me again and again, "*It is going to happen first in the faith realm*."

Meanwhile, the contagion spread further. A global financial meltdown had been ignited. Japan officially entered into recession. In 1998, Russia and Brazil saw their economies enter a free fall. Global stock markets plunged and hit record lows.

I said, "God, what is happening?"

Again the Lord said, "*By faith!*"

Then God began to show me and others on the church board that He was going to use the current situation. In fact, this was God's moment for us. This time, when prices were down, would be the best time for us to buy property. Therefore, we had to legally position ourselves for God's leading. We had to be ready so that when God opened the door, we would be able to step through it.

In May 1998, I called for an Extraordinary General Meeting (EOGM) asking our members to endorse a special resolution: To empower the church board with the ability to purchase properties for up to three more regional centers. It was out of the ordinary, because I did not have any specific locations or terms or prices to present to them.

At the meeting, I challenged them to believe: "God is preparing us for a new season of harvest in Singapore and beyond. New opportunities for growth abound and we need to seize them at the right moment. The future belongs to you and to your children. Therefore, now is the time to position Trinity Christian Centre for the new millennium."

You must understand, all this took place during a time of economic upheaval and uncertainty. Despite the challenges, Trinitarians rose up in faith and in unity to affirm our call in God as a breakthrough church. The special resolution was passed. It was a huge vote of confidence and a gesture of trust in me and in our church board.

An Unprecedented Opportunity

Then the miracle happened. In 1999, the Lord opened the door for us to buy the old Shell Recreation Club on Paya Lebar Road. What a journey of faith that was! When Danny Yeo and I first spoke with the Shell people, the land area was huge, but it had declined in usage and was not of any real benefit for their members. We were progressing in our discussions when they abruptly stopped contacting us. Almost a year went by and there was no news.

Then suddenly they called us again. We went back to their office and discovered they had gotten permission to change the title on part of the land. This allowed them to sell off a large portion to a property developer. However, they still had 3.7 acres available for tender. Now that may not seem big to many people, but in Singapore that is a big space.

In October 1999, after much deliberation and prayer, our church board put in a tender of S$19.1 million. Later, we were told that our bid was just a whisker higher than the next highest bid. In other words, we didn't pay any more than was necessary to win the tender. The managing agent said, "Surely the God you serve has given you this figure to win the bid!"

I was amazed at the way God worked. Considering that we had bought the 5,000-square-foot property at Lavender for S$10.5

million, now to be able to buy 3.7 acres for less than S$20 million – I mean, this was a miracle. The contrast was huge. This was a freehold, commercial property that could have been bought by a listed entity or by a company – and we were a church. Unbelievable!

Then one Sunday as I was walking across the platform preaching, the Lord spoke to me even as I was speaking: *"Because you were obedient to go where others would not go, now I have given you this."*

> *"Because you were obedient to go where others would not go, now I have given you this."*

I knew He was referring to Paya Lebar. Now we had the land, but it was only the beginning of another journey. Although the club did not have a large enough space for worship, we could use the swimming pool, badminton courts, restaurant, and some space for offices. So we used the space for training, youth camps, Divine Exchange Weekends, and various events.

During this time, I continued to challenge the people to sow financially into the spiritual future of their children and their children's children, to build something for a multigenerational blessing. Praise the Lord for a congregation that shared that kind of vision! Everyone had a part: The Chinese ministry, the children, the youth and all the different language congregations were committed to the miracle.

A Miracle Needed

The next miracle we needed was government approval for a change of use. The property was zoned for 'sports and recreation.' Without submitting a rezoning request, we drew up plans on how we would use the land and submitted it to the government authorities.

Several months passed before they called us in for an interview. At that meeting, they informed us that we could not build a church.

"Okay, but can we use it for the purposes we have indicated on our outline submission?" I asked.

After some discussion, they sent us away, asking us to come back later. Again we waited several months before they called us in again. At this second meeting, the first question they asked me was, "Are you building a church?"

I said, "No, because you told us we cannot build a church."

"So what will you build?" they queried.

"We will build according to the plans we have given you, if you approve them," I replied.

"But will you have church services there?"

My response was, "Well, we are a church and we do own the property, so we will probably conduct some activities in the new building."

Again they sent us away. Many months went by and we heard nothing. We began to wonder what was happening. I shared this situation with the congregation, urging them, "Come on church, let's pray. We don't know why the delay."

Finally a call came for us to see them again. We walked in and, after some greetings, sat down. The smiles stopped. They gave me a very stern look and said, "Okay, this is it. We have taken this all the way to the top and this is it; take it, or leave it."

I was a little taken back by those words, so sternly spoken. It is at this point in the process that the authorities will either reject your request, or give you a list of conditions that you must comply with. If you comply with their conditions, your request will be approved.

"Well, all right, what is it?" I asked.

Anxiously, I and those with me waited for them to speak. The government representative said, "Okay, this is it. Condition number one: You *must* build a church."

He continued on down his list, but honestly I did not hear the rest of it. I was still stuck on condition number one. When he finished, I said, "Excuse me, did you say that we must build a church?"

"Yes," he replied.

I said, "But I thought you told me, we could not build a church?"

He quickly responded, "Look, this has gone all the way to the top – take it, or leave it."

They indicated that the whole area could not have the same zoning, so I asked to see the lines for zoning and the area approved for a church. Quickly calculating what my eyes were seeing on their drawings, I realized that the area allotted for the church was very small. The size was typical of the land parcels that they released for churches to bid on. Trying to choose my words carefully, I slowly began, "Okay, we accept the offer to build a church on this property, but... I want a larger allocation of land to be zoned 'church.'"

God had answered our prayer. We now had permission to rezone part of the land for a church and then develop the whole complex.

But now a new miracle was needed: Would they enlarge the space allocated for the church? Let me just say, it took many trips to the relevant government offices, many meetings stretched over almost two years, before an agreeable compromise was reached. We are thankful for a reasonable government who is open to consider situations that are 'out of the box' and different from ordinary applications. The journey tested our faith and the resolve of a faithful congregation.

More Miracles

During some of those final discussions with the government agency, I discovered what the real issue was. They were afraid that if they allowed us to have just one zone for the entire property, we would be able to resell the property for profit. They thought this way because they already knew about future redevelopment plans for the area, which we were not privy to. I told the officer, "Sir, God gave us that property. It is for our children and our children's children. It is not for sale; even you cannot buy it."

This took place in May 2004. At the same time, our request for a higher plot ratio was also approved, paving the way for us to maximize the use of the land. But that was not all. We were about to discover just how perfect God's timing was. In the case of any rezoning or plot ratio increase, a development charge or tax is usually due. However, it is not a fixed rate; the authorities adjust development charges every six months, according to market conditions. This development charge for our property was initially estimated to be S$4.5 million, but as it turned out, the development charges when we applied in June 2004 were zero. We did not have to pay any development charges at all. It was God's perfect timing.

Though the application process was behind us, it took us another two years to select an architect, prepare the architectural drawings, submit them, get all the needed permits, and form the team to oversee the building project. As these were being done, I knew that the church needed our own representative on that building team to protect our church's interests as different decisions would need to be made.

That was when I contacted Pastors Steven and Margaret Tay, who were then based in India. Pastor Steven is a trained civil engineer. We discussed the need for them to return to Singapore, so he could help me in the building project. In prayer God confirmed it to them, and he returned to undertake the huge building project while periodically going to the nations on missions assignments. If you are around Trinity much, you will soon learn that everyone is expected to multitask. Steven and Margaret are great examples of this culture in the church.

The Paya Lebar complex would comprise a community wing, an education wing, and a place of worship. The community wing would house Care Community Services Society and our offices, youth hub and a restaurant area, along with a large function room for wedding receptions, badminton and other activities. The education wing would house TCA College, including a 1,000-seat chapel, lecture theaters, childcare facilities, nursery rooms, and a hostel for our international students. The place of worship would comprise a 3,000-seat sanctuary and two 400-seat meeting halls. In all, the complex would have over 500 car park lots.

The building project at Paya Lebar was in full swing when I handed the church over to Pastor Dominic Yeo in March 2005. This meant that he would inherit the oversight of the building project as well. Dominic had not been involved in our earlier building projects, so I told him, "I am passing the building project to you now. This way you can learn what this project is all about, and how to do it. I'll still

Naomi (extreme left) with her grandmother, auntie, dad and baby cousin.

Naomi at seven years of age.

Naomi with her dad. He is wearing his truck driver uniform.

Naomi with her cousins.

Naomi with her high school basketball team (sixth from right).

Naomi in her high school band uniform.

Naomi (extreme right) with her mother, stepfather and stepsisters

Naomi during her high school years.

Learning golf while working in Washington D.C.

Naomi during her high school years.

Naomi (middle) as part of the singing trio that performed at various churches.

As a missionary in the Marshall Islands.

With Florence Beck

Sam & Florence Sasser with their children.

Baptizing new converts in the Marshall Islands.

Hosting a 'Welcome Home' party for Wayne, Judy and their newborn daughter after an emergency birth on Kwajalein. Chris Bangert (front row, extreme right) came up with the idea of a prefabricated church.

Directing the radio evangelism ministry in the Marshall Islands.

Singing was a big thing with the islanders. A girl choir dressed in matching outfits.

The island missionary.

Building the A-frame prefabricated church.

Students going on mission trips to the other islands.

*Naomi (extreme left) with Sandra Duncan
and Judy Cagle.*

Building the seawall. Naomi is on the extreme left, pushing a wheelbarrow.

Brother David Thompson and his wife Vivian. He served as captain on those boat evangelism trips.

Naomi's first trip to Singapore in 1972, with her co-worker Iris Brown (third from left), at the invitation of Howard & Rosella Ridings.

Preaching in Singapore in 1972.

Naomi setting up a missions booth at the churches in the States, where she preached to raise funds for missions.

Firm friends (from left): Deborah, Barbara and Naomi.

Naomi with Deborah.

With Pastor Emil Balliet and his wife Gladys in Singapore in 1977, six months before he went to be with the Lord. Standing (from left): Chris Ang, Bertha Ang and Ang Beng Siong.
Seated (from left): Ng Buck Chua, his wife Kim, Rosie and Paul Gan.

Praying at an opening ceremony in Singapore, wearing her custom-made robe and stole.

Naomi with Bertha Ang

With Trinity church members. Tang Seng Foon (extreme left) was one of the early church board members.

At church camp with Choo Lai Ying, in the late 1980s. Behind them is a MG convertible, the type of car Naomi used to drive when working in the States.

With Beatrice Kang and Choo Lai Ying in 1986. Beatrice is carrying Lai Ying's newborn son, Jin Yian.

Naomi (extreme right) with her mom Mama Wilson, and her stepsisters, in the States.

Groundbreaking ceremony at the church's first property in 21 Adam Road.

With Angelina and Eu Yat Wan and his mother, at their wedding in 1982.

At the Singing Christmas Tree in 1987.

Front row (from left): Anita Chia, wedding couple Janie and Jeffrey Wong, and Naomi in 1990. Back row (from left): Chee Kang Seng, Steven Tay, Tan May Ling and Derek Tan.

Dedicating Raymond Choudhury's baby Daniel in 1991 in the new Adam Road auditorium.

Naomi with her mom in Singapore.

In Colombia for the first time in 1991, with Esther Milian.   *With David and Getziel Mohan.*

Breaking a deadlock in traffic in Fusa, Colombia in 1991.

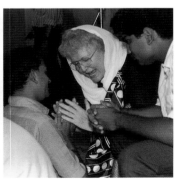

Preaching at an evangelistic rally on a beach in India.   *Praying for a man in India.*

Praying for a little girl in Romania in 1999.

With Singapore's founding prime minister Lee Kuan Yew and his wife Kwa Geok Choo at the Istana.

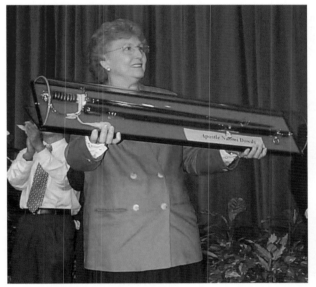

Being recognized as an apostle in 2000.

Preaching in Ghana in 2000.

Teaching in Japan in 2001

With John Kelly in 2001

Training pastors in Poland in 2001

With Laurie Vervaecke in 2002, all dressed up for Trinity's Missions Convention.

With Les Bowling in the early 2000s, and with Sheila Bowling in 2010.

Presiding over the graduation ceremony as Chancellor of Theological Centre for Asia (now TCA College) in 2004.

Groundbreaking ceremony at 247 Paya Lebar Road in 2004.

Change of Command service at Trinity Christian Centre on 10 March 2005.

Getting an update on the Paya Lebar building project from Thomas Lee and Steven Tay in 2006.

Trinity@Paya Lebar: From a vision to a reality.

Teeing off at the annual charity golf event of Care Community Services Society.

With Daniel and Deborah Cheah and the congregation of His Sanctuary of Glory in Kuala Lumpur, Malaysia in 2011.

Celebrating the eighth anniversary of Apostolic Generation Church in Jakarta in 2011, with Indri Gautama

With Ong Sek Leang and Cynthia Figueroa in Colombia in 2011.

On the road with Laurie Vervaecke in 2014 near Pebble Beach, California.

Women in Strategic Leadership mentoring roundtable 2014.

Topping off over two decades of ministry in Colombia in 2014.

From left: With Esther Milian, General Reinaldo Castellanos and his wife Martha in Colombia in 2014.

With Dominic Yeo and his wife Chin Inn at Trinity's Staff Dinner in 2015.

With Lana Heightley and Janet Mangum (right) in 2014.

Classic Naomi Dowdy in action.

be around and if you have questions, you can call me." The building team was in place but there was still much work to be done, including the main sanctuary.

It was important for him to learn this because all future building projects would be totally his, not mine. However, I was confident that he could handle it. I was also sure that the church would be able to pay off all loans and building costs in an extremely short period of time. Why was I so sure? Because God had always supplied in the past – such that we paid off all loans ahead of schedule – and He would do it again. Furthermore, I knew that once we had begun services at the Paya Lebar location, the church would grow in number. An

Why was I so sure? Because God had always supplied in the past and He would do it again.

increased congregation who also embraced the vision would ensure an early payoff. I had faith in God and in God's people.

Father Knows Best

It happened just as I expected. When we started the services at Paya Lebar in 2007, the numbers were not too many. But as people realized that our new location was up and running, those who had wanted to be a part of our church earlier, but who had stayed away because of the shortage of parking facilities at Adam Road, now began to make a commitment to our new location. New facilities, new people and new families resulted in growth. Soon we began to fill the 1,000-seat chapel at Paya Lebar, even as the 3,000-seat sanctuary was being built. It was completed in time for our Christmas services in 2009.

There were more surprises yet. When we purchased Paya Lebar, we had no clue what the authorities had planned for the area. In 2008, the master plan was unveiled to the public: The Paya Lebar area was designated to be one of the nation's commercial hubs outside the city center, as part of a nationwide decentralization strategy. This meant new homes, hotels, offices, malls, and industrial parks would be built all around our new location, bringing more people within a five-mile radius of the church. In 2010, a subway station within five minutes' walking distance of our church opened. This made the church accessible to many more people via the public transport system. We could never have foreseen this magnitude of development when we looked at the sleepy Shell Recreation Club ten years before this.

We had positioned ourselves by faith in a time of crisis, and God had opened a window of opportunity to us at the strategic time. It proved to be a *kairos* moment. Since then the value of land and property all over Singapore has risen exponentially. Buying the land and developing a similar property today would probably cost at least triple the price, if not more.

Today, Trinity@Paya Lebar is the largest Christian complex in our nation. Freehold land like ours is hard to come by in an island city-state like Singapore. Knowing that God has blessed us beyond measure, we have opened up our facilities at Paya Lebar and Lavender Street and made them available for other churches to use. We have been blessed to be a blessing.

CHAPTER 19

Success & Succession

SUCH BOLD MOVES would not have been possible without a church board who believed in the vision and worked to make it a reality. I believe that church boards should work as enablers of the senior pastor's vision. I know that many pastors have experienced great challenges working with their church boards, so much so that some have decided they do not want to have boards in their church structure.

However, I am here to declare that I love our church board. In almost thirty years, I have never had negative experiences with our church board. The men and women who served on our church board were discipled sons and daughters of the house. They shared the vision, and contributed generously in areas of their training and expertise. They were valuable team players, and a great help and support to the senior pastor. This wonderful working relationship still continues under the leadership of Pastor Dominic Yeo.

Over the years, I enjoyed great support from our board secretary, Doreen Lee. Doreen had joined us as a young adult, and over the years she has served several different pastors as a secretary. While serving she married and is now a mother of four. She is proactive and relates well with our board members, and has become a trusted partner in the process.

To have strong administrative support is critical to the fulfillment of the vision. After Patsy Chan, my first full-time secretary, became a pastor, I often found myself overloaded because the different ones who would work as my secretary would end up being called by God to do other ministries. This was one area of frustration for me. Each of these gals had a wonderful heart and spirit – but God had other assignments for them. Then an answer came.

In 1998, Joanna Tam joined our administrative team to work on the LoveSingapore project. She assisted Pastor Dominic who was then helping me to manage the project. At this time I had no personal assistant and often looked over in envy at Pastor Dominic and the level of secretarial support he was getting! When the LoveSingapore project came to an end, Pastor Dominic graciously released Joanna to serve me. She has now served as my secretary and personal assistant for many years, and still faithfully serves with me today. She supports me not only as a personal assistant, but also as a powerful intercessor, always quickly adapting to the many changing challenges that the Lord places before me.

God knows the one to connect you with, for you to be able to fulfill your assignment from Him.

me. Praise the Lord, she is flexible and adaptable. God knows the one to connect you with, for you to be able to fulfill your assignment from Him.

It was a divine provision, just like in 1995, when God brought into my life an armor-bearer to travel with me. Laurie Vervaecke and her husband Joe were based in Singapore, but she 'happened' to be in Canada when I went there to conduct a pastors' training. After sitting through the training, she was convinced that this was what pastors around the world needed. Back in Singapore, she and her husband began attending our church.

One day, she asked to see me. When she came into my office, she shared that she felt the Lord telling her to serve as my armor-bearer. She was willing to do whatever needed to be done, including traveling with me. I was a little surprised as I had never had an armor-bearer before, and wasn't sure how that would work out. After a few days, I called to tell her that I had a month-long trip to India, and if she wanted to join me, she could. I figured if she could survive one month in India with me (she had never been there before and it was not as developed then as it is today), then maybe the arrangement could work.

That turned out to be the first of many trips. Laurie accompanied me on many trips to just about every continent, including Africa. She helped me with research for my training and sermons, created Powerpoint slides, and assisted in just about every way. Her husband Joe was very supportive and released her to travel with me, sometimes for several weeks at a time. Both of them relocated back to the States in 2002, and from there, Laurie became our Global Leadership Network coordinator for the US. She continues to be a part of my mentoring roundtable and travels with me when I am in that part of the world, including Colombia.

Success and Succession

All over the world, I saw the need for the baton of leadership to be passed to a new generation. Something that I observed troubled me deeply: I saw notable leaders building ministries of significance and then simply giving them over – releasing everything into untutored hands – and walking away into the sunset. Often the ministry splintered, people lost confidence, and there were many casualties, or the ministry lost its original vibrancy and became a shadow of its former self. I did not want either scenario to happen.

I felt God saying, *"Enough is enough. We have wasted money, time, energy, and lives with this model. It is a new day. Now I am calling a generation of leaders who are older, wiser, and more experienced. I am calling them to step out of their comfort zones and to release their churches and organizations over to Me. Train, disciple, and equip a younger generation to take your place so that you will be free to serve as My ambassadors to the nations—to help, encourage, and upgrade other leaders in the ways of God just like Paul did when he went to the city of Ephesus."*

As a leader, I had to plan for the future of the organization beyond my tenure – and to build a team of leaders and a successor who would continue God's work after my exit. This is seldom taken seriously nor done intentionally. Most pastors and leaders I know love their work and have never really paused long enough to seriously consider an actual succession plan. Sure, they know it must happen someday, but it is not something they feel an urgency to plan for at this present time. In their minds, there is still so much more they want to do, so many new things they want to see happen. They still want to initiate so many new endeavors and expand in so many new areas, and cannot imagine the day when they will no longer be doing this kind of thinking and planning.

However, the world is changing. We live in a time of rapid, drastic, and sometimes disorientating change. A new world demands a new anointing, new approaches to ministry, and new methods. The vision does not change, but the expression of that vision must be updated with each changing generation. It must change, because your successor will be leading in a different season or era. I see myself as a Moses. God helped me to take a people who "were not a people" (1 Peter 2:9-10) and to make them a people with a shared calling, vision and identity. I established them, but my successor would lead them and build them into a mighty army for the Lord.

Too often, pastors and organizational leaders underestimate the time taken to complete the succession plan. I understood that this was a lengthy process that could take years. That being the case, I felt it was better to plan early than to leave it till it was too late. It was far too important a matter, one that would impact thousands of people. Hence I could not wait till I was ill or incapacitated to do this. I could not assume that I would always be able to function the way I did.

Therefore I was convinced that I had to start planning and preparing for my successor. I knew that how I transitioned would determine whether I would actually finish well. I had to work intentionally towards the goal of passing the baton and commissioning the next generation of warriors who would go forth to take the land.

> *I knew that how I transitioned would determine whether I would actually finish well.*

Mentoring Potential

In the mid-1990s, I took the church through a period of restructuring. Sometimes God's new direction and season will demand that we restructure, because old structures will not facilitate God's new thing. During this restructuring, I set in place another platform for the final development of anyone who would become my successor. I did not tell them that finding a successor was part of the objective; they only knew it was part of their leadership growth and development in ministry.

I handpicked a six-member leadership team as part of my succession plan. What this meant was that I had a plan, a process, and a platform where I could develop and test these potential successors. Dominic was one of these six, and he was growing and becoming a 'son of the house.'

As I worked with all six members of the leadership team, I was keenly aware that I was mentoring a team of potential successors. I felt the weight of responsibility in assessing everyone. I wanted to be sure before God that I did not play favorites, so I gave each of them equal opportunity to make their calling and election sure. I needed to test them in other areas as well, including their character, prayer life, relationships with other leaders, views and practices concerning money, family life, values, and especially their concept of power. The next senior pastor had to be a person who could develop team players. Additionally, they needed to have a God-given ability to take the church and its vision farther in the future. They also needed to be able to communicate and train others in our Carecell model.

I also needed to enlarge my team's vision of how they should function and how they should see the church from an overall holistic perspective, rather than just being concerned for their own personal departments and scope of responsibility. In other words, I needed them to function in true team ministry. First of all, the leadership team should be a team that represents the different gifts of the fivefold ministry. Secondly, they should think, pray, and plan together for the overall church – not just for their specific department. They needed to make that shift in their thinking, from a narrow perspective that is limited to one or two specific areas, to seeing a wider view of how the entire organization can move forward. Suffice to say, there was a lot to work on during those years.

Over the years, as I planned for this issue of succession, I looked for possible models of the transition process, but I could not find any acceptable models for us to learn from or follow in our journey of transition. Yes, there were pastors who had left their churches and gave the leadership over to a new pastor, but none of them fit into what I considered to be a strong model we could follow. I talked to other leaders; I tried searching for books that might help us, but I found nothing that could serve as a model. It became very clear that God wanted us to create or establish a new model that could serve other pastors and churches in the future.

I prayed over this for many nights, asking God for revelation concerning my transition out of Trinity Christian Centre. I knew that this would be not just for Trinity, but would become a model for other churches and leaders to follow. There was an awesome weight of responsibility on my shoulders during this time.

CHAPTER 20

Letting Go

IT WAS EXCITING TO SEE each of my potential successors grow in their leadership. They were all good. They all had a heart for God. Each of them was faithfully committed to each assignment given to them. Still, there was always the nagging question: which one has the spiritual gifts and capacity to take the church forward? All of them could preach, prophesy, and lead ministries but... who was God's choice? This required me to look beyond personal relationships, their longevity in the church, their outward personalities, and their charisma in the pulpit. In the midst of many, there was the challenge of knowing God's choice of the one who would take the church forward.

While every one of the potential successors had outstanding qualities, I made my choice through much prayer and the leading of the Holy Spirit. Since my choice would impact many people, and knowing the delicate situations that I needed to navigate, I felt there was no one I could share my plans and thinking with at that time. I could not risk the person hearing about my thinking. This was an intense time of prayer for me.

Looking at the kind of church we had become, it became evident to me that Trinity Christian Centre needed a leader who walked and functioned with the mantle of an apostle and prophet. Whoever took over the church would also have to lead the other entities—the Bible college and the community services organization. It was a multiple portfolio, a complex creature. In business terms, the church was more akin to a multinational corporation than a typical local church.

Although he was not aware, it was evident to me several years prior to the actual transition that Pastor Dominic Yeo was going to be my successor. Dominic had been saved in the church and mentored by spiritual parents in our carecells. He had grown and developed as a spiritual son and leader. However, there were some areas he needed to overcome, and I was waiting to see him grow in those areas. Thus I did not make the fact known to him until the time was right.

Transition Time

That time came in 2002. I spoke to him and asked him to pray and hear from God, regarding becoming the new senior pastor of Trinity. He had to be convinced that this was God's calling for him. I encouraged him to pray and to talk to his wife Chin Inn, since taking on the leadership role would be a joint commitment.

They came to talk with me and told me that they accepted this as God's direction for them. However, Chin Inn had a question. She was a very successful business woman in the marketplace and she was involved in different ministries in the church as well. Now she wanted to know, "Must I quit my job and become primarily a pastor's wife?"

I totally understood her anxiety. I smiled and told her, "No, you need not resign your job. Stay in the marketplace and continue as you always have, being supportive and involved in ministry along with your husband." She was relieved and was affirmed to walk through this change in their life.

Dominic affirmed that he was willing to accept the challenge of the new position. However, he asked for time for him to get used to the idea and the responsibilities of being a senior pastor, and for the congregation to also have time to adjust to the impending change. I agreed, and told him, "When you are ready, I am ready!"

The first group I shared the news with was our church board. This was a time of prayer and consensus building until there was full agreement among this level of leadership concerning my choice of successor. I gave them time to get used to the idea that I was really going to step aside and release this organization to a new leader.

Next I shared this with the next level of leaders, i.e. the leadership team, and then the pastoral staff and the church staff. I met with them, sharing my heart about passing the baton and about my choice of successor, and why. Next I met with our sectional leaders, and then our carecell leaders and spiritual parents.

Each of these times was an opportunity to answer questions and clarify doubts. In each meeting, I gave the group time to pray for Dominic and to release words of prophecy as the Lord moved. This allowed for a special time of bonding and affirmation. All these meetings took time, but they were the necessary first steps in actualizing transition.

This process of communication, level by level, continued until the entire congregation had heard about the transition from me personally. (The congregation was the last to hear the news not because they are of lesser importance, but because they were the largest group, and without the prior affirmation from all of the other groups, I would never have reached this point in the process.)

When the announcement was released to this largest group, it was a time of celebration and the beginning of a new season of expectation. Dominic was given the title of 'Senior Pastor Designate.' This made it very clear that change was happening, and that time was being given to both the new person and the church or organization to get used to the idea of change. This period where the successor is appointed 'designate' is a transition time between the outgoing and the incoming leader. Change was being set in motion.

Historically, pastors of long tenure are hard to follow, because of the many and long attachments formed over many years. Although I was not the founding pastor of Trinity Christian Centre, I was the one God brought in to establish the work. We had been on a long journey of change and development for almost 30 years. During that time, I had seen most of the congregation come to Christ, receive water baptism, grow in the Lord, and become leaders in the church. Then I had the privilege of marrying them, dedicated their babies to the Lord, and counseled many of them through difficult seasons in their life. Naturally they were attached to me.

Thus extra effort and time were needed to allow for emotional adjustments to be made, for the people to also embrace a new pastor with loyalty and commitment. It is not a transfer of trust – it is really an expansion of trust. This is just the reality of human nature.

It is not a transfer of trust – it is really an expansion of trust.

During this period, I sought to give Dominic and the congregation time to see each other with new eyes. I was frequently on trips overseas for ministry, and sometimes I would deliberately lengthen my times away from the church. This also gave the space for him to work with his new team and develop plans for the future, so that everything would be in place for acceleration once the transition was complete.

It also took time for the new leadership team to adjust, and for the reality of the weight of their new responsibilities to hit home and become a settled fact. Old habits die hard and it does take time to get used to the idea of being in the driver's seat. One day, in a meeting, a member of the new leadership team (handpicked by Dominic, not by me) asked me, "Pastor, what is your vision for the next ten years?" I replied, "Wrong question. The issue is not what my vision is, but 'What is *your* vision?'"

Change of Command

The duration of the transition period was not cast in stone, and we did not publicly commit to any time frame. I had told Dominic, "I am ready when you are." I was waiting for him to feel ready and prepared, because the congregation was a large one, spanning many age groups. In slightly less than two years, Dominic felt he had everything in place, and that the team was ready for the completion of the transition.

In 2005, after almost thirty years, through the process of intentional leadership development, all the pieces were in place and the timing was right. I had found the right person to become the senior pastor of Trinity Christian Centre, and he was now ready to lead the church onward into her prophetic destiny.

On March 10, 2005, we had a 'Change of Command' service and commissioned Rev Dominic Yeo to be the new senior pastor of the church. God had promised that "the latter glory of this church would be greater than the former" (see Haggai 2:9). I released and claimed that Word. I was confident that under his leadership, working with all the other excellent staff and leaders in the church, Trinity Christian Centre would experience the best and finest years of her ministry.

I felt strongly that Dominic should not try to fit into my shoes. He was to walk in his own shoes and be 'his own man,' but he could start by standing on my shoulders! He did not need to start from scratch; instead, he was to begin from the vantage point of all God had done through my leadership, and move on and move up to the next level, taking the organization forward into God's new seasons.

God is raising a new breed of leaders, a new generation of Samuels who will lead in such power and anointing that the spirit and perception of God's people will shift into high gear, and entire nations will be impacted. Succession is not merely a transfer from the older to the younger. In reality, the changing of the guard is a time to release a fresh wave of God's glory and power, and to stir up a fresh vision for new possibilities.

Letting Go

Although I had been working toward selecting a successor, there were many things that needed to be aligned for the actual transition to take place. When all these fell into place, I knew it was time for me to let go. However, it is never easy to let go. It is like a father walking his daughter down the aisle to be married to a young man. You know it is right, you know it is time, but it hurts to let her go.

Doing this takes courage. Now I had to voluntarily step aside and release them – and step into God's new season for me. No, I was not retiring. No, I was not too sick to lead and minister. Rather, it was time

Now I had to voluntarily step aside and release them – and step into God's new season for me.

for the new team to lead the church so they could all continue to rise in their calling and destiny. For this to happen, I needed to step aside and open the door for them. Transition was an emotional roller-coaster ride. It was a potent mixture of sorrow and joy all scrambled together.

Following the transition, Pastor Dominic and the church board asked me to continue to be involved in Trinity. I am not involved in the planning nor the running of the church, but I serve as a mentor and advisor to the new senior pastor, as well as to the church board and all the stakeholders in the church. There is a reversal of roles. In the beginning, Dominic served on my team, but now I serve on his team. It is still team ministry but with different roles and responsibilities. My role is to make myself and my counsel available to the new team so they do not make the same mistakes I did. I am privileged to have Pastor Dom as a friend, a golf buddy, and as one of the prophets who speaks into my life.

To date, it can be said that the handover to my successor has been successful – not perfect, but successful. Under the capable and anointed leadership of Rev Dominic Yeo, Trinity Christian Centre has continued to grow in every aspect. It has grown numerically, financially, and spiritually. In fact, the church – not only the senior pastor, but the pastoral team, leaders, and congregation – is continuing to enlarge.

Under Pastor Dominic's leadership, Trinity Christian Centre has continued to grow and presently touches over seven thousand people every week, in addition to the thousands more through our missions program, which has touched more than thirty nations.

God has kept His promise. Not only are we seeing greater glory in the house, but the journey we have undertaken has also now become a model for others to follow.

CHAPTER 21

An Attitude Problem

THE DIVINE ASSIGNMENTS God gives us are often really stepping stones to the greater things He has in store for us. Leadership transition and succession did not mean that I would not continue doing what I loved. More likely than not, I would still be using my gifts, but in a different expression or in a larger capacity. I would say it this way: Same mission, different expression. God always has something more ahead for us.

During my time as Trinity's senior pastor, I always had a ministry that extended outside our local church. There was always a Macedonian call to train pastors and leaders in other nations, to help them build strong churches. God said that there was a breakthrough anointing upon me that had to be imparted to others. All this was exciting. Yet the reality was, there always seemed to be more churches and organizations to be helped than I had time for.

With the leadership transition process in full motion, I knew it was time for me to shift into a new level of ministry, to do the things God had placed upon my heart. I had some ideas and thoughts about what I might be doing. In the past, my focus had been on the development of leaders; how to disciple, mentor, and release them. Now God was opening up a whole new level of leadership development – where I would not just work with leaders, but with leaders of leaders. My vision had not changed, but I was to pursue and fulfill it at a new level.

My vision had not changed, but I was to pursue and fulfill it at a new level.

God strongly impressed this upon me: Whom do leaders talk to? Who can they share their struggles and heartaches with, as they face the challenges of leading in these turbulent times? Here is where God began to use the combination of my age and my many experiences in life and ministry at a new level and in new ways. He has positioned me such that I now spend more time with leaders of leaders.

Accepting the Label

Over the years, every now and then, people had called me an apostle. Once in a while, someone would come along and say, "What you are doing... is what an apostle does!" However, I shied away from the title as I did not feel that I needed another title. I felt that it would not make a difference.

Then God said, *"The title isn't for your sake; it is so you can help bring credibility to the office."*

At this time the AG was not embracing the apostolic and prophetic offices. They were wary of the abuses and the excesses, because there were people going around as self-appointed apostles and prophets. They called me to Springfield to discuss this. I told them my stand: "You can fight it, you can deny it, but if it's God, it's going to happen. You and I can choose to fight it, or choose to engage it and have an influence on its proper development. For me, I have chosen to engage it."

Now they have not officially called anyone an apostle, but they did say to me, "You have an apostolic track record." This was a huge step for them to take. They have become much more open, though cautious.

I myself went through a process of learning to accept the title and to embrace the office of an apostle. It took a while. But embracing it was the first step towards a new level in ministry. Now not only did I know it, but others began to see the evidence of God's grace upon my life and recognized it. This became an encouragement to me and gave me greater confidence in who I am in God. It has also opened the door for more women to embrace the gifting God has placed in their lives and to be similarly recognized.

Being able to interact with and minister alongside other apostles from different parts of the world brought further affirmation. A key platform for this has been the International Coalition of Apostolic Leaders (ICAL), previously known as the International Coalition of Apostles (ICA). I was on the original council and I continue serving on the council today. The convening apostle is John Kelly, who has become a dear friend and a great encouragement to me in this phase of my life and ministry.

When Peter Wagner first introduced me to John, he thought there would be friction, because of John's earlier concept about women apostles and leaders. However, God divinely arranged our meeting in such a way that just the opposite happened – we bonded in the spirit and have served together ever since. I highly respect him as a true apostle.

A New Assignment

Throughout the years, despite being a woman leader, I rarely accepted invitations to speak at women's meetings because I did not want to be stereotyped and pigeonholed as a woman who only ministers to women.

The prevailing mindset in denominations and churches was to make a token acknowledgment of women by creating a women's ministries department in local churches as well as their national headquarters. Naturally, they had a woman leader as head of that ministry. The scope of that ministry was usually limited to women reaching other women. They would organize women's Bible studies and lunches, and then channel their energies towards missions, children, or other activities to keep the women busy in the local church.

The attitude seemed to be, if you are a woman called to ministry, your ministry would naturally be to other women or children. So women were in charge of hospitality, prepared the food, and organized the meetings. This presupposition actually limits women. It was assumed that a woman would speak on Mother's Day or Women's Day in the church, but not at any other time.

This was a far cry from my own ministry, which had started on skid row, preaching to drunken men! In fact, from the time I was in the marketplace, I had always worked mostly with men colleagues. The early days of computer development and its use in commercial industries was mostly male-dominated. When I began ministry, it was always to a mixed group. I felt called to the Body of Christ, male and female. Therefore my spirit rejected the idea of allowing myself to regress from ministering to the whole Body of Christ to being limited as one who only ministered to women.

At the rare women's meetings that I did agree to speak at, I knew my messages would not be directed towards topics that women seemed to want to hear about: Stories about marriage, children, heartaches and how one dealt with those issues. As a single woman, I had no babies to talk about! Instead I preached on topics like spiritual warfare and developing your full potential, discovering your identity in Christ. It was not a gender issue; it was a gift issue.

An Invitation

The first notable invitation I accepted to preach at a women's conference was in January 2002, when Indri Guatama from Jakarta had one of her speakers canceling on her. It was her first women's conference. Because it was so close to the date of the conference, she was in urgent need of a replacement. She was asking around in Indonesia for a speaker when someone gave her my contact details. When the invitation came, I asked, "Who is this?" My instinctive reaction was to decline. Besides, I did not know anything about her.

However, before I responded, I showed the invitation to our leadership team, and asked them to pray about it, to see if they felt that I should do it. After a couple of days they said, "We really feel like you need to go – God has some reason for you to be there." Man, that was definitely not what I wanted to hear, but because we were a team and I trusted them to hear God, I rearranged my schedule and agreed to join her.

After I preached the first night, Indri, who was then an evangelist, asked me about my ministry. I shared my journey from being an evangelist to making the transition to pastoring. I discovered that she was struggling with the same issues. She would preach and people would come to Christ, but the following year when she returned to that same church for further meetings, the converts from the year before could not be found. The new babies in Christ had disappeared. She was becoming increasingly frustrated that the fruit of her ministry was mostly being lost, because the pastors did not know how to disciple those new converts. Yet at the same time she was resisting starting a church and becoming a pastor – for the same reasons that I had struggled with in the past.

We spoke about how Trinity was helping churches to make disciples through training and consultation. She said, "Teach us about discipleship. Forget the topics I gave you earlier; we need this new message on discipleship." So I put aside everything I had prepared and taught them about God's plan for disciple-making. It was good that Janice Chng, one of our younger pastors, along with another person, were with me on that trip, because I was able to involve them in the new schedule of training.

During this conference and further meetings, Indri and I developed a strong relationship. She became a formidable spiritual daughter. She has not only established a powerful church in Jakarta, but she has also birthed several new Kingdom businesses with her members to bring transformation to other parts of Indonesia. God has released through her an apostolic anointing to touch hundreds of churches and thousands of believers in the nation. Today, I am honored to serve and support her as she continues to do things never done before, to bring transformation to her nation.

An Attitude Problem

Some time later, towards the end of 2003, God began to wake me up in the middle of the night, telling me, "*You have an attitude problem.*"

I was not used to being awakened in the middle of the night. I was a sound sleeper. After several nights of this happening, I wanted to know more. "Okay Lord, what is it?" I asked.

God answered, "You have an attitude problem about women."

After some consideration, I agreed with the Lord and said, "Okay, I'm guilty. I repent." So I asked for forgiveness. I assumed that was what God wanted me to do. Naturally, if it was a sin in my life, I wanted it out as well.

But He had more in mind. The following week He woke me up again. That night, he said, "*Get up and get a pen.*"

So I got up and went into my home office, found a pen and paper and returned to my bed, and sat down. "Okay Lord, I have my pen."

Then the Lord said, "*I want you to write down some names.*"

He began to impress upon me the names of well-known women speakers in the States. With each impression, I wrote down their name. These were all women with international ministries. After writing down these names, I asked, "Okay Lord, now what?"

"*Now call them and tell them they have an attitude problem.*"

"What? Surely I can't just call them out of the blue and tell them they have an attitude problem!" I knew them, and they knew me; we had each other's phone numbers, but we were not in the habit of calling each other.

"God, what will they think? Won't this offend them? Surely they will become angry with me. Who am I to deliver a seeming rebuke to them and their ministry?" I struggled, trying to reason with God...but nothing worked. He did not change His assignment.

Finally I stopped struggling with God. Reluctantly, I picked up the phone and called the first woman leader. She was out of the office, so I just left a message that I had called. "Phew, that was good," I told myself, "because I did not actually have to talk to her." Then I decided to call the second one. She answered the phone. After the usual greetings, I stopped and said, "God told me to call you.... and He told me to tell you that you have an attitude problem – regarding women."

There was silence. I quickly continued, "He told me I had the same problem."

As we talked, we soon discovered that her reason for shunning invitations to speak at women's conferences was the same as mine. The same was true with every one of these powerful women leaders I called. We did not want to be pigeonholed or stereotyped as women who only spoke to women. All of us had valid ministries to both men and women, and we wanted it to stay that way.

Shortly after that I called a meeting of these nationally known women. Some were already scheduled in meetings elsewhere, but several of them flew to Michigan and we spent two days talking and praying about the implications of what God was saying.

In the time between my phone calls and our gathering, God woke me up again. He said, *"The world sees men at one level and women at a lower level. Yet I made it clear in My Word in the book of Genesis, what My plan was from the beginning."*

God continued, saying, *"I am calling you and the others to bridge the gap. You are to teach women to recognize the gifts I have given them and release them from the bondages of man and society's systems so they can rise up to a higher level. Men think they have achieved their highest levels in ministry, but they have not – and they cannot rise higher until the women break free and rise up, until there is a convergence, where men and women are equally joined together in ministry, as I designed in My Word. Then I will raise both the men and the women to a higher level."*

> *Men think they have achieved their highest levels in ministry, but they have not – and they cannot rise higher until the women break free and rise up.*

God also said, *"You and the others have achieved a measure of success and recognition by My grace working in your life. But the success I have given you is not for yourselves, it is for you to now use and release other women."*

The next morning I reread the early chapters of Genesis. The assignment was clear. I, along with the others, was to begin ministering to women, breaking off the old mindsets, ministering healing to their wounded spirits, and empowering them to rise up and join ranks with the men. I had always mentored both men and women in ministry, but now I had to make a shift and expand my ministry. I had to be more intentional in finding and mentoring women leaders so they could rise to the level that God intended for them to achieve.

CHAPTER 22

The Journey Continues

THIS REVELATION that God dropped in my heart resulted in a deep commitment to change my attitude and to also change this same attitude in the minds of many others. Out of the original group of women I had contacted, several of us – Barbara Wentroble, Indri Guatama and I – shifted our schedules and committed ourselves to a priority of reaching women. We began to organize meetings under a new banner which we called Apostolic Women Arising (AWA), where we challenged women to arise in their calling and destiny. Pastor Indri would organize and fly her music team from Indonesia to the States to lead worship for these conferences, and they were an amazing blessing.

At times, Jane Hanson, head of Women's Aglow international, Barbara Yoder and Pamela Anderson would be with us. God began to awaken an army of women as they responded to His call to arise in their anointing and do the work He had called them to do. As we conducted conferences in Australia, Indonesia, and several cities in the States, there were many powerful testimonies of deliverance, a shifting in their self-image and the assurance of God's call.

While the conferences were having an impact, I felt that they were not accomplishing enough, because there was no way we could actually follow up on these women and walk them through their various transitions. I felt God directing me to focus on gathering selected women leaders and mentoring them in smaller groups.

I felt the Lord impressing upon me the needs of these 'successful' women in ministry: Whom do they talk to? Whom can they share with concerning issues or challenges in their life and ministry? How can they grow to a deeper level in God? These impressions soon led me to know that I was to work with women who are already leaders of leaders. They, in turn, could form their own mentoring groups with others within their sphere of influence.

I felt this was more the strategy of Jesus, to spend time with a select group of world changers, and that was the way I should develop my mentoring group.

> *I felt this was more the strategy of Jesus, to spend time with a select group of world changers.*

Women in Strategic Leadership

In the past, I had received requests from many women, asking me to mentor them. God had also been dealing with me about mentoring for several years. But I had resisted it because I always wondered, "What is it that I have, that others might want?" Besides, I had never been to a mentoring roundtable and didn't know how to actually do it!

So by faith and with fear and trembling, I convened the first mentoring roundtable in Salt Lake City, Utah, in 2004. In the first couple of years we met twice a year and we now meet annually. The roundtable developed into what we would now call Women in Strategic Leadership (WSL). I wanted to keep the group small, not more than 20-25 peer level leaders, because with too large a group, it becomes difficult to interact meaningfully. It has been challenging to keep it small, because someone always knows someone else who needs to be there!

In these sessions, I share my insights on God's perspective of women, both in the Spirit and the Word, as well as in the church and in the marketplace. We talk about attitudes they need to have in ministry, and practical ways to overcome challenges that they face. We even address the need for them to prepare for generational impact and transfer. This is not just one-way teaching; there is dialogue, prayer and ministry time.

I have come to realize that these women leaders need to draw from a well of wisdom and experience of others who have paid the price, who have gone ahead of them and are able to help them get into their destiny. At times they need encouragement, at other times they need breaking of bondages and mindsets. Some of the women have now begun to join together to lead mentoring roundtables within their circles of influence.

In obedience to God's leading, while not ministering exclusively to women, I have done more in the realm of ministry to women in the last few years than I have done my whole life!

Time for Convergence

In my ministry I had always worked with and mentored both men and women. In fact, some of the guys and husbands of these women began to feel left out because it was a women's roundtable and they could not attend!

However, this restoration of women isn't just about the women. It is about the Kingdom. The mandate to rule the earth and subdue it was given to both male and female (Genesis 1:27-28), and we will be able to fulfill the mandate when men and women rule and reign as equal partners in His Kingdom. Men think they have achieved their highest levels in ministry, but they have not. There are greater levels of anointing to be unlocked. That is why God wants women to rise up in leadership, and to enable, train, and empower other women to do the same. Only when there is a convergence of men and women at the same level, can both men and women rise together to a higher level of anointing and effectiveness in God's Kingdom.

Sad to say, many mainline denominations and independent churches are progressing faster than the AG in this area. Although our leadership has taken steps to try and give some 'face' to women, they (especially single women) are still largely limited in certain positions of leadership.

Some women resent younger women who are being used by God. They quote old mindsets or teachings to try and disqualify them. They reason, since they themselves had not been allowed to minister in the past, why should these young women feel they have a right to preach or minister? As women, we are often our own worst enemy.

But this is changing. The old walls are coming down, faster in some areas and more slowly in others, but they are coming down. Many male leaders are rising up to champion women, and to encourage and support them. One of God's male leaders in this area is Lee Grady, formerly the editor of *Charisma* magazine. God spoke to him and challenged him to defend, protect, and empower women regarding their worth and calling in God. He also challenges men who are abusing their wives to stop and honor them as God intends. The altars are full of men repenting and changing their marriages. Now a large part of Grady's ministry involves mentoring a younger generation of men who are joining him in this ministry in many different nations. It is awesome.

The restoration and recognition of the fivefold ministries (Ephesians 4:11-12) has also contributed to the release of a larger number of women in ministry and their acceptance in leadership roles. People's attitudes towards women in leadership are changing. Change is taking place. Women are beginning to be more valued, and seen as equal partners. I see a movement that is escalating across nations, governments, business, and even within denominations.

God is breaking old mindsets and stirring His people to fulfill His calling and purpose, not only in their homes but in all other spheres of society. The end times are upon us. God is pouring His Spirit on all people and wants to mobilize all of His army – men and women included – for the work of His Kingdom.

The Journey Continues

Yes, the journey continues. In fact, I am actually busier these days than I was as a senior pastor! I love the fact that I can still serve the Body of Christ in so many different ways, and across denominational lines.

However, I do need to make a confession. I realize now that I have not taken good care of my physical body all these years. While I was physically active and played sports, I was not resting enough. According to the doctor, I have traveled across too many time zones too quickly and too often, not taken vacations to get a break, and not gotten sufficient sleep. I have to admit, I am guilty on all counts! I loved what I did, and to me it was not work; it was the Kingdom of God. Since then, I have sincerely repented before God, but I must now deal with some of the consequences of that overly gung ho mindset and lifestyle.

What consequences, you might ask? Well, they all seem to be happening in rapid succession, perhaps because they were accumulated or compounded over the years. Some of the things that have surfaced, almost back-to-back, are knee problems, breast cancer requiring surgery and radiotherapy, then total hip replacement. While my hip was healing, a growth on my left thigh developed into skin cancer and required surgery to get it all out before it did major damage.

When the enemy comes in like a flood, the Lord lifts up a standard against him. Well, God has surely shown Himself to be powerful in my life. I have continued in my ministry schedule regardless of these events. I have been preaching under all circumstances and I can testify that in my weakness, His strength is made perfect (2 Corinthians 12:9). The services have been awesome. The response to the Word has validated His presence. All I can say is, to God be the glory. Like Paul, I say, "... I consider my life worth nothing to me, if only I may finish the race and complete the task the Lord Jesus has given me – the task of testifying to the gospel of God's grace" (Acts 20:24).

Through all this, I learned more about trusting God at a deeper level for myself. At the same time, I have sensed a greater authority and anointing, a wisdom that comes from a lifetime of hearing and walking with God.

I have shared my journey in this book not because my life has been perfect. On the contrary, I have made plenty of mistakes. I have been hard of hearing, at times. At the threshold of new seasons, I have often struggled to grasp what God wanted me to do. Yet I have shared all this, in the hope that as you see the fingerprints of God across all the different seasons of my life, you will be encouraged that God is faithful – and you will pursue God and His purpose for you with greater intentionality and intensity than ever before.

Your life journey may be different from mine, but one eternal truth remains: Your life can be mighty in God's hand. Your *beginning* does not determine your *end*. It does not matter if you are single or married, young or old, rich or poor, introvert or extrovert. It does not matter whether you come from a whole family or from a broken home, like I was. Perhaps, like me, you have been bullied, or have had negative words spoken into your life.

> *Your life can be mighty in God's hand. Your beginning does not determine your end.*

Whatever has happened to you does not determine the outcome of your life. You can break out and you can break free by the power of God. If you will rise up in your spirit and let God take hold of your life – surrendering all to Jesus – there is no telling how He will use you and where He will take you. Yes, these things may have held you back previously, BUT GOD!

God has a vision for your life – a life of destiny, purpose and power. Seek Him for your divine assignment. Listen to His voice. Be filled with His power. Embrace fully who He has made you to be. Follow where He leads – and let *your* adventure begin.

On Women in Leadership

REQUIRED READING FOR BOTH MEN & WOMEN

Here are some foundational principles that form my perspective on women in leadership. Men should read this too, because it is not 'just a women's issue' – it is a Kingdom issue.

Foundational Principles

1. Look for the gifts, not the gender.

My approach to the gender issue is essentially to make gender a non-issue. This is my guiding principle: Look for the gifts, not the gender.

John Wesley believed that a woman's gifts would make way for her ministry. He was the first within his movement to authorize women to preach. He did not push women into ministry but affirmed that women could be in ministry, and it would be their gifts that would open the way to ministry.

Likewise, I believe a woman's role should not be determined by her gender but by how God has gifted her, by His calling on her life. I do not believe every woman is called to be a preacher, just as I do not think that every man is called to be a preacher. Women must look to their calling.

I remember preaching in the church of Pastor J. D. Middlebrook. We were discussing something when he made the statement, "I don't have women preach in my pulpit."

I asked him, "Who's preaching today?"

"Well, you are!"

I was puzzled. "But you just said you don't let women preach in your pulpit..."

"Well, I didn't mean *you*!"

Amused, I responded, "If I am not a woman, then what am I?"

I believe he saw God's anointing, God's calling upon my life. He did not see it as a gender issue. If the calling is there, if the anointing is there, it makes the way for the ministry.

2. Let your ministry or work speak for itself

While there were people who had issues with women in ministry, no one actually came up and said it to my face. I have had challenging questions thrown at me only a few times in my ministry, during the early days. Once we were in Michigan, and there was a Q&A session during missions training. Someone asked whether God could use women in missions. My quick reply was, "If God can use a jackass,

God can use a woman! God can use anyone He wants to." (Let's just say I was 'quick-triggered' in my younger days!)

I realized that if God wanted me in the ministry, He would have to open the way and make it happen. Therefore I was determined not to fight my way into it. For this reason, I have never fought for women's rights in ministry. I have never preached to defend them. I did not teach on women in ministry; I did not try to justify it. I held no debates and no classes about the topic even in the church I pastored. I felt the ministry should speak for itself. This was a deliberate strategy. The ministry should bear fruit, and the fruit will be the evidence. That is my philosophy.

3. Know your identity and assignment.

Here is a fact: People are tougher on women leaders than they are on men. As a woman leader, I have had to work twice as hard. Others may never see you or acknowledge your hard work, but God sees you.

Yes, I had men reject me because I was a woman, but I did not let it bother me. I tried never to put a lid on myself and never to allow others to put a lid on me. I chose to obey God and let the results speak for themselves. I learned to be still and let God fight my battles for me. Often I made the choice to do what I knew was right at the risk of being misunderstood.

It is very important to maintain a right attitude, coming back to knowing that God has called you and asked you to do it. Our spirit must never be one of rebellion or arrogance, but one of determined dependence on God, seeking His guidance for decisions, plans and strategies to be carried out.

To be a woman leader is to go against the grain. Therefore your perspective of who you are, and your certainty about your calling and your role, are very important. Always go back to your calling and identity in God—know who God has called you to be and what He has called you to do. If you know your identity and assignment in God, criticism cannot throw you off.

Believe that if God has put you in a position or given you an assignment, His presence and favor will make a way for it to happen. I have often told God: "You asked me to do this; If You don't bail me out, it's not going to happen."

Practical Pointers

Here are some practical pointers which will help you as a woman leader, or as a man who works with women leaders.

a) **You don't have to become a man to lead**
   Some women feel they have to compete with men to be a leader. They try to steel their emotions and, as a result, appear demanding and domineering. A woman can be a strong, effective leader without becoming masculine.

b) **You will come up against traditional stereotypes.**
   Traditional stereotypes of both men and women run deep, beginning in the cradle, with the distinctions of pink or blue baby clothes. One of the challenges a woman leader will come up against is the long-held perception that women run and function on emotions rather than on rational, practical logic.

   Female leaders will initially face the prejudice and bias of these old stereotypes. People will view them through the lens of these stereotypes. However, if women leaders persevere in what God has called them to do and demonstrate godly leadership, these naysayers will come to see them as God-called, God-anointed leaders – gender notwithstanding.

c) **Learn to work with men.**

Women leaders need to learn how to work with men. Many singles do not know how to comfortably relate to men in the ministry or workplace. They have only learned to view men as romantic figures, which obscures their ability to work effectively with them. Some women turn on their feminine charm to get their way rather than appeal to the logic of their male coworkers. This crosses the line, confuses the roles, and can lead to emotional entanglements.

As women, we need to appreciate the unique strengths of the men we work with. We must also understand that men do go through mood swings. They do know it when it happens, and if we do not fight back, ultimately they will have a greater appreciation of our strengths. When both men and women have a healthy self-image, and have no need to prove themselves, a healthy work partnership can be achieved.

d) **Assign tasks according to giftedness, not gender.**

Sometimes we come up against the mindset that "That's a woman's job". Women often have their job scope defined for them. They are expected to do things like teaching other women, ministering to children or counseling. They are typecast into a supporting role and tend not to lead, preach or vision-cast. They are expected to be a helper rather than a peer in ministry.

When assigning responsibilities to various team members, we need to recognize the spiritual gifts God has given to every member on the team, whether male or female. The men do not always need to be the ones leading the committee or standing in front of the ministry, and the women do not always have to be the ones providing the administrative and back room support.

e) **Embrace every learning opportunity.**
In my ministry, I have had times when men would 'dump' on me the jobs and tasks that they did not want to do. I chose to see these occasions as divine opportunities to learn something I did not have prior experience in.

These things do happen, but we can choose our response to them. We can receive these things as rejection or a downgrade of our self-worth and allow them to become a root of bitterness in our spirit. Thankfully, there is a better way: we can choose to allow God's grace to give us an attitude of learning and, thereby, add new skills to our resume and repertoire. It boils down to our spirit, attitude, and posture.

f) **Dare to dialogue**
When one is at the forefront of change, we sometimes step into opportunities and scenarios for which no written policies exist. There were missionary policies that seemed to discriminate against single missionaries. In those early days, there was one key discrepancy regarding salary: Single missionaries (mostly women) only received half of the salary of a married couple. This put singles at a severe disadvantage with regard to their living conditions.

We all lived with this seeming injustice without rebelling, but I looked for an opportunity to bring up this issue. When the chance came up, I highlighted the inequity of the salary policy, asking, "If our salary package has a housing allowance, but that housing allowance is cut in half because we are single, how do we rent half a house or buy half a car or pay half a utility bill? Whether you are single or married, some expenses are the same."

Within a few short months, the salaries of singles increased. No longer was it one-half, but now 70 percent of a married couple's salary was offered, which was fair, taking into account that one person would not consume as much food as two persons. I am happy to say that the AG did make room for me. They did try to accommodate the uniqueness of my ministry that did not fit into the box. They did this not just for me, but for others too.

When faced with seeming injustice or outdated policies, we can labor under a sense of injustice and rebel against authority, bail out and quit, or suffer in silence. I chose to speak out, to engage in dialogue. When we experience unreasonable policies, it is all right to question them and to engage in dialogue. We live in a changing world where conditions on the field remain in a constant state of flux. We should not fear raising these issues for reasonable dialogue. Rules are made, and rules can change.

Take, for example, the inheritance law in the Bible. The five daughters of Zelophehad went to Moses who was the lawmaker (Numbers 27:1-11). Moses in wisdom took their case to God in prayer. God told Moses to change the rules. Moses the spiritual leader heard from God and changed the rules – and changed history. I believe that we should engage the issue of injustice or inadequate policies in the same way.

g) **Do not place limits on girls.**
If you are raising a daughter or mentoring a group of girls, do not place limits on them because of their gender. Rather, give them opportunities and mentor them according to their gifts, not their gender.

A key influence in my childhood years was my grandfather. He never said I could not do something because I was a girl. This was a key influence in my formative years. Because I did not grow up with any lids placed on me, I simply did not know that these lids existed. I did not try to be like a boy, but there was nothing I could not do. I was always ready to try new things and was given the opportunity to do so.

If more parents, teachers, and pastors would nurture and mentor girls according to their gifts and not their gender, girls would not grow up thinking that they have limitations in serving God just because they are female. When that happens, we will see more women in leadership and missions, simply because they can be who God has called them to be. Then both men and women can reach a point of convergence and rise together to a higher level of anointing and effectiveness in God's Kingdom.

It's about the Kingdom

The mandate to rule the earth was given to both male and female (Genesis 1:27-28). When men and women rule and reign as equal partners in His Kingdom, we will be able to arise to greater levels of anointing and fulfill that mandate.

The end times are upon us. God is pouring His Spirit on all people. He is ready to mobilize all of His army – men and women – for the work of His Kingdom. Will you respond and say, "Here I am, Lord... I surrender all. Send me!"

An Adventure Around the World

COUNTRIES WHERE NAOMI HAS MINISTERED

Argentina
Australia
Barbados
Bulgaria
Canada
Colombia
Denmark
Ecuador
Egypt
Fiji
French Polynesia (Tahiti)
Germany
Ghana
Guam
Hong Kong
India
Indonesia
Israel
Japan
Kiribati (Gilbert Islands)
Macau
Malaysia
Marshall Islands
Mexico
Micronesia

Nauru
New Zealand
Nigeria
Norway
Palau
Palestine
Papua New Guinea
Philippines
Poland
Romania
Samoa
Singapore
Solomon Islands
South Korea
Sri Lanka
Taiwan
Tanzania
Thailand
Venezuela
Vietnam
United Arab Emirates
United Kingdom
United States
Zambia

Reflections

BY VARIOUS CONTRIBUTORS

Contributors

Alan Wharton 242

Alistair & Marie Petrie 245

Alton Garrison 247

Antonio & Ruth Cortés 250

Barbara (Liddle) Cavaness Parks 253

Beatrice Kang 258

Beth Grant 266

Deborah Ong & Daniel Cheah 270

David Grant 274

David Mohan 279

Deborah Gill 282

Dominic Yeo 287

Edgardo Peña Arenas 292

Esther Victoria Milian 295

Eu Yat Wan 300

Gary & Cindy Panepinto 303

George Wood 306

Gerald Tan 309

Indri Gautama 314

Contributors

Janet Mangum 317

John Kelly 321

Joseph Mattera 323

Lana Heightley 324

Laurie Vervaecke 326

Les Bowling 334

Margaret Court 336

Ong Sek Leang 338

Pamela Anderson 341

Pang Ek Kwan 350

Peter Loo 352

Philip Lyn 356

Raymond Choudhury 359

Ray & Judy Rachels 362

Reinaldo Castellanos 364

Steven Tay 366

Wayne & Judy Cagle 369

Yang Tuck Yoong 374

Onwards and Upwards

ALAN WHARTON

My first meeting with the dear Apostle was towards the end of a Conference in Argentina, being hosted by Ed Silvoso in 1999.

At the end of the last evening meeting of the conference, there was a 'fire tunnel'. Delegates entered the tunnel, in order to receive prophetic and encouraging words from the speakers, before returning home the next day. At the end of the tunnel was a smartly dressed lady, who gently and graciously prayed for each delegate, anointing them with oil. When I became aware of my surroundings again, I found I was under the platform, having been moved by the stewards. Being so impacted by the power of God, I joined the tunnel queue again – with the same result.

The following morning, at breakfast, I 'happened' to sit at the same table as the apostle. This became the longest breakfast meeting I have yet experienced, from 8.15am-11.30am. I came away with many table napkins, used to illustrate a mixture of what I have later come to know as 'Seven Steps', 'Spiritual Parenting' and 'Carecell Leaders Training' material. This was my first major download of practical teaching from Naomi, whom I am now privileged to know as a friend and mentor.

In 2001 I attended the full Seven Steps programme at Trinity Christian Centre, having been dissatisfied with some 'home-grown' small group leadership training. This second encounter with the apostle's incisive and perceptive teaching style, included what felt like being put on the rack by a caring friend. She wouldn't let go (metaphorically speaking), until I had put into words what I was going to do having heard from God. She wanted to hear the details – not the generalities of how hearing from God had impacted me.

Concerning leadership development, I remember asking, on one occasion, "How do you minister so accurately to so many people as they come down from the congregation?" Her answer was memorable – "Next time, come and stand behind me and see." It sounded so New Testament. At the next available opportunity, I was up on the platform being given a personal master-class.

Apart from the anecdotes above, I can personally testify that this lovely lady, always careful in her presentation, both in dress and in the content of her teaching, walks the walk, as well as talks the talk. Her international standing is without doubt; the meaningful way in which she communicates across the breadth of denominational streams, is awesome.

If I were to catalogue her strengths as I have witnessed them, the list would include:

- being ready and willing to invest time and resource to up-skill and empower the weak
- being equipped to see beyond the visible, in order to draw in a preferred outcome
- being sure-footed out in front as a leader, relying on her Master's leadership

- gifted in problem solving, spiritual or temporal, then discerning strategies to deal with them
- being graced, "for such a time as this", with a Breaker anointing for the benefit of the 20th and 21st Century Church

Being human, Naomi is still seeking after perfection. However, based on my experience over the last 15 years, in terms of a model in Church leadership, she is golden. Thus, I am honoured to congratulate her on these first 50 years of anointed and very productive international ministry.

"First 50 years?", I hear you ask. Well, the vast amount of printed material will benefit readers long into the future. Whereas many authors reach their zenith with a first book, I rate *Moving On and Moving Up – from Succession to Significance* to be the best so far.

In apostolic significance, then, dear friend "Onwards and Upwards".

Rev Alan Wharton
Connect Groups Overseer, The Vine Relational Mission Church
Maidstone, United Kingdom

Moments of Life with Naomi Dowdy

ALISTAIR AND MARIE PETRIE

My wife and I have known Naomi for a number of years. She has been a colleague, a friend, and a counselor to us in ways she is not even aware of! She is a leader of leaders who has understood the power of servanthood within leadership. She mixes wisdom with compassion in a manner we rarely see within leadership.

We have found her to be a true friend who lives her life and ministry with a genuine depth of integrity and transparency. She listens to people; she does not simply hear and then move on to another conversation. Naomi has the amazing ability to process what is being said, put it into simple yet meaningful action, and then basically say, "Now get on with it!" She mixes faith with reality in a compassionate yet businesslike manner!

I have yet to meet with her on the golf course, though many promises have been made in that direction. I hear she is clearly an Apostle in that area of "field work" – and is always out in front!

For Marie and I personally, there was an occasion in 2003 that will always stay with us concerning Naomi's profound way of pastoring and being a friend in need. We had just moved to the city in which we now live. Shortly afterwards, a fire began to rage in the area causing one-third of the population to be evacuated and housed elsewhere. It was a highly concerning time and the fires were nearing our home. Smoke and debris was everywhere and we had to leave our home twice. Even after we were permitted to return, the smell of smoke had permeated every part of our house: every dish, all the cutlery, and all our clothing, never mind the fabric of the house.

Out of the blue Naomi called us from Singapore and wanted to check if we were fine. Immediately she sent us a financial gift that took us through the next two months which otherwise would have been hard for us. We had both our sons with us – one who was married, and the other who was engaged, and a menagerie of pets! It was over a year until our home was 'clean' – but Naomi was there for us, even before we had asked!

She is an amazing woman of God and we thank Him for having brought her into our lives.

May the Lord bless her with many more years of ministry – and may all her rounds of golf be at par!

Love and blessings

Rev Dr Alistair & Mrs Marie Petrie
Executive Director, Partnership Ministries
Kelowna, British Colombia, Canada

A Life of Kingdom Advancement

ALTON GARRISON

Johanna and I express our heartfelt birthday blessings to our longtime friend, Rev Dr Naomi Dowdy.

The first time we ministered at Trinity was in 1981 when our daughter Lizette was just four months old. Our trip to Singapore was memorable (but not in a good way) because we attempted to take Lizette on the flight without her having her own personal passport. I had experience as a world traveler, but it was not demonstrated that day.

We had some close friends with us, and my friend's wife was convinced it was a sign from God we were not supposed to make the trip. She, Johanna and baby Lizette had to stay behind to obtain the proper documentation. The only conceivable solution was for the husband and I to fly on to Hong Kong because the dates of the crusade were not flexible, and we did not know how long it would take to obtain the passport. We had planned to be in Hong Kong a couple of days before proceeding to Singapore.

Without my going into all the details (boring now but pretty frantic then), some good friends took the ladies into their home and helped

Johanna get the passport in record time. The two ladies and the baby met us in Hong Kong, and we all arrived in Singapore on schedule.

This may be the first time Pastor Dowdy is learning how close I came to disrupting all her plans and organizational expertise! However, a relationship that began with so much disorganization has endured for all these years.

Pastor Dowdy's leadership, earmarked by organizational efficiency, was apparent from the beginning of our relationship. A plethora of details were necessary to conduct a meeting of that dimension – among them:

- My picture on city buses advertising the meeting. I had never had that happen.
- Outlines that had to be approved by government officials. That was also a first for me.

Even then I knew Pastor Dowdy had a leadership gift but had no idea how that gift would serve Trinity or the larger body of Christ so dynamically. While giving credit to God, Dr David Mohan from India told me years later how instrumental the teachings of Pastor Dowdy had been in helping develop the small group ministry that was foundational in the growth of that great church to over forty thousand people in weekly attendance.

As Trinity grew and new buildings were built, it was apparent God had blessed Pastor Dowdy with extraordinary abilities and gifts. While her personal skills were apparent, God also gifted Pastor Dowdy with an anointing of a prophetic voice and ministry thereby blessing thousands around the world.

Pastor Dowdy's passion for missions was transferred into the DNA of the church. Few churches have committed as much to missions as has Trinity Christian Centre. The faith promise approach was begun because of her vision and still continues today.

The mark of a great leader is not measured just by that leader's accomplishments but also by the exponential impact of those mentored. It takes a secure leader to unselfishly empower those around them to become successful and flourish. And that is exactly what she has practiced throughout her ministry.

Pastor Dowdy's desire for an effective succession plan was not only implemented by her but also executed with precision and God's guidance. Passing the leadership baton too early, too late, or so reluctantly that the successor has limited opportunity for success frequently mars the legacy of an anointed leader. Pastor Dowdy set an excellent example of how succession should occur. The growth, health, impact and reach of Trinity after Pastor Dowdy handed the baton of leadership to Pastor Dominic Yeo is a testimony of God's obvious blessing upon the process of transition.

I have ministered at Trinity several times since Pastor Dominic became the lead pastor; and the honor, love, and respect between those two great leaders are palpable. God continues to bless both with phenomenal effectiveness.

Johanna and I would like to thank Dr Dowdy for her life, ministry, and prophetic voice. May God continue to grant her an expanded role in kingdom advancement for years to come.

Rev L. Alton Garrison
Assistant General Superintendent, Assemblies of God USA
Springfield, Missouri

An Apostle Called by God to Serve the Nations
ANTONIO AND RUTH CORTÉS

In 1988, I (Ruth) was invited to Singapore by Haggai Institute for training in advanced leadership. One of our instructors in that seminar was Dr Naomi Dowdy, who taught on Church Mobilization. During the seminar she gave us insights into her ministry, but what impressed me most was the knowledge and authority with which she spoke. I never imagined then how Rev Dowdy would affect my life and the influence she would have on Colombia through her apostolic ministry.

On returning to Colombia I continued to work with Haggai Institute, organizing seminars for key Christian leaders. In 1990 our director Dr Hernando Avila, asked his wife Claudia and I to organize the first international ten-day seminar. We prayed that God would guide us to bring teachers who could impact the lives of the leaders and challenge each one to do great things. We considered many names.

Rev Dowdy was one of the persons we really wanted to have at the seminar, but we considered this to be almost impossible. However we wrote to Rev Dowdy inviting her, and explained our economic situation at the same time. She answered very graciously, assuring us that she would be delighted to come without being a burden to us financially. In October 1991, she arrived in Colombia for the first time and continued to do so for the following 23 years, coming once or twice a year to teach and preach in the land of Colombia. (It was at this first seminar that Rev Dowdy met Esther Milian.)

I was very impressed by Rev Dowdy's life and her desire to reach the unsaved for Christ. She wanted them not only to come to Jesus and be saved, but to become a disciple, grow in Christ and bring others to the Lord. During the initial years I assisted in distributing her books and training materials to the different churches, and travelled with her to different cities and churches on a few occasions. I enjoyed the challenge of working with Rev Dowdy and listening to her teaching. I realized that God was able to use her because she held nothing back.

As the ministry grew, it became clear that the ministry needed a dedicated full-time worker. Though I would have loved to have continued serving with Rev Dowdy, I felt that my place was at the side of my husband, who serves as the director of the national denomination, Christian Crusade Church.

Then Rev Dowdy came to teach on raising up biblical apostles and prophets. As the leader of our denomination, my husband Antonio Cortés encouraged the main pastors and leaders to attend the three seminars that were taught by the apostles and prophets, Rev Dowdy and her team. They were a real blessing. We were admonished and made to realize that to receive blessing through these ministries, we had to obey the Word and not do anything that was not in the Bible. The authority of the Word was essential in these particular ministries and in any ministry!

In June 2005, the Christian Crusade Church commissioned the first apostles and prophets of our denomination. We had the great privilege of having the Apostle Rev Naomi Dowdy preach at this ceremony and commission my husband as an apostle, along with other apostles and prophets. This was the first ceremony of its kind in our denomination and in the country. Since then Rev Dowdy has commissioned other apostles in different missions and denominations throughout the country.

Rev Naomi Dowdy's legacy is that of authority, of a life consecrated to God, of service and love. This legacy was given through conscientious teaching and consecration. Her words of counsel and admonition will not be forgotten; we will continue to put into practice what we received.

In Colombia we were able to observe and experience the authority God has given her to minister as a woman. This has served to show the missions and denominations that God's call and delegated authority are not limited by gender. Many women have been encouraged to use their gifts and ministries for the glory of God, under the authority established by God. Many have been challenged to change their way of thinking and allow God to work through their lives for the glory and honor of His wonderful name.

Personally I have benefitted greatly from Rev Dowdy's ministry of teaching and her wise words of counsel. I love to sit under the teaching of the Word given with authority. May Rev Dowdy be able to continue this ministry in a deeper and lasting way.

We praise and thank our dear Lord for allowing us to know and learn from Dr Naomi Dowdy. With all our love we say: "Thank you very much and our gratitude is to God and to you, Rev Dowdy. Thank you!"

Rev Antonio & Ruth Cortés
Directors, Christian Crusade Church
Bogotá, Colombia

A Cherished Friendship Through the Years
BARBARA (LIDDLE) CAVANESS PARKS

Naomi and I seemed to have an instant connection when we first met in Springfield, Missouri, in June 1974. Some of her friends from Michigan had come to see her there and introduced us. She soon began sharing her stories from the Marshall Islands and I recounted my adventures in West Africa. Naomi needed my help in filling out some forms that first day, and thus began my "paperwork ministry" to her that was to continue for many years. I was impressed with her Marshallese and she taught me some greetings. The five of us laughed and prayed together. I remember being impressed that she prayed "with authority" and I wanted to do more of that too.

We both attended the School of Missions that year plus an extended seven weeks of classes at the newly established Assemblies of God Graduate School. In that class we formed friendships that have lasted these 40 years! I was itinerating to serve in Indonesia, another island nation. She raised funds in Michigan and California, while I traveled mostly in Wisconsin. I used some of her island stories and curios along with my African ones, since I had not been to Indonesia yet. One in particular that I remember had to do with God's miraculous provision in Ebeye. She was building a big seawall out into the lagoon in order to enlarge their property to build the church. The wall was constructed but they did not have the sand needed to fill up the hole created by the wall. She and the people were praying for a miracle. Then as they slept – trusting God to provide – an unusually strong wind blew all night. In the morning a sand bar had miraculously appeared, stretching out into the sea. They were able to haul in the sand and had plenty to finish the project. A challenge became an opportunity for a miracle!

After attending the General Council meeting in Denver the following August, we said our farewells and headed for the East Asian Conference in Taipei, Taiwan. The taxi driver from the airport spoke no English and drove us all over trying to find the address. Missionary Jim Andrews was a most welcome sight and rescued us from the unfair price being demanded. I recall how cold it felt in the dorm rooms at night, the hard beds, and the shock of eating 'authentic' oily Chinese foods. We also made our acquaintance with some of the great-granddaddies of all cockroaches. But we did not despise the days of those small beginnings (Zech. 4:10), and what we now call 'networking.'

One thing people don't realize about Naomi is that she is by nature a very shy and private person. It's the Holy Spirit that enables her to reach out and minister with passion and power. Without Him we can do nothing. But with Him, we can do all things!

Missionary Florence Beck had mentored Naomi in California and traveled out with us – next stop, Singapore. It was her first trip back since her husband's passing. She wanted to take us to every spot that she and Ed had visited. She would say, "Ed and I sat over at that table there and we ate the most delicious mulligatawny soup. Have you ever tasted that soup? Let's order some!" And so we would. Some things measured up to the memories, some not so much. She took our teasing and eye-rolling with good humor. Since the passing of my first husband, R. B. Cavaness, I understand much better. Some wisdom comes only with experience.

We visited Trinity services at the Equatorial Hotel, meeting the Hugh Bakers and Wes Weekleys, fellow missionaries. After seeing some of the sights, I went on to Jakarta and language school in Bandung. Naomi visited Malaysia, intending to begin evangelistic meetings in the Asia-Pacific region. But God had another plan: "In their hearts humans plan their course, but the Lord establishes their steps" (Prov. 16:9).

Following language school and my move to Malang, I was invited to join Virgie Cruz and Naomi as speakers at the Calvary Church (KL) camp on Pangkor Island, near Penang. We stayed in little thatched A-frame huts on the beach. Thank God for mosquito coils! At another camp in Port Dickson, we tried our hand at sailing with Dan Anglin, but we went out too far once too often and capsized the sailboat we had rented trying to head back to shore. I think Naomi lost one of her contacts and we all lost some of our pride as we tried repeatedly to get that water-logged sail upright again. We were so grateful to God, who enabled us to get back to dry land.

I also went to Singapore for a Christmas break in 1976. I got pressed into a "cooking and baking ministry" – traditional American turkey dinner and special cookies. We had an open house, which became sort of an annual tradition, and then Family Communion for New Year's. I directed the choir,' more of a girls' chorus that year, in a Christmas presentation. What we lacked musically, we made up for in enthusiasm – "a joyful noise to the Lord"! I began teaching block courses at Trinity School of the Bible, speaking at retreats, helping with the singing Christmas tree and other events. In these ways, I had the privilege of speaking into the lives of many who later became leaders of the church in Singapore.

What stands out about the next year was discovering a huge lump in my throat, the size of a small egg. When I came to Singapore to escort my parents into Indonesia, the doctors told me it was malignant and I needed to be admitted for surgery right away. This was my pastor father's first trip outside the US, and I had arranged three weeks of evangelistic meetings for him to preach around Indonesia, and I was going to interpret for him. Before they arrived, I went back to Naomi's and prayed. God poured His sweet peace over my troubled heart and told me it was going to be all right, *whatever* happened. So I told my surgeon that I would be carrying out my plans and would return for the surgery in three weeks. When they did operate, none of the dire predictions the surgeon had made came to pass. The tumor was removed and it was benign. To God be the glory!

So many visitors came to see me in the hospital that the head matron came in one afternoon and shooed everyone out. You see, I wasn't supposed to talk for six weeks – a tough assignment! We took some time to work on Naomi's studies and recuperate in the cool weather and quiet of Cameron Highlands. Satan wants to discourage God's children and cause them to turn back, but what the enemy intends for evil, God intends for good, to strengthen our trust in Him and testify of His faithfulness and goodness (Gen. 50:20).

My contribution to this collection of reflections is already too long; we have shared so many testimonies of God's goodness over these 40 years. I will include just a few more highlights. In 1979, Naomi and I went to speak at the HKBP church in Medan. Some of the church elders were a bit dismayed, because we were the first women they had ever invited to speak from the high pulpit. The solution was for us, Naomi as preacher and me as interpreter, to put on our jackets before ascending the stairs. God was faithful to move on hearts that day and afterwards we joined in fellowship around a pig roasted in our honor.

We were supposed to carve it – but that was never covered in our schooling! Our friend came to our assistance.

Later that year Naomi and I toured through Athens, Greece, and then met friends of mine who drove us around Israel on a personalized tour. I stayed in the US for nine months to itinerate and move my parents to Missouri, while Naomi had only a few services before returning to Singapore.

My second term was in Jakarta. After that I was assigned to FEAST in Manila. In the 1980s both Naomi and I became active in what eventually became the Asia Pacific Theological Association (APTA). We met several times a year to evaluate accreditation bodies and procedures, eventually developing standards, a self-study guide, visitation instruments, and a number of documents to encourage the upgrading of the Bible training institutions in the Asia Pacific region. These early documents have been adapted and used in virtually every other region in AG World Missions. Up until 2010-11 both of us served on visiting teams and the APTA Accreditation Commission.

After 20 years as a single missionary, I married R. B. Cavaness in December 1989. Naomi was my maid of honor and Beatrice Kang came as soloist. We welcomed them with snow and sub zero temperatures. In July of the following year, R.B. and I were back in Singapore as coordinators of the Decade of Harvest. We shared many good times, ups and downs. One of the 'downs' we laughed about was the day R.B. decided to try to jump the cement drainage ditch in front of Naomi's apartment. He didn't quite make it and skinned up the whole side of his face, arm, and leg, breaking his glasses. He came to her door and with blood streaming down his face, said, "Does anyone have a Band-Aid?" We shared good times of fellowship and food with Naomi and her mom Mama Wilson during those years. I taught at what had become the Theological Centre for Asia (TCA) and also the Bible Institute of Singapore (BIS). In 1994 we relocated to Springfield to serve at the AG Theological Seminary and AG World Missions.

I count it a privilege to have ministered to Naomi and with her through the years. Two of her mantras would be: "There is nothing too hard for God!" and "Just because it hasn't been done before doesn't mean it can't be done now!" She encourages those around her to move toward excellence in all they do, but especially to develop their strengths. She is a visionary and has faithfully led others to make the vision a reality. Her legacy will not be the properties and buildings, as awesome as those are, but rather the many lives God is helping her to impact around the world. Only heaven will reveal that!

Dr Barbara (Liddle) Cavaness Parks
Missionary Educator, AG World Missions
Springfield, Missouri

Naomi Dowdy: A Leading Servant
BEATRICE KANG

We often use the term servant leadership, but I would like to describe Pastor Dowdy as a 'leading servant.' Back in the 1980s, I went with Pastor Dowdy on a missions trip to Seremban, Malaysia. We didn't stay in a hotel, but in someone's home. In those days, female senior pastors were very rare, so the people were in awe of her. They would have her sit on a chair, not a stool, because she was a woman of God.

We had breakfast in the home of our hosts. After the meal, Pastor Dowdy proceeded to collect the crumbs from the table. Our host freaked out: "You cannot do that. You are a senior pastor!" But Pastor Dowdy went on to keep the food and wash the plates (I was making myself useful by wiping the table). She did it all very nonchalantly. She was not trying to show off in any way; she was just doing what she would normally do. She was simply being herself.

On that same trip, before we headed home, the front grille of her old Volvo car was stolen. This was dangerous because things could catch on to the engine while we were on the road. Before leaving, we went to a hardware shop, bought some chicken coop wire gauze, and tried to bend and fix the wire gauze onto the front of the car. By the time we were done, both of us were drenched in perspiration, and our clothes were covered with grease.

I went in to shower and left my greasy shirt and shorts outside, thinking I would get to them later. However, when I came out of the shower, I realized, to my horror, that Pastor Dowdy had picked up my dirty clothes and scrubbed them when she went in for her shower! The thing that amazed me was, she had no qualms about doing it at all. That's the Pastor Dowdy I know.

A Pastoral Heart

To hug a hawker, or to pat a petrol attendant who is drenched in perspiration and reeks of oil, is no big deal to Pastor Dowdy at all. Most of us would cringe and go "eek" but she doesn't even think that way. It's no issue for her at all to simply serve. This is one thing about her that I'll never forget. She has such a pastoral heart. If you catch it, you will notice that not everybody does it. I've seen pastors be very officious about things – but not her.

My uncle always reminds me about how Pastor Dowdy prayed for him when my auntie passed away. Pastor Dowdy had just come back from overseas and unexpectedly, she turned up at the funeral and asked, "Where is your uncle?" She walked over to him, knelt on her knee to comfort him, and prayed the most powerful, comforting prayer he had ever heard. It was a three-minute prayer at most, but it impacted him so much that he remembers it till today. Whenever she preaches at his church – even if it's a women's conference – he will sneak in just to hear her!

I've also seen it happen when we were in India. The situation was like in Mark 10:13-16, where people were shooing the children away. There was this mother who came carrying a half-naked baby. Pastor

Dowdy, wearing a most beautiful sari, reached out and touched their hair. Some people around us said, "She should have checked if they have lice." But that was the furthest thing from her mind. Then the mother asked her to pray for the baby. More than just praying, Pastor Dowdy decided to carry the child to pray – and at that very moment, the baby decided to pee! Pastor Dowdy did not flinch. She laughed and said, "Oh, that's a good flow!" She did not holler "Get me a towel!" Rather, she said calmly, "Let's carry on..." That was the posture of a leading servant. Many people can function as a pastor, but she really carries that heart.

What Business Are We In?

Once I received a call at Adam Road. Someone had called the church to ask if we could conduct a funeral for his uncle. "I am not attending your church. My uncle just passed away but he has not attended church for many years." I brought this request to Pastor Dowdy.

She looked at me and asked, "What business are we in, in the kingdom of God? Are we not in the business of reaching out to anyone?" That is one of her most powerful legacies till this day. We never ever say, "But it's our day off" or "It's a public holiday" or "We can't do it because you are not a member of our church." We should never have borders, fences or walls; just be there to minister the presence of God.

Once we ministered at a funeral at Circuit Road, and we brought some church members along. The team asked, "Who is this family? How did we know them?" I could only reply, "I don't know" because that was the truth. We had no prior connections with them; we were only meeting them at their point of need.

This attitude has really extended the love of God and the ministry to people who would have never stepped into a church. That is how she sees ministry: Never calculated, and never calculative.

A Strong Maternal Personality

Pastor Dowdy has a strong maternal personality. Once I was with her at a pastor's house in Kuala Lumpur. The pastor just had a newborn baby girl, who was being looked after by the pastor's wife upstairs. From the time we stepped into the house, we could hear the baby wailing. After twenty minutes, Pastor Dowdy told the pastor, "Bring your wife down." She greeted the wife, swaddled the baby in a cloth and put her against herself. The baby went quiet!

She told the new mother, "Go upstairs, bathe and rest." She prayed for the mother, who was in tears, and told her to go upstairs to rest. Then Pastor Dowdy said, "Let's continue our discussion." The next thing I knew, she put the baby on her thigh, started swinging her thigh to rock the baby, and continued with the discussion we were having – just like that!

Pastor Dowdy was the one who introduced me to durians. I had an aversion to durians and was terrified of trying it. On one of our mission trips to Malaysia, we went to a plantation belonging to the grandmother of a church member. Wanting to provide a gentle initiation for me into the world of durians, she tasted like 15 seeds of durian before she found a suitable one for me. I ate maybe two seeds, while she devoured the rest. I would have missed out on so much in life if not for her initiation into durians!

A Scientific Mind

I would say that Pastor Dowdy has a scientific mind. The strength of her mind is incredible. She has an ability to digest, unpack, analyze, and size things up. Men gravitate towards her because of her strong mind. They find that they can engage with her. This impacted Pastor Mohan greatly because he had never seen it in a woman. The women want to emulate her, to be a strong leader without losing their femininity, to assert authority without losing that warmth.

Pastor Dowdy does not like to deal with conflicts but if she has to do it, she will. She confronts issues without weakening down or crumbling. She does not mince her words; she is not afraid to say it as it is. Over the years, she and I have had disagreements. She would say certain things, and it would get to me. But give me a couple of hours and I would realize that what she said makes a lot of sense. If she were to mince her words and sugarcoat it, it wouldn't hit home. I just didn't like the uncoated version!

In a sense, it can be highly paradoxical and very confusing. On one hand, you see that she is highly pastoral and warm. On the other hand, if you don't know her heart, she can sound demanding because she is a strong personality.

She has such strong convictions about the Kingdom of God – the ministry, life and embodiment of the Kingdom of God. She does not believe in diluting things, in watering things down. She does not believe in half measures. She believes we have no business doing things that way. We can't make an impact by doing three things out of ten. This is how she has demonstrated the Kingdom of God to me. She has taught me how to bring the Kingdom into the lives of people.

An Innovative Leader

As a leader, she has demonstrated to me the ability to be innovative, to recover and bounce back. During my early days at Trinity, we were meeting at the Singapore Conference Hall. It was Good Friday and it was an illustrated sermon. After the Crucifixion scene, she got up to preach. At this point, the curtain was supposed to close, but it got stuck, and we could all hear it. We had three men still 'hanging' on the cross! Pastor Dowdy knew that 'Jesus' and the two thieves were shivering in the cold. So she made an emergency altar call right in the middle of her message: "With every eye closed and every head bowed, from the front row to the back row – if you have anything, let God deal with your heart..." She wanted to make sure that everyone had their eyes closed! As every eye was closed, she gestured for the three actors to get off their crosses. Her recovery skills are incredible! She is the master craftsman of altar calls.

A Distinct Fragrance

Pastor Dowdy wears a strong identifiable perfume. When you enter a room, you would know that she has been in the room because you can literally smell her. When we entered the toilet at World Trade Centre, we would sniff and say, "Pastor Dowdy is here!"

It became a standing joke among us. She often prayed with people and hugged them. So when we could detect her perfume on someone, we would say, "You have been 'pastor-ised!'"

A Wild Horse

There are many more stories I could share, but let me close with this one. At a leadership conference in India, a question was posed to Pastor Dowdy about selecting leaders. In answering the question, she said, "I would rather work with a wild horse than a dead mule." When she said it, she looked straight at me (I wonder why?) I knew she was referring to me. She has always felt that I was like a wild horse.

One day I read a book which said, "You don't tame a wild horse, because when you tame a wild horse, it loses its personality and spark. Instead, you *work* with the wild horse and transform it."

Pastor Dowdy understood this principle instinctively. Indeed this wild horse has not been tamed, but by God's grace and through her ministry, it has been transformed for the Master's use.

Rev Beatrice Kang
Executive Pastor, Trinity Christian Centre
Vice-President, Care Community Services Society
Singapore

A Legacy of World Changers

BETH GRANT

When David and I married 38 years ago, one of the special gifts in his life he shared with me was a friendship with Pastor Naomi Dowdy. David had already ministered with Pastor Dowdy in different countries for several years. From the first time we were together, it was apparent that this was a great lady and a woman of God. Only over the years have I been able to appreciate what that meant and the extent to which it was true.

One of my earliest and most enjoyable memories of Pastor Dowdy was at a ministers conference in South India. Pastor Dowdy was one of the guest ministers and the only woman preacher at the conference. Two missionary men were seated in front of us as Pastor Dowdy took the pulpit and began to minister powerfully with great spiritual authority. It was not long before the two men were smiling in surprise at this woman preacher. One leaned over to the other and whispered, "When God called that woman to preach, some army lost a great general!"

Yes, Pastor Dowdy is a great woman preacher and a woman of extraordinary spiritual authority. But she is also a great friend to her

266

friends, and is willing to walk with them through not only the times of celebration and honor, but also the times of suffering and battle.

Thirty-one years ago when David and I were expecting our second daughter Jennifer (now Jennifer Barratt), I developed a very dangerous condition which threatened the lives of both mother and unborn baby. I spent three weeks in the hospital in Maryland, USA, unable to leave the hospital until the baby would be born. During that time of serious crisis and waiting, Pastor Naomi was itinerating in that area of the US. To my surprise, she showed up at the hospital, prayed with us, and spent time with us as a family as we trusted God through those uncertain days and hours. She is a great woman of God with heavy responsibilities and schedules. I was deeply touched that she would find time to come wait with us for God's answer and Jennifer's safe birth.

During this past year when my husband David was facing great challenges, one of the first people I texted when security, confidentiality and powerful intercession were needed was Pastor Dowdy. She responded immediately and walked with us through the spiritual battle in the weeks and now months that followed. Like Old Testament prophets, she understands the political and spiritual times and speaks God's vision and victory into them with confidence.

In the past fifteen years, as God opened doors for me to encourage and equip women in ministry, Pastor Dowdy has inspired and coached me by her example as a powerfully anointed woman minister and leader in the church. Paving the way for women ministers and leaders, she walks with boldness and relentless courage where many fear to go – because she knows God is calling her there.

As a great minister and leader, Pastor Naomi models for men and women what it means to walk in the Spirit and in supernatural authority to accomplish God's mission and build His church. She is a strategic leader who convenes women in leadership and helps them to develop in their God-given calling more effectively than anyone I have ever met. She has been groundbreaking in coaching women leaders to plan generational transfer as she herself has done so strategically. She gleans best practices from the corporate world, integrates them powerfully with God's Word, and pours generously into the lives of leaders – including myself. In my personal journey, Pastor Naomi has played a unique role in spiritual prophetic leadership that no one else has played. I will be eternally grateful for her friendship and for the times that she has spoken into my life.

At this point in her extraordinary life, Pastor Naomi continues to amaze and inspire. She has not allowed herself to become fixated on one generation or season of success in ministry. In fact, just this week while I was writing this reflection, I saw her picture on FaceBook looking very edgy and contemporary – a whole new Apostle Dowdy! I suspect that when she goes into heaven one day, she will still be pushing forward in faith and vision, all too ready to try something new in a new season!

Recently, David and I attended the World Missions Congress of the World Assemblies of God Fellowship. As we watched and listened to these global church leaders who are sending missionaries to the nations, I realized just how many of these great leaders had been personally mentored in their ministry by Pastor Dowdy. I can think of no one else who has had that kind of deep spiritual influence over a region of the world by raising up great men and women of God to boldly fulfill God's call. Those into whom she has poured her life are taking Jesus to the nations and literally changing the spiritual landscape of missions in our world today. What an extraordinary legacy!

Dr Beth Grant
Co-Founder, Project Rescue
Executive Presbyter, Assemblies of God
Faculty, Assemblies of God Theological Seminary

Naomi Dowdy: A Gift of God

DEBORAH ONG AND DANIEL CHEAH

In our journey as ministers, we had the great privilege and honor of getting to know on a personal level a few outstanding Christian ministers who are listed in the Who's Who of the Christian world.

These great men and women were not just speakers who ministered God's word from our pulpits, but they were and are our personal friends too. Dr Naomi Dowdy is one of these few outstanding servants of God, whom God graced and gifted us with.

About seven years ago, Dr Naomi Dowdy came into our church life and her wise apostolic leadership working through friendship shifted us into another level. The very first weekend she came to minister for us was memorable and significant. During the very first night, she delivered a powerful message which we received with absolute faith and exuberant obedience as the Word for the hour. That released Word was to become the fuel to fire up again our hunger and passion to move upward.

Subsequently, a private coffee time with her ended with her asking what our vision was, and the question of "When are you going to take the next mountain?" We knew instantly what the Holy Spirit was speaking to us. At that point we were comfortable, we had what we needed for the current moment in church life, ministry and global missions. We were going to build slow and steady and take our time to do the next thing, especially with regard to the physical facilities and staffing!

But God had another agenda and He sent His revelatory directive through His apostle! The mountain in question was literally taking the next piece of land for church expansion, buy more land for the church, something we were not ready to do – not just yet anyway –though we knew it was something that would come!

However, after that coffee time, our spirit rose with faith and we knew that our time in the comfort zone was up.

The following year, we bought the piece of land next to our existing properties. Though it was rather expensive, we paid cash for it and literally moved the church forward. Concurrently, we began to upgrade and expand the existing facilities to prepare for growth – taking another mountain in every way.

As the physical mountain was being taken, so did we begin to take on the spiritual. The challenges were numerous because we were taking two pretty big mountains. The physical changes that took place provoked strong reactions with repercussions from governing authorities. We steadily overcame each obstacle because we had the One who moved mountains on our side!

Comparatively, the spiritual mountains were less daunting though there were also numerous obstacles and challenges. However, it sure helped when 'the sent one' continued to stand with us. Through the months and years that followed, her very regular engagements and presence at our church, and her rich experience in the ministry, especially in building a strong local church, added depths of wisdom, strength and courage to us.

One of the significant things about her, especially in speaking and and training, is her choice of words; her skill and grace in stating hard sayings with choice words without coming across as harsh, demeaning or judgmental. The way she phrased or said strong stuff came across as gentle nudges and suggestions. She is able to lead people into rethinking and even resetting a whole course of actions or directions without them feeling beaten down. That's the coaching skill of Apostle Naomi!

Though at the apex of her ministry, she comes in as someone who submits and serves the leadership of the local church. A true Servant Leader indeed! Dr Dowdy is high in IQ, SQ and EQ but never abrasive, superlative or assertively aggressive, and never religiously over-spiritual. Her down-to-earth spirituality is refreshing and exemplary!

In recent years, whenever she comes to our church, we have the joy of hosting her at our home. Having her stay at our home enhances the friendship factor and takes it to another level. The personal private downtime at home and over meals gives us precious and privileged insights into her heart, passion and integrity for the kingdom of God. She works tirelessly to network, bringing Christian leaders together for a greater common cause. Apostle Naomi is among the very rare breed of selfless Kingdom minded leaders in Christianity today.

As an individual, she is really a very nice and down-to-earth person. She loves good popcorn and Coke during the very-far-in-between movies nights. Her energy level is another surprising discovery. There was a time after a busy weekend, she went from Sunday service to golf course then to dinner and to a movie! Sitting beside her in the comfortable movie theater for a late night movie, her younger companion who was not at the golf course earlier zoned out, while she herself was wide awake and enjoying the movie. Amazing woman with youthful valor!

Her positive outlook on life coupled with a pragmatic spirit flavors her response and approach to life circumstances. No challenge seems to be able to hold her down or delay her. Her capacity to rebound and her can-do attitude of "let's do what needs to be done and get on with life" is admirable and inspirational! She's the picture of the song:

Onward Christian soldiers, marching as to war
With the cross of Jesus going on before.
Christ the royal Master, leads against the foe
Forward into battle, see His banners go.

We have figured that God must love us a lot because He sent and gave us Naomi Dowdy! Amen.

Rev Deborah Ong and Daniel Cheah
Senior Pastors, His Sanctuary of Glory
Kuala Lumpur, Malaysia

My Friend, Naomi Dowdy

DAVID GRANT

My friendship with Naomi Dowdy goes back over four decades. I first met her in the Marshall Islands of Micronesia. Fellow missionary evangelist David Daniels and I surprised Naomi in the Marshall Islands when we landed in the military base of Kwajalein. Although we did not have a permit, they allowed us to land as long as we promised to immediately take the boat to the neighboring island of Ebeye where Naomi lived. They called Naomi and said, "There are two American men who have come to see you. We are sending them to you on a boat to Ebeye." She was totally surprised and delighted when we stepped off the boat!

The Lord used her in a miraculous way among the Marshallese people. They are big people, and I remember a water baptism service where she baptized a 300-pound Marshallese brother in the Pacific ocean. What a fitting picture! Pastor Naomi Dowdy has never shied away from big challenges. She has always carried a big vision of God and of His mission for her and the church.

The Lord led her from the Marshalls into a broad ministry of missionary evangelism throughout Asia. Then she was approached by the World Missions leadership and asked to take responsibility for Trinity Christian Centre in Singapore. She struggled with this because she felt the calling to be a missionary evangelist. But feeling confirmation from the Lord, she accepted the pastoral position which launched a powerful new direction for her life and ministry.

The Lord has used her miraculously in the establishment of Trinity and a missionary vision that has reached throughout the world. The church has grown from a handful to several thousand. The missions giving skyrocketed from a few hundred dollars to several million. The leadership conferences for national leaders from the nations impacted the whole world. Pastor Dowdy's personal ministry took her beyond Asia to Europe, North America, South America, and the regions beyond. As Trinity grew, its leadership developed and its staff multiplied, she poured her life into developing young men and women to whom the leadership responsibilities would be transitioned in the decades to come.

Today, thousands of national leaders are serving in all parts of the world who have sat under the teaching and mentoring of Pastor Dowdy and the staff of Trinity.

For me, the most important contribution that Pastor Dowdy and Trinity has made is in the nation of India. Pastor David Mohan, David Stewart Senior and myself had the joy of launching New Life Assembly of God in Chennai, India, 40 years ago, beginning with seven people. Within 15 years, the church was running over 3,000. Pastor Dowdy and Trinity leadership staff revolutionized the church and Pastor Mohan's ministry with the small group concept and organizational methods that had been developed at Trinity. Where New Life had plateaued at 3,000, suddenly the growth trajectory went through the roof.

Today, the church has over 40,000 in attendance and continues to grow. Hundreds of churches have been planted out of New Life. Almost

200 missionaries have been sent out of the church to the unreached parts of India, southern Asia and the world. Much of this explosion of evangelism, revival, church growth, I attribute to the influence of Pastor Dowdy and later, the influence of Pastor Dominic Yeo and the staff of Trinity. Hundreds of Indian pastors have been impacted by Pastor Dowdy and the leadership conferences held at Trinity. If there is one person that could be identified as the most powerful influence in India in the last 30 years for church growth, it would be Pastor Dowdy.

My wife Beth and I married 38 years ago, and we have had the joy of visiting Trinity almost every year since, as we were coming and going to India from the U.S. This has brought incredible encouragement and inspiration in our own life and ministry. We feel like members of Trinity.

Twenty years ago, Beth and I partnered with KK Devaraj in founding Bombay Teen Challenge. Out of the ministry of Teen Challenge in the slums of Mumbai emerged a new powerful ministry called Project Rescue. Project Rescue was birthed with the specific mission of rescuing and restoring young women who had been exploited and enslaved. There were 100,000 girls who had been trafficked into the brothels and red light district of Mumbai.

Pastor Dowdy and Trinity partnered with this ministry from its very inception. Thousands of young women and their daughters have been liberated, spiritually and physically, through the efforts of Project Rescue – not only in Bombay, but in Delhi, Calcutta, Nagpur, Nepal, Bangladesh, Central Eurasia and Europe.

Trinity has sent teams for spiritual warfare, intercession and deliverance ministry to every Project Rescue site in India. Under the inspiration of Pastor Dowdy and now the leadership of Pastor Dominic, Trinity has been deeply involved from Project Rescue's beginning until now, with every aspect of the deliverance and healing ministry to the girls who have been victims of this terrible slavery.

Our daughter Rebecca, who was deeply involved in Project Rescue in Bombay and Dehli, has experienced the times of personal renewal at Trinity in Singapore under the ministry of Pastor Dowdy and the staff. In the midst of our daughter's greatest spiritual challenges in launching Project Rescue work in Dehli, Trinity staff came alongside her and provided spiritual strength and balance that was so desperately needed in her life and ministry.

Beth and I consider ourselves extraordinarily wealthy individuals not from a financial standpoint, though God has always provided resources for the vision He imparted. We are wealthy in friendship because of great people like Naomi Dowdy who have invested their leadership strengths into our lives, transferring spiritual emotional resources over the last four decades. We are enriched by her contribution to our life, ministry and family.

We see her as a world-class missionary evangelist; an anointed, gifted mentor and teacher; a powerful, effective pastor; an apostle within the worldwide Church of Jesus Christ. The apostolic anointing that rests upon her life and ministry has blessed the nations of the world, and our life and ministry. She has had great suffering, incredible success and a marvelous apostolic ministry which we recognize and are impacted by.

As we celebrate her 80th birthday and her 50th year in international ministry, we anticipate another decade or more of anointed apostolic ministry. The Lord has given her amazing health. We have witnessed a growing strength and wisdom in the last year or so as she has developed healthy margins in her life.

She is poised to pour herself into a truly apostolic role of enabling generational leadership transitions. She has role modeled apostolic and pastoral leadership transition in Trinity, and her responsibility is now to take this role model to the world, where scores of ministries and churches are facing that exact chapter of their life. That is the future. As I turn 70 this year, she has been urging me to plan for my own transition in ministry. She is the apostle and I am her student, her disciple, her follower.

Beth and I love her as a godmother. To our daughters, she is a god-grandmother. We have one grandson and three grand daughters; these are her great-grandchildren. She is part of a four-generation family. We honor her and our family is her legacy.

Rev David Grant
Eurasia Area Director for Resource Development,
Assemblies of God World Missions
Co-Founder, Project Rescue

Naomi Dowdy: Perseverance, Love & Generosity
DAVID MOHAN

By God's grace, New Life Assembly of God in Chennai grew from a house church of seven people to an urban church of 2,000 people.

Through the gifts of evangelism many people were drawn to the church. However, we had no relationship with them or any insight into who they really were.

Her Contribution

In 1991, Apostle Dowdy visited our church and gave us a vision of what the Great Commission was all about, explaining to us the purpose of the church from the book of 1 Peter. She emphasized that the most important thing in the Great Commission was making disciples and helped us develop leaders in the church.

She conducted a Lay Leaders Institute training, and then she taught us about Christian Education during Sunday services. She laid a structure for the church and gave us a strategy for church growth. Personally she helped me to develop my associate pastors at different levels. She taught us the need for and the role of the spiritual parent for the newcomer and new believers.

She did this for ten years and invested her money, time and energy to teach us. She willingly stayed with us in our small apartment and developed this ministry. She was like a doctor who diagnosed the disease and gave proper treatment. Whenever she visited our church, she immediately discerned the problem in the church. She taught us all the right things – what to do, and how to do it. As our church grew to 20,000, we were able to develop 8,000 leaders.

Her Perseverance

When Apostle Dowdy took up any task, she would commit herself wholeheartedly and wholly to the work until she completed it. She would get up very early in the morning and keep working till past midnight, without taking time to rest.

She would teach in a seminar the whole day, preach an evangelistic meeting in the evening and then spend time praying for the other people. She would be there for meetings, and be punctual for all meetings. She has a vast knowledge about all areas of ministry and knew how to deal with any problem that anyone was facing.

She related with everyone and had a real love for people. She was a very simple lady who loved even the downtrodden. She kissed them, embraced them and prayed for them without any partiality.

She brought my wife out of the kitchen to the pulpit. She said that anybody could do kitchen work, but not everyone was called into ministry! She always encouraged my wife and boosted her morale. My wife was not very outgoing but Apostle Dowdy trained her very well. She enticed her to visit Singapore, made her stay in her own apartment and trained her to be a minister. My wife became encouraged to be a pastor for a few care groups and then became a regional pastor developing care cells. Now she is going all around the world teaching and preaching!

Her Nature

Apostle Dowdy is a generous woman, giving and sharing all she had. She always kept ministry ethics. She always understood the heart of the one she ministered to. She obeys authority and encourages others to do so. She loved and cared for all our children, and attended all their weddings. We are very grateful to her and bless her for all her help.

When Apostle Dowdy came to our church, we had 2,500 believers and after her training on discipleship, we reached twenty thousand believers and now we have reached forty thousand believers.

We thank God for Apostle Dowdy and her ministries.

Rev David Mohan & Family
Senior Pastor, New Life AG Church
General Superintendent, Assemblies of God India
Vice Chairman, World Assemblies of God Fellowship
Chennai, India

My Barnabas, "Pasta Dowdy"

DEBORAH M. GILL

Naomi R. Dowdy has been a Barnabas to me.

What do I mean by that? Barnabas, the buddy of Paul, was a model mentor. His story is found in the Acts of the Apostles, chapters 4, 9, and 11-15, and in the later Pauline Epistles. What was he like? What makes a model mentor?

Barnabas was exemplary in generosity—not only financially, but with his life's energy. He invested himself in others: in the congregation in Antioch; in the young convert, Saul of Tarsus; in the gentile believers; in his nephew, John Mark; and in many others all through his life.

Barnabas's life was equated with encouragement. Though his given name was Joseph, the apostles called him "Barnabas" (Acts 4:26), i.e., "son of encouragement" or "one with the attributes of an encourager." Everywhere he went he was encouraging others.

Barnabas was endued with goodness, the Holy Spirit, and faith. That's what the Bible says about him. What higher description could be desired!

Barnabas was intentional in initiative. He didn't wait for things to happen – he partnered with the Spirit to make them happen. He didn't always have to be told or even asked – he took the initiative. He saw a hurt and healed it; saw a need and met it. Saw potential and nurtured it; saw a minister and mentored him.

Barnabas was courageous in leadership. He was no wimp: in the midst of persecution he still took leadership. Nor was he afraid to lead, even though Paul, his mentoree, was so well qualified. He refused to be intimidated.

In 'being', Barnabas was a person of virtue. In 'doing', he advocated for the underdog, strengthened the souls of the disciples, encouraged their continuance in faith, commended them to the Lord, and invested himself in others – he was a spiritual nurturer.

As I describe this biblical man of God, I think of my own Barnabas, who in so many ways resembles the biblical Barnabas. This present-day woman of God, whom I affectionately call 'Pasta Dowdy', has been a great encourager and mentor to me..

The year was 1979. I had just graduated from the Assemblies of God Theological Seminary (then called the AG Graduate School) in Springfield, MO, with an M.Div. and was finishing a M.A. in Biblical Languages. As a recently licensed minister with the Minnesota District of the AG USA, I was required to preach at least 15 times a year. This is a great idea – but was a great challenge to me for several reasons: I was a full-time seminary student at AGTS; a full-time college teacher at Central Bible College; lived in a city of hundreds of veteran ministers whose preaching would be preferred over a young, recently credentialed minister; and I am female – and some people didn't believe women should preach. How would I ever meet the annual preaching quota as a licensed minister (and eventually the quota of 25 if I ever got ordained). How was I going to get my start? Who would give me a chance? No one seemed to believe in me.

Enter my Barnabas, my mentor in ministry, whom you already know and love, the Reverend Dr. Naomi Dowdy. We had met at Seminary through mutual friends, Helen Stauffer and Barbara Liddle (now Barbara Cavaness Parks) and really hit it off well. One night at 3am, I received a long-distance call from Singapore, after Naomi had returned home to Trinity Christian Centre, the church she had been invited to pastor a few years earlier – a struggling little church that was just starting to take off. That night she called and asked me to come and spend the summer of 1980 working with her at Trinity. She believed in me, she wanted to give me a chance. And, she promised to help me reach the annual preaching quota that summer!

The Lord enabled me to raise sufficient funds in order to accept that invitation which grew into so much more. I absolutely loved Singapore, the Singaporeans, Trinity Christian Centre, and the wonderful people on the team and in the congregation! They were so welcoming to me and so hungry for the Lord! These wonderful folks are 100-fold soil (cf. Matthew 13:23)! Though I had never been there before, Singapore seemed immediately like my home. Learning from the life and ministry of 'Pasta Dowdy' (the local pronunciation of her title) was an unbelievable gift from God. Sitting under her preaching, sensing the Spirit's anointing as she prayed, working side-by-side with a modern-day apostle right out of Acts 29 were unparalleled treasures to me! And Pasta Dowdy kept her promise, not only did I reach preaching quota that summer, but she let me preach over 15 times each month. Twice that summer I made the annual preaching quota within one week!

Pasta Dowdy let me preach, let me pray with folks, let me drive her Speed-the-Light car, let me speak at camp meetings with her, traveling in ministry out-of-the country, let me assist her in counseling, and let me teach at the Bible school. Wow, that was exactly my heart's desire – an opportunity to stretch my wings in ministry. What an incredible gift! But, what's even greater is that Pasta Dowdy coached me after my preaching, counseled me on my calling, prayed for me, and talked with me into the wee hours of the morning. When I was in a discouraging ministry setting the next nine months following that summer, she came to my aid by giving me perspective, encouragement, and friendship through the trials.

Pasta Dowdy was a model, a coach, and a mentor. She believed in me – the greatest encouragement I could ever ask for! After one year of overseas ministry (from summer 1980 to spring 1981), I returned home to the US to pursue the Ph.D. in Biblical Studies at Fuller, but our personal friendship has continued through all of the years since! Especially when I was a pastor – and that of a cell-based church – my mentor has continued to pour into my life and ministry.

I know that my story has been repeated over and over in the lives of many men and women who are serving the Lord with confidence today because of the generous kindness of our precious Pasta Dowdy. I always thank God for her investment in my life; I tell this story to my students; I pray that they will have such quality mentors; and I pray that I will be such a quality mentor to others as well.

A final recollection comes from one ministry trip together. I think it was to Port Dickson, Malaysia, for a Trinity church camp. While I was walking down the street with Pasta Dowdy and Sister Florence Beck, a stranger on the street addressed us as a three-generation family, thinking Pasta Dowdy was my mom, and Sister Beck her mom. Of course it wasn't the case – in the natural – but I wonder if there might have been a spiritual resemblance. As for me, I just beamed remembering Luke 6:14 – a disciple when fully formed is just like her mentor.

Dr Deborah M. Gill
Professor of Biblical Studies and Exposition
Assemblies of God Theological Seminary
Springfield, Missouri

A Hug That Changed My Life
DOMINIC YEO

In June 1980, I accepted Christ at an evangelistic meeting. The next day, my friend brought me to church. I walked in sporting long hair and torn jeans, and still reeking of smoke and alcohol. The Red Sea parted that morning – the crowd of people parted around me as I walked into Trinity Christian Centre. I did not look like a Christian, and I certainly did not smell like one.

An American preacher was preaching in church that day. When she made the altar call, I responded and went forward to be prayed for. No one but the preacher herself came forward to pray for me. Rev Naomi Dowdy put her arms around me, engulfing me with the strong fragrance of her perfume and prayed for me, allowing God's love and grace to flow through her to touch me. The man who had been shunned by others was given a new beginning in God.

That was the beginning of my journey with Pastor Naomi Dowdy. I call her Pastor because she will always be my pastor – a mentor who looked beyond the physical shell and saw who I could become in Christ.

Catching Her Heart for His Kingdom

When I was part of the staff at Trinity serving Pastor Dowdy's vision, I was blessed to be one of those who travelled with her on overseas trips. Traveling with her gave me a close-up view of her humanity and her heart for the things of God. I learnt many invaluable lessons and received an impartation of godly values from her. These principles have helped me form many of my own values for ministry.

Kingdom Mentality

Pastor Dowdy is always prepared to give generously and sacrificially of herself to see the Kingdom of God established.

On a trip to Central Java in 1985, I witnessed how she would remain in the altar area praying until the last person left the worship hall where she had preached in hours ago. By this time, she was soaked in perspiration as the hall was not air-conditioned. Yet despite the discomfort, she had a big heart to see that every individual encountered God.

On another occasion, I saw that she would work beyond our denominational lines. I asked why she was doing so, and her response to me was that rather than be myopic, we should have a large heart for the Kingdom. She said, "This is Kingdom and we need to do Kingdom work with Kingdom mentality."

This Kingdom mentality is pivotal to her ministering effectively across denominational lines, cultures and people groups because she believes that the kingdom of God is never limited, but always has an all-encompassing circle.

Having a Kingdom heart simply means that we should be a blessing to others. Pastor Dowdy has always selflessly given of herself and Trinity's resources to others to help them succeed. Her thoughts are never about what would happen to us as a church, because she believes that God will take care of Trinity while we are busy being a blessing to others. This has set the path for Trinity in investing monies, time and both pastors and leaders into churches beyond our shores to assist them and see them succeed in their ministry.

This Kingdom mentality and heart has become a hallmark of my life and ministry. Trinity is a global church and not a local church because we inherited this value and lesson.

Be a Mentor

This is an area that best describes Pastor Dowdy. She constantly desires to see people around her learn and grow.

Every time I was with her on those many ministry trips, I always saw her engaging with other pastors and leaders. She would always challenge their status quo so that they would step out in faith to try something new.

I too was not left out of this challenge. There was one day she called me into her office and told me that for my ministry to grow, I had to learn to administrate. Now, I never thought much of administration when there were souls to be saved and Christians that needed discipling. Pastor Dowdy issued a strong challenge: If I wasn't going to buck up, I would have to contend with mediocrity in my life and ministry. That was a wake-up call for me and it drove me to learn new skills and scale new heights in the ministry. Had I never learned and grown in administration, I would not be capable of running Trinity today.

When I took on the role of Senior Pastor from Pastor Dowdy, I had huge shoes to fill. I was rather intimidated by her legacy and I remember telling her that her shoes were too big for me. Pastor Dowdy said, "Dom, you are not taking my shoes. You will wear your own pair of shoes. You will be standing on my shoulders as you step into your place as Senior Pastor, and you are going to take Trinity to another level." That was a powerful lesson. She didn't want me to be another Naomi Dowdy, leading Trinity the way she did. She knew God had something more in store for me and for Trinity. She released me to be the person God has meant for me to be.

Never Too Old to Learn

Pastor Dowdy's love for durians and salted vegetable duck qualifies her to be a true blue Singaporean. Besides food, her other passion and hobby is golf. She is an avid golfer, but you'll never guess that she only learned to play golf in the latter part of her life.

It was in the year 2000 that she first picked up golfing. I remember that day vividly. We talked about sports and the times we used to play squash every Sunday night after service. As we reminisced over those times, we turned our attention to golf and she said she was keen to play. The next thing I knew, we were on the way to a golf course in Malaysia.

I remember her saying that she had to take lessons on how to swing the golf club. A group of us challenged her to tee off from the first tee – she did, and that began her journey in golf.

As I reflect on this, I realize something new about my pastor. She is one amazing lady – constantly challenging herself, picking up new skills and even learning a new sport. She is such an intense golfer now, and will not even allow herself the grace and latitude to move her golf ball should it fall into a bad lay or even when it is sitting in between tree roots. Like a true professional, she will hit the ball. She can also be so focused on the game that she can get ahead of her flight.

From Pastor Dowdy, I learned the value of being bold in learning new skills or picking up hobbies, no matter one's age or education level. This is an extremely important value if one is to be the leader of any organization. It's easy to say 'I don't know' and 'I don't need to'; it takes true courage to step forth and learn new things.

Can't Say Enough

You will always be my pastor. Thank you for the hug that transformed me more than thirty years ago. Thank you for sharing your life with me. Your mentorship and love have been pivotal in how God's plans and purposes have unfolded for me. Here's wishing you many more years of giving and serving the Lord.

Rev Dominic Yeo
Senior Pastor, Trinity Christian Centre
General Superintendent, Assemblies of God Singapore
Chairman, Asia Pacific Assemblies of God Fellowship
Executive Council Member, World Assemblies of God Fellowship
Advisory Council Member, Pentecostal World Fellowship
Singapore

Rev Naomi Dowdy – Apostle of Jesus Christ

EDGARDO PEÑA ARENAS

I met Rev Naomi Dowdy at a seminar about church growth in 1996, a number of years ago. The truth is that the training became a good "divine excuse" to meet this woman of God who has touched my life for good at different times.

I remember her teachings on the subject of the seminar, but I remember more the messages in which she revealed her heart and deepest convictions. At some points her preaching brought me even to tears, and this has happened again many times since.

I did not even think that I could have a close relationship with Rev Naomi Dowdy, but I tried to be close to everything she did in Colombia and to be present in every area of her ministry in my land. To my surprise, the passing of the years God has joined our journeys closer to her beyond what I would have imagined.

I have had the great privilege of being part of the team led by Rev Dowdy and traveling with her to many cities in Colombia, working alongside her in the training about "The Five-fold Ministries". On one of those trips, in the beautiful city of Santa Marta, the 'Caribbean of Colombia', I had a brief but intensely personal conversation with her.

Previously I had heard her challenge the leadership of Colombia to rise up with an apostolic attitude. During our conversation, she said it again, but this time something was different. It was more profound and urgent, and her eyes shone with intensity. What made the difference was her sense of responsibility and love for Colombia. There was a deep and intense cry in her spirit for Colombian leaders to take their place of radical commitment to the nation.

Her words also showed a poignant sense of legacy and inheritance. It was then she said something that has remained in my memory over the years: "How much time do you think I have left?" That reverberated inside me with great force to the point that it became unforgettable; I came to understand the strength of her passion for my country and her commitment to fulfill her commission among us.

This incident revealed to me several things that are evident in the character of Rev Naomi Dowdy:

- Her deep love and commitment to the work of God and His people, particularly in Colombia
- The intensity of her sense of legacy and inheritance, her hunger for emerging leadership
- Her respect for God's design for my country and for the leadership that God wants to raise in Colombia
- Her dedication to service to our land over many years, without ever seeking to widen her own ministry.

I admire her ability to accommodate to the different public scenarios that receive her. Her ability to 'read' the time and the place is so amazing; she knows how and what to say from a pulpit. She is not seduced by large gatherings but seeks small spaces, the innermost circles where she can deliver deeper things of the heart to people in need of her experience and anointing. This has asserted in me the importance of strategic intimate circles and small meetings, and reminded me of the value of what God does within the intimacy of a few.

I admire her life and career. I admire her desire to give legitimacy and credibility to the apostolic and prophetic ministry. I admire her tireless dedication to service, her pursuit of excellence, her transparency, her sense of legacy and her ability to release and delegate to emerging leaders.

I have had various encounters with her. Sometimes I have been confronted in a strong and very direct way. Many times I have been treated with love, maternal care and sincere concern for myself and those around me.

Today I join with others in this tribute to Rev Naomi Dowdy for her 50 years of international ministry. My perspective of her life is summarized this way: that she is a genuine Apostle of Jesus Christ.

Edgardo Peña Arenas
The House Christian Church
Bogotá, Colombia

Naomi Dowdy: Daughter of God, Mother in Zion

ESTHER VICTORIA MILIAN

I first met Dr Naomi Dowdy in 1991 in the town of Fusa, Colombia, when I was chosen to be her interpreter for a Haggai Institute training seminar. The organizers of the event had been very careful in selecting her translator. They wanted someone with high standards not just in interpreting the content of what she said, but also the anointing that she carried.

I was greatly impressed to see a lady who carried such authority and the presence of God, and to witness her skills in teaching and impartation. I was surprised to discover that she loved the Colombian people, even though she did not speak Spanish, and did not know exactly what our nation was like.

She came into my life at a very critical time. I was in the midst of a struggle in my life and ministry. I found myself frustrated as a young woman in ministry, wanting to do more for God. She saw in me potential which I did not see in myself.

She arranged for me to come to Singapore for my theological training. This was my first time in Asia, and the experience of living in multicultural Singapore, with a host of students from many different nations, greatly broadened my horizons. Besides studying at Theological Centre for Asia, I was involved in Trinity Christian Centre as a cell and sectional leader. This gave me a strong foundation in the cell model.

After I returned to Colombia, I ministered alongside her as her 'voice'. I found her to be a leader in every sense of this word: In the way she relates to others, the strength and wisdom that she carries, her vision and strategic thinking, and her deep love and compassion. She is a strong leader of great vision, depth and insight.

I have witnessed her helping a minister in the process of restoration. I have seen her give direction and wisdom to organizations and business people. I have watched her confront unflinchingly character issues and other areas that were not right. In each of these scenarios, I saw a different facet of her. Working and serving under her ministry has been a powerful learning experience – different every time, but with the same power and impact.

In all these settings, I glimpsed a heart filled with passion for God and for leaders. Here is a person who is consistent in her character, who has built such a strong foundation in God's Word and presence that she is able to stand in front of any challenge, to confront people and to confront the powers of darkness. She is unique as a true leader of transformation – a woman with the voice, authority, presence and power of the Kingdom of God here on earth. And yet there is this sweet side of her that really cares deeply for others!

All this has been a journey of personal growth and challenge for me. From her I have learnt:

- "Never assume anything" – a statement that has helped me in my leadership skills and growth

- "Train them and trust them!" – one of the statements she repeats and imparts to help the older generation to discover, develop and deploy people for their destiny.

She is driven by a passion for God and for leaders. Traveling from Singapore takes two whole days, including transit time. We are like 'the furthest end of the earth' and yet she has fulfilled God's call and invested so much love – her time, treasures, training and talent – in us over the years. Thank you, Pastor!

I believe Apostle Naomi's legacy will be:

- **Generational Transfer**: She understands clearly the need to raise up the next generation to run for God. She understands that if there is no generational connection, there will never be generational transfer. She has never withheld her wisdom, resources, skills, revelation, and anointing from others. Like Naomi in the Bible, she has served the next generation and, in so doing, has found great fulfillment in her own life. The next generation has now emerged, and we will press into all of God's plans for us.

Apostle Naomi: Like Naomi in the Bible, you have discovered that your destiny was to work with the next generation. Through you God has released an anointing to train, release and nurture the children of tomorrow. I believe each of your spiritual sons and daughters, including myself, will pass the baton to the next generation.

- **Leadership for Transforming Nations**: She has a strong vision for reaching nations and transforming nations. Colombia is one nation where churches and leaders have been transformed because she had a vision for what we could become in God. She believed in us when no one else did.

I would like to share an amusing incident that took place in that little town of Fusa, where it all began. It is a prophetic picture of what she has accomplished in Colombia. During that very first training seminar, I brought her and her companion out, to show them around and to have a drink. When we got to downtown Fusa, there was a very bad traffic jam. A donkey chariot that was carrying fruits had become stuck in the middle of the road. There were many cars and people trying to go down that same road but the donkey was stuck in the middle of the road, and creating a very bad traffic jam. Everyone was shouting but nobody would give way. It was a deadlock situation.

Suddenly a lady opened the car door and with all authority – without speaking a single word of Spanish – stood in the middle of the jam and started directing the traffic. The most interesting thing was that everybody followed her hand signals and respected the authority she exercised – even the donkey! Everyone soon got untangled from the jam and applauded the lady who had stepped up as a traffic marshall to get us out of the deadlock. That lady was Apostle Naomi.

This is a true story which I believe has become a prophetic picture of Apostle Naomi's ministry in the nation of Colombia. As we have journeyed with her through the years, I have seen her exercising authority to lead leaders and churches onto a path of order, credibility, and most of all, character.

Through her training and mentoring over the years, she has brought order, credibility, protocol and process for leadership development and recognition in the nation. Our nation has been able to move into new levels of leadership, establishing and recognizing the apostles and prophets God has raised up in our land to lead the nation into our destiny.

Apostle Naomi, you are truly a Daughter of God, a Mother in Zion. Thank you.

Rev Esther Victoria Milian
Global Leadership Network
Bogota, Colombia

Naomi Dowdy: Living the Abundant Life and Becoming the Proverbs 31 Person

EU YAT WAN

Proverbs 31:10 asks a pertinent question: "Who can find a virtuous woman? For her price is above rubies."

So often when people read the description of Proverbs 31, they feel discouraged as such a description seems out of reach, making it an impossible dream.

However, in the life of Naomi Dowdy, I have found keys that can make this a reality for each of us.

Becoming a Proverbs 31 person starts with A Solid Foundation of Faith.

I first came to know of Pastor Dowdy as she was affectionately called in 1977 when I first attended Trinity Christian Centre (TCC) which was meeting at Equatorial Hotel. I was intrigued by her dynamic preaching and her passion for God. Having church worship services at a hotel was a very unusual move for a local Singapore church at that time. Having to set up and strike set every Sunday was something I became familiar with as I began serving in the worship, logistics and ushering ministries. It was probably the place where I grew some muscles too!

A clarion call to purchase our own church property (after many years of meeting at hotels, cinemas, the World Trade Centre, RELC and PUB auditoriums) was a call to faith! Naomi's trust in God and belief that we will own our church property propelled the church to envision the future together. It became a reality in all the current properties (Adam Road, Lavender Street, Paya Lebar) owned by Trinity Christian Centre today.

Without faith, nothing else really matters. Faith is the firm foundation of Pastor Dowdy's ministry. Like the woman in Proverbs 31, she was faithful in little things and God has blessed her with much.

Becoming a Proverbs 31 person means Living the Abundant Life.

I had the privilege of being part of a TCC Missions trip to Batu Pahat and serving as a TCC Board member in 1979. Pastor Dowdy conducted our marriage ceremony in 1982. All this gave me an insight into Pastor Dowdy's personal life. I saw her enthusiasm and competitiveness in basketball, squash, and swimming. She loved her durians (her eyes still sparkle when you say that magic word!) and her rib eye steak. She would hang around us at Newton Circus and Adam Road food stalls. Such was her zest for life, that she was very much part of our local food scene and locale. There was no distinction of her as a missionary pastor and us locals.

John 10:10 (NKJV) says, "I have come that they might have life, and that they may have it more abundantly." Pastor Dowdy certainly exhibits a zest for life – the abundant life.

Becoming a Proverbs 31 person means Living Life with Purpose.

Mentoring and radical discipleship is what Ps Dowdy lives for. She is intentional about raising future generations of church leadership.

This means crossing denominational boundaries and bringing change to how the church functions and serves the community at large.

Having known her since 1977, this zest for living in Christ has influenced how I mentor and disciple future generations of Spirit-filled believers. She has impacted the lives of thousands by her principled beliefs and her devotion to God. Her passion for missions has stirred many into serving our Lord, and this will be seen and felt for generations to come.

She has lived a life of purpose, and continues to pursue that purpose with passion.

Pastor Dowdy, we honor and love you for the way you have been obedient to God's call to serve. Thank you for being faithful and for empowering generations of believers to pass on your legacy of service and love for God.

Rev Eu Yat Wan
Senior Pastor, New Life City Church
Perth, Western Australia

Our Fond Reflections & Tribute
to Apostle Naomi Dowdy

GARY AND CINDY PANEPINTO

I (Cindy) first met and began to foster a relationship with Apostle Naomi in 2007 after attending an Apostolic Women Arising conference in Atlanta, Georgia. Attending this conference and sitting under the teaching and stirring messages of Apostle Naomi truly catapulted me toward my next level in ministry.

After attending that meeting, I was fully persuaded that God had just arranged a divine encounter and relationship in my life. I received great impartation from this conference and the evidence of a lid coming off of me was obvious to many around me, including my husband. This newfound freedom helped me to impact many in the region where my husband and I were at the time, leading in a regional church.

Apostle Naomi invited me to her Women in Strategic Leadership roundtable meetings. I continue to attend these roundtable meetings till this day, always sensing a great deposit in my life after spending time with this leader of leaders.

I (Gary) was first introduced to this icon of a woman, when Cindy invited Apostle Naomi to our church as the keynote speaker for our annual women's regional conference and to preach at our Sunday

303

services. I immediately recognized the gift God had sent to our church, and more personally, into my life. My hope, somewhat selfish, was to get in on a good thing by also having a relationship with Apostle Naomi.

I first saw Apostle Naomi in action in an advisory role when I was transitioning in my function at a church where I had been serving for over 20 years. Apostle Naomi introduced me to her book, *Moving On and Moving Up, from Succession to Significance*. The book outlines practical principles for legacy management and leadership transition. Apostle Naomi was available to assist in the transition and challenged leaders to think through the process. I have never seen anyone navigate difficult circumstances this way. Apostle Naomi carries and conveys great wisdom! She was able to read my strengths and weaknesses, as well as the rest of our team without exception. She truly is an amazing, insightful woman of God.

Apostle Naomi also stood with us and walked us through a very difficult season in ministry and gave us both a new perspective on moving forward with our destiny in God. She invited us to attend the Cell Church Conference at Trinity Christian Centre Singapore in 2009. Again, this was a life-changing experience. We had a chance to experience firsthand the impact of the carecell model and training. We also had a chance to see this wonderful church body in action. We attended again in 2013 and continue to see the lasting fruit of her years of ministry poured into Trinity.

From the first time we met her, Apostle Naomi has always emanated a Kingdom mindset. She is a great impartial leader, always looking to see both men and women advance with God's purposes and potential.

We admire her character. Although she has ministered and helped countless people through her ministry and continues to touch many lives for the glory of God, she is humble and transparent and not pretentious. She is also a lot of fun, very real and amiable. I (Cindy) so enjoyed the time when Apostle Naomi announced at one of the WSL roundtable meetings, that we were going to have some fellowship after dinner. When we were all gathered together, she brought out the game called Farkle. This is a game of dice, simple but a blast! We gathered at a few tables and began playing. We laughed all night and had a great time. Apostle Naomi was in the middle of it all, making sure we were all enjoying our time and having fun. I still play this game with family and friends to this day.

Since our first interaction with Apostle Naomi, we have always coveted our time with her whether by Skype or in person. No matter how busy she is, she always seems to find the time to pour into our lives.

We celebrate Apostle Naomi, whom we consider a high-level General in God's army, for being the extraordinary woman that she is. We often thank the Lord for the gift that Naomi is to us and for the divine connection that He brought into our lives. We remain grateful to this day for her involvement in our lives. We honor her and count it a privilege to call her friend and mentor.

Gary and Cindy Panepinto
Upward Call Ministry
Charlotte, North Carolina

A Life Well-Lived

GEORGE WOOD

Naomi Dowdy as pastor, evangelist, and apostolic leader has been an example and mentor to a great host of leaders over the past 50+ years. From San Diego to the Marshall Islands to Singapore to the nations she has been very successful in every phase of life.

Naomi began her journey of faith as a young successful career woman working for Convair aircraft in San Diego, California. She came to Christ in First Assembly of God during the ministry of Rev. Emil Balliet, and while there she was filled with the Holy Spirit and called into missions service.

While serving in the Marshall Islands, Naomi worked with Sam and Florence Sasser in founding Calvary Bible Institute in the 1960s. She was one of the early faculty of CBI which was a high school and Bible school as the Marshall Islands had a shortage of high schools. The young people who attended CBI were saved and filled with the Spirit during the early outpouring of the Holy Spirit that occurred in the Marshalls during the 60's. Pastors and leaders were trained in this school which at one time had as many as 325 resident students.

Other missionaries joined Calvary Bible Institute, including Wayne & Judy Cagle, David & Sondra Duncan, Rev. Namo Hermios (a high king of the Northern MI chain and first superintendent of the new work), missionary Jill Clark, Darlene VandeVelde and Rev. Erakrik Samuel (part of the royal family, graduate of Southern California College and present superintendent of the Assemblies of God), along with other Marshallese leaders and missionaries who joined the faculty and workforce in the maintenance and establishment of the developing ministries.

Naomi moved to the island of Ebeye in the Kwajalein atoll of the Marshall Islands, but continued to serve on the Board of Directors of Calvary Bible Institute. From Kwajalein, she undertook boat evangelism to many of the 32 atolls in the Marshall Islands, developing materials and was involved with radio evangelism as well. She trained local co-workers who assisted her in the rigorous boat evangelism ministry. She was an outstanding evangelist and was fluent in speaking Marshallese. Naomi played an important role in the developing national church of the Marshall Islands, instituting the Missionettes and other discipleship ministries. She was a mentor and role model for many of the young pastors and leaders. The Assemblies of God grew to include approximately 25% of the population of this island country.

From the Marshall Islands Naomi went to Singapore in the mid 1970s and pastored Trinity Christian Centre which became a major center for evangelism and the discipling of thousands of Singaporeans – Indians, Chinese and other Asian nationalities during the outpouring of the Holy Spirit in Singapore, as people from many Asian racial groups and churches received the Baptism of the Holy Spirit.

Again, Naomi became a mentor of young men and women who were raised up in ministry. She formed a training school within the church and was a key figure in the discipling and conservation of the tremendous harvest in Singapore. She eventually set her goals on surrounding nations, encouraging younger leaders to pastor the church in Singapore and she evangelized in India, Sri Lanka, Indonesia and many other areas of Asia and beyond.

An indication of her outstanding success has been seen through the exceptional growth of Trinity Christian Centre after the installation of Dominic Yeo as senior pastor. The congregation has more than doubled to over 8,000 attendees under the leadership of this young dynamic leader who is counted among those mentored by Naomi. In addition to leading this great congregation, Dominic is currently serving as General Superintendent of the Singapore Assemblies of God.

Naomi Dowdy has been recognized by many missions leaders, including Peter Wagner and others, for her vision, apostolic anointing and evangelistic efforts. She has lived her life well, filled with faith and the power of the Holy Spirit enabling her to accomplish wonderful feats for the Lord Jesus Christ, her Savior.

Rev Dr George O. Wood
General Superintendent, Assemblies of God USA
Chairman, World Assemblies of God Fellowship
Springfield, Missouri

Serving with Apostle Naomi Dowdy

GERALD TAN

I had the privilege of serving with Pastor Naomi Dowdy, especially through the years of 2003 to 2010. We travelled and ministered together in Colombia and other South American nations, as well as Indonesia. The years of ministry with her have shaped much of my ministry philosophy and imparted to me God's heart for people and the nations.

Three things that I would like to share about Pastor Dowdy are Learn, Love, and Lead.

Learn

Starting on a lighter note, one of the most impressive things about Pastor is that she is willing to learn! I have been called her 'Tech Support' for years, and have seen her learn new technology that many would cringe at the thought of having to adapt to. From the advent of Palm OS to PDAs, from Windows Mobile Phones to iPhones and iPads, from Windows to Mac – she has mastered them all! She has always initiated the use of these devices, and is always keen to discover and master new technology that will keep her connected and effective in ministry.

This learning journey for her has sometimes been amusing to watch but has shown me that there are no limitations to learning. No one is 'too advanced' to learn the basics again. Most importantly, when it comes to serving God, our choice to be on the cutting edge is clearly reflected in our posture and attitude towards embracing change and learning new ways of doing things.

Love

Pastor Dowdy has a heart of love. Out of the depths of her love for God flows a reservoir of love for the leaders that God brings to her. Time and time again, I have seen how people are drawn to her because of her anointing and ministry – and how they are especially blessed when she ministers to them in love!

She has a wealth of wisdom from years of ministry, an anointing that releases God's power, and yet she has a heart that will compel her to fly thousands of miles to minister to someone who is broken and in need of spiritual advice. Every time after she ministers in meetings, she looks forward to moments when she can spend with the pastors to encourage them, pray for them, challenge them and build them up. That is truly God's love flowing through her.

She often says that she does not like to be called 'Mommy', because she is not one who will be soft and gentle. But she truly espouses the love of God: tough yet tender love that builds lives and causes people to grow. Hers is a love that nudges the eaglet out of its nest to soar, a love that tends to the wound but will stop you from licking it, and will in fact push you to face the very same circumstances again so that you can be an overcomer.

As a young minister traveling with her, I thought I would simply be carrying her bags and Bible, and learn from the sidelines, watching her and praying for the ministry. I quickly realized that it was not going to be so easy. On many occasions, I would be thrown into a 'spot' to step out and minister. Yet those were some of the best learning opportunities.

Another personal experience of her love and care was the time when I was hit with food poisoning while we were in Colombia. After several days of purging, I was totally dehydrated and at the end of the trip, my body finally gave in. I was running a high fever and becoming delirious. When we got back to the hotel, she prayed for me and waited for the doctor to come. She made sure I took all the medicine and drank all the hydrating salts so that I would be able to fly home to Singapore the next day.

Lead

Leading is the very essence of apostleship, and Pastor Dowdy is truly a leader. I have witnessed her leading people, ministries, organizations and denominations to weather the roughest moments and to navigate through the toughest transitions. Her leadership qualities cause her to be one of the first names that come to mind whenever pastors need someone to help them in their times of need or transition.

A beautiful aspect of leadership that I have learnt from her is that true leaders release others. It is always a multiplication of yourself to release others, not as a clone of yourself, but into their calling and destiny in the Lord. I have seen so many leaders who have truly stepped into higher heights because of her ministry and faith in them. I have seen many leaders restored and healed because she chose to see in them who they could truly be.

I honor Pastor Dowdy because she has truly allowed herself to be a 'push-off' block for many to soar into their ministries and anointing,

311

as she comes alongside them and helps them. I believe there are countless leaders today who would attribute a certain measure of their success to the ministry of Pastor Dowdy into their lives.

Treasured Moments

Over those years of ministering with her though, the times I have treasured most are the times when we were able to sit down to have a meal together, and to hear her reflect and share on her personal life stories. Most of the time, we would be busy preparing for the meetings and looking through the programs, notes and ministry arrangements. However, every now and then, she would begin to share about her life. The little stories of her growing up in the United States – coming to the Lord, working in an IT firm, taking part in car rallies – are truly inspiring.

One of the things she shared was that she was faithful in her giving because she wanted to show that she could 'out-give God.' It was not till many years later that she discovered how her faithfulness could not be outdone by God's mighty provisions in her life.

She told many amazing stories of being called to missions and serving in the Marshall Islands; of how she would travel to meet the locals and preach to them; of her love for coconuts, even using coconut juice for communion! Stories of how she would pray and see the Lord miraculously provide everything needed to build a church, from sand to wood. Stories of the crazy 'goonie' bird in the islands that flew so graciously in the sky but would crash land every time, tumbling over and rolling in the sand. She shared about her journey of being called to Singapore and pastoring Trinity, and from there, building the church for a good thirty years. To hear all this has truly been a blessing.

Her ministry perspectives, her passion and burdens truly make her the exceptional person we all know as Pastor Dowdy. In the midst of her busy schedule, she is never too busy to give a call and ask how I am, how my family is, and how the ministry is coming along. She is not waiting to shoot some advice or truth, but she truly just wants to listen. She is never too busy for some durians or to share a meal to catch up.

Thank you, Pastor. I truly appreciate you.

Rev Gerald Tan
Senior Pastor, Calvary Assembly of God
Singapore

A General in God's Kingdom

INDRI GAUTAMA

Apostle Naomi is a woman of God with inner strength and stability. That was my first impression when I first invited her to Indonesia. She walked into the conference hall with confidence, and she spoke with such authority which I had not yet seen in the male leaders of my country.

The terminologies she used in her opening speech that evening which really struck my heart and mind were Purpose, Strategy and Vision. That night I invited her and her assistant to explain to me a very specific thing that my heart was searching for ever since I got saved: What is a local church? She spent two hours in the coffee shop with me. I was so hungry for the revelation, I decided that night that she was not going to preach on women in ministry during the conference. Instead, I asked her to preach on "What is the local church, this rock, that the Lord Jesus builds upon, against which the gates of hell shall not prevail?"

I went to her 'Seven Steps To Transforming Your Church' seminar in Singapore. I was not a local church pastor then, but I was so hungry to be what Jesus called me to be. I went back to my country and immediately started the basic foundation of a local church philosophy: the apostolic community of GOD called c.a.r.e.cell.

We experienced the Acts 2 community after the Pentecost in our small dingy old office of my late father. There were seven of us led by me as I served them to be filled by the Pentecost power. This small group soon grew to 300, and we were forced by the local authorities to report to the Department of Religion to declare that we were a new church. Having been continuously trained by Trinity pastors in my new young local church, the name Apostolic Generation Church was born.

I have been so privileged to have been honored by Apostle Naomi as one of her mentees. She does not know that her life so inspires me greatly that I dare put my life and my everything to see the young believers dream big and to carry the Great Commission mandate across my city, my country and internationally.

I love Apostle Naomi dearly. She is our big asset in our local church life. We call her a General in God's Kingdom and an Ambassador of Christ. A woman of strength and a mentor for men and women in leadership. She demonstrated her significance in her boldness to pass on the baton to her successor successfully. Local churches across the world need her as God's strategist to realign them back to God's original intent. The local church is God's *ekklesia* – the sent ones to introduce, infiltrate and infect the world with God's kingdom culture as agents of change.

We find such completeness in her teaching. We are not leaders because of title but because we influence others to imitate Christ through the transformation in our lives that we model.

315

She is a matriarch, but not a mom. She does not coddle us. She doesn't raise wimps but leaders with a backbone of steel in the local church. She is faithful in God's calling for her life. We love her dearly. I will still need her for a long time to come!

Apostle Indri Gautama
Senior Pastor, Apostolic Generation Church
Jakarta, Indonesia

Naomi Dowdy: An Amazing Woman of God
JANET MANGUM

I met Apostle Dowdy in 2000 as a bystander. I was in a significant decision-making time in ministry. My friend and mentor, Lana Heightley, had a meeting with her in Singapore on our way to India. Apostle Dowdy graciously welcomed us into her office and conference room. I was pleasantly surprised at her very gracious and humble acceptance, and her willingness to give us her time. I was struck with the thought, "Where are the books that share this woman's massive experience and wisdom?"

She answered Lana's questions and then turned to me. She wanted to know who I was and what my focus in ministry was. I had just been asked to consider an associate pastor position by my senior pastor. At the same time, I was thoroughly enjoying my most recent ministry in evangelism and discipleship around the world. Her advice was simple. It came in three sentences, giving me a plumb line for discerning God's will and effective ministry. It not only changed my perspective then, but it has continued to be a guide for decision-making.

Her Leadership
One day, a few years later, I received a letter inviting me to a

317

gathering she was leading for women in the U.S. I was shocked. I couldn't believe that such a successful minister would include me! Of course I said yes. At the first Women in Strategic Leadership (WSL) gathering, as she began her topic on leadership in pastoral ministry, my heart began to beat faster. I knew I was hearing from the Lord and gleaning wisdom from years of experience. It was as if she had been in our church board meetings and had been listening in on all my pastoral conversations.

She began to unfold the scenarios to expect when decisions were being made. At one point I must have had an odd look on my face. She asked, "Are you okay, Janet?" My answer: "Yes, I feel like my hair is on fire!" It was the fire of the LORD. The power and presence of God was so evident in her sharing, it was astounding. The accuracy of her leadership wisdom was dramatic for me in that moment.

When I returned home, I told the board what she had said. Before the week was out, we saw the evidence of her practical experience. The situation unfolded exactly as she said it would, leaving the church confused and in pain. With gentle friendship and willing service, she volunteered to come and speak with the leaders of the board and offered ministry aid to everyone, to bring the situation to a positive closure. I was then asked to take the interim senior pastor position. Again she offered herself and her church to help bring healing and speak truth into the difficult situations that lay ahead.

She gave me practical simple advice on how to sit, how to speak, when to speak, and wisdom on various leadership variables a pastor would encounter. She never told me exactly what to do when it came to important decisions, but instead gave the practical considerations and scenarios that I would encounter, so I could make a quality informed choice.

Throughout the years her willingness to be a voice of reason and Spirit has aided me in strategic decision-making, both in my personal life and in ministry, and I am deeply grateful for her.

Her Wisdom

On one occasion, I debated about attending the Women in Strategic Leadership gathering. It would be held over one evening and the following day – so short. Was it worth the cost and time needed to travel there? Yet, when my friend and I exited the meeting, we were trying to assess what it was we were sensing. Then my friend said, "That was just wild in the Spirit. I actually feel taller!" I laughed and we marveled how something significant had transpired in the short time we spent with Apostle Dowdy.

One of the areas I respect, among many, is her ability to perceive where people are in character, ministry and anointing. I have seen it multiple times when she prophesied to someone, or gave them a word of wisdom without knowing them, or barely knowing them. She seemed to be able to pinpoint their weaknesses as well as their strengths, all with the Holy Spirit's input, and to say it to the person in an instructive and gracious manner. Working with others, I have now followed her model of gathering my leaders and joining with other ministries, for iron sharpens iron.

The Way She Relates

"Hey gal!" Her greeting always brings warmth to the heart and a sense of peaceful welcome. I have never once felt unwelcome in her presence. Her grin, slightly deep voice, and bright eyes make you want to step closer and give her a big hug! I cannot resist, sometimes even giving her a big kiss on the cheek!

Certainly this lady is no ministry snob. When the invitations for the WSL gatherings went out, it appeared that the selection wasn't all about numbers or power ministry, but heart passion, calling, and God's timing. Sometimes the person invited was deep in ministry to massive numbers around the world, or in power ministry to a select few. Other times the person would be in a transition season, with no apparent ministry at the time. The diversity of the women she invited, the diversity of the seasons of their life, and the diversity of age, shape and size was a continual delight to behold. She is a God-ordained, life-giving, gracious and Jesus-focused expression of His goodness to each of us. And the best part is, she is our friend too.

When I struggled to write my first book, I knew I needed some help from a therapist who had worked with children before. Naomi recommended someone to me. When I asked the therapist, she replied, "Absolutely, because Naomi asked me. I would do anything for her."

Who doesn't love and appreciate this amazing woman of God? I haven't met anyone who doesn't. Even if there might be someone out there who doesn't agree with her opinion, I'm convinced they would respect and love her anyway.

She perseveres in relationship to such a degree that she would allow her own life to be harmed just to keep covenant with someone she is committed to. That's not what you normally expect, especially from someone who is always giving to you while getting little or nothing in return. Her goal: To see you succeed! Truly unselfish to the core.

Happy Birthday!

Janet Mangum
CEO, Partners for Transformation
Director, Aglow Transformation
Apostle Naomi Dowdy's Friend

Tribute to Apostle Naomi Dowdy

JOHN KELLY

I love Naomi Dowdy! She is a great friend, a strong woman of God and an apostolic matriarch who loves people and the Church. Naomi has forged paths few would ever attempt. She is an excellent example of a practical teacher/preacher/apostle. She provides a place for people to grow in their gifts and talents, and she develops leaders around the world! She is a woman of courage, great anointing and skill whom God has blessed with lasting fruit.

Naomi Dowdy made a believer out of me! Many people thought we would not get along because of my views on women in ministry. Many years ago, I led an apostolic network that believed women could be in ministry but not in government, not leading a ministry or church. However, as I traveled the world, I was seeing something different that I could not deny. Many women were successfully leading churches and ministries and I had to agree it was God's plan because of the obvious fruit of their efforts. I took my experience and God's word back to my network, but few were open to change.

Then along came Naomi, an American whom God had planted in Singapore – it was love at first sight! It was a God moment, a divine connection that would lead to great admiration and appreciation. I love to hear her views, even though sometimes it is like iron sharpening iron – we have a great time doing it! She is smart, witty and gracious, a rare combination.

I honor Naomi Dowdy yesterday, today and forever. Her work for the King and His Kingdom will be honored for eternity.

Thank you Naomi for being my friend, inspiration and hope for the future of the apostolic movement and the Church.

Building together with Him and you my friend,

John P. Kelly
International Apostolic Convenor,
International Coalition of Apostolic Leaders
President, John P. Kelly Ministries, Inc.
Fort Worth, Texas

Tribute to Naomi Dowdy

JOSEPH MATTERA

Dr Naomi Dowdy is one of the most brilliant, practical apostolic leaders in the global church today. Her ministry has made a huge imprint not only in Singapore but in the nations of the world!

She understands the biblical principles regarding discipleship, spiritual parenting, the nurturing of indigenous leadership, small group ministry, city church networking and the kind of revival that leads to societal transformation.

The local church she founded is a model for the whole Body of Christ, but perhaps her greatest legacy will be that she is a person who has fully surrendered herself to the Lord for the sake of His Kingdom.

I join everybody else in celebrating her life.

Dr Joseph Mattera
Convener, US Coalition of Apostolic Leaders
Brooklyn, New York

The One Thing I Remember

LANA HEIGHTLEY

Where would one start? Dr. Naomi is like a finely cut diamond that has many facets, all of which are brilliant and beautiful. She is certainly a multi-faceted woman who makes it almost impossible to narrow down a primary talent or gift.

Possibly I could write about her passionate, articulate preaching; her great presence in a room; her many accomplishments as an apostle, teacher or pastor; or perhaps even her influence on the nations. All of which are clearly commendable. All of the above is certainly true, but I found her most remarkable trait is her humility.

When I think of Apostles, I think of one who has incredible authority, one who has suffered much and one who has humility. I have discovered her to carry immense humility.

I met her in 2000 while traveling around the world (with Janet Mangum) as we went from nation to nation, conducting women/pastors training conferences. As part of our travel plans we needed a room in Singapore for several days. Ever mindful of our 'missions' budget, I wanted a room which was safe, clean, and most of all, reasonably priced! A mutual friend told me about her and suggested that I call to have her get us a room. I did as advised.

When we arrived in Singapore, we went to visit Dr. Naomi at her church. To my great embarrassment, I was stunned to see the large, beautiful church where she was the senior pastor. Did I really ask her to get us a room? Indeed I had! When we entered her office, she was extremely welcoming and kind. We shared about our trip, and she told us a little about herself.

After we visited for some time, I asked her if she would consider letting me include her in a book I was writing. She reluctantly said "yes." I then asked for her biography, thinking perhaps someone had written a book about her, or perhaps she had written an autobiography. I was shocked when she replied, "Why would anyone want to write a book about me? I don't have one, but we do have information about the church." She also informed me that she had never written an autobiography. She did hand me the church promotional material.

That was just the beginning of our many years together, and I soon discovered this was her pattern and attitude. She never brags on herself, she is never filled with pride and her character is one of complete humility. To me, this is the most commendable thing I can think of. We live in a world of extreme pride and exaltation. I have learned immeasurable things from Dr. Naomi, but none that encourages me more than her immense humility. She has the attitude of leaning into Jesus, but His glory is forever displayed when she shows up!

Dr Lana Heightley
Founder, Women With A Mission
Colorado Springs, Colorado

Life & Times with Naomi Dowdy

LAURIE VERVAECKE

I remember the very first time I met Pastor Naomi Dowdy. My husband Joe and I had moved to Singapore in April 1990. In August that year, we were invited to attend Trinity Christian Centre's dedication service of their Phase I building completion at Adam Road.

We visited Trinity that Sunday in August with some AG missionaries from India. We spoke briefly with Pastor Dowdy after the service, and I remember being impressed that this American woman was pastoring a growing vibrant church in Singapore.

The second time I met her was in passing, at a Women's Conference hosted by Church of Our Saviour in 1993.

I would never have guessed that within two years after our second meeting, I would have the opportunity to begin serving and assisting this awesome woman of God.

Let me take a few moments and share how God connected Pastor Dowdy and I. In early June 1995, I was scheduled to minister in a church in Vancouver, Canada and then to stay over a few days for some rest and relaxation. Three weeks before I was to be in Vancouver, I received a phone call from the pastor. He wanted to let me know that the day after I finished ministering, Pastor Naomi Dowdy would begin a three-day Cell Conference. This caused me to go "hmmmm".

What no one knew then was that my husband and I had begun to pray about making a move from the church we had been working with for the past five years. Knowing that our season at our current church was coming to an end, we made a list of churches we wanted to visit – and Trinity Christian Centre was right at the top of that list.

I knew it was no coincidence that Pastor Dowdy would be at the same church in Vancouver. I told the pastor in Canada that I would like to attend the Cell Conference and hear what Pastor Dowdy taught about small groups.

Before Pastor Dowdy arrived in Vancouver, I was sitting in the church office answering my emails. A staff member came into the room where I was working and asked me if I knew where Pastor Dowdy's seminar workbooks were. I told him I did not have any idea where her workbooks were. A few moments later, this same staff member returned and asked if I had Pastor Dowdy's PowerPoint slides that she would be using during the training. Again I replied that I did not have her PowerPoints, nor did I know where they were.

A few minutes later, it dawned on me: This guy thinks I am with Pastor Dowdy! I am from Singapore and she is from Singapore, so he assumed I had come to Vancouver before Pastor Dowdy arrived – to prepare the way. I went out into the hallway and asked this young man if he thought I was with Pastor Dowdy. He said, "Yes, because you are both from Singapore!" I told him it was just a coincidence that we both happened to be from Singapore. We both had a good laugh about it.

As I listened to Pastor Dowdy teach the Local Church Breakthrough Seminar, I could not take notes fast enough. By this time, I had been in ministry for almost 18 years and had worked in a number of churches. I knew what I was hearing in her seminar was the answer many pastors were looking for. To hear that all but one of her pastors at that time were homegrown was amazing to me. Here was a process that could take a pre-believer and nurture them into a growing reproducing disciple in nine to twelve months. The Carecells laid a foundation for the spiritual growth of every believer.

After the seminar, Pastor Dowdy and I went for dinner at the pastor's home. While the pastor and his wife were preparing coffee and dessert, Pastor Dowdy and I had a chance to talk. I was really surprised to find her traveling by herself, so I asked her, "Do you always travel alone?"

Pastor Dowdy replied, "Not always. I do try to bring a pastor with me as part of mentoring and equipping. For this particular trip, schedules did not work to bring someone with me."

Little did I know, our meeting in Vancouver and this one question I asked Pastor Dowdy would be the beginning of an amazing ministry relationship and lifetime friendship.

By September 1995, Joe and I began attending Trinity Christian Centre. I prayed and asked the Lord, "What is it that You want me to do in Trinity?" I heard the Lord say, "I want you to serve Naomi Dowdy."

As Pastor Dowdy and I talked in those early days of attending Trinity, I shared with her what I sensed the Lord had spoken to me, about serving her. I shared that I was willing to do whatever she needed done, that would help her do what God was asking her to do – whether that meant taking her mom Mama Wilson to get her hair done, or running errands, doing research for sermons or creating powerpoint slides. Through the days, weeks, months and years since, I have done all of these and much more.

At one point, I mentioned to Pastor Dowdy, that if traveling with her would help her, I could also travel and help in any way needed. I will never forget our first trip together. We would be going to India for one month. While Pastor Dowdy had traveled many times to India, this would be my first trip there. I knew this trip would be a test. If we could survive one month in India together, then we could probably handle traveling together in the future.

While in India, she would be teaching the Local Church Breakthrough Seminar in three different cities, teach at Southern Asia Bible College and minister in local churches on the weekends. The test came the very first week we were in India. Pastor Dowdy had just begun the first seminar when she became very ill. She had picked up a parasite. Pastor Dowdy learned quickly that I knew how to pray and to be instant in season. I could not teach any of the seminar. She would teach, and I would pray. She told me, "If I give you this look, you need to jump up and do an ice breaker; put the participants into small groups, do something!" This meant that she had to make a dash for the toilet.

At the end of the seminar, one of the pastors asked me, "How long have you been assisting Pastor Dowdy? The two of you really work well together." I smiled and thanked him. I did not tell him this was our first trip together. Thank God for the anointing!

Since 1995, we have traveled to 30 nations and have flown over 1 million miles together. We have ministered in small groups, Bible schools and churches of various sizes, to tens of thousands on the beach in India.

As we traveled the world and interacted with pastors, ministers and leaders around the world, there were times when some women pastors and leaders would ask Pastor Dowdy if she would mentor them. I remember one time as Pastor Dowdy and I were talking, she asked, "What is it that I have to give to all these ladies who ask me to mentor them?"

I could have swallowed my tongue when she made this statement. By this time she had not only been a missionary for ten years in the Marshall Islands, she had been the Senior Pastor of Trinity Christian Centre for twenty years, plus all the various ministries she had started and directed. And she wanted to know what it was she had, that she could pass on to other women!

As a result of Pastor Dowdy being obedient to God's 'rebuke' about ministering to women, the Women in Strategic Leadership (WSL) mentoring roundtable was born. Naomi now mentors women around the world. Each woman that has been touched through this relationship has grown, and their ministries have gone to new levels, with each one moving toward fulfilling their destinies set before them.

After living in Singapore for twelve years and serving Pastor Dowdy for more than six of those years, Joe and I returned to the United States in April 2002. I discovered that when God connects you with people, distance does not make a difference. I continue to travel with Naomi when she comes to the US and South America for 7 Steps training, church consultations and ministry, apostolic roundtables, WSL gatherings and last but not least, to play golf every chance we get.

As a result of the many hours we have spent together, my life and ministry have moved to new levels. My spheres of influence are continuing to expand. Besides working with churches involved with the Trinity cell model, I am working to protect children on multiple fronts from child abuse. I equip churches to implement child protection policies to prevent child abuse. I am a Project Rescue ambassador and am becoming certified to train caregivers of human trafficking survivors.

As part of the Utah Chapter of Childhelp, the oldest US non-profit that deals specifically with child abuse prevention, I am working with others to implement a child abuse prevention curriculum in elementary schools statewide.

As a result of my growing expertise on the topic of child abuse, I now have a voice in the Government mountain. I am part of the CWIC-Child Welfare Improvement Council for the state of Utah, a multi-agency council which examines state policies, procedures and practices on child protection. I am moving into my destiny!

Being in relationship with Naomi Dowdy, I have learned many lessons and have grown in a myriad of ways.

One area that has impacted my life greatly is learning the power of words. As I journeyed through all my Psychology courses, I became attentive to words and phrasing – the art of asking the right questions, and phrasing statements systematically to guide a person to discovery and solutions.

I became even more conscious of the power of words and terminology when Trinity began broadcasting from a radio station in Batam, Indonesia. The broadcasts could be heard in Singapore and Southern Malaysia. Pastor Dowdy had this desire in her heart for years and she knew that one day, she would be on the radio in Singapore.

For the first year of broadcasting, Pastor Dowdy recorded all the radio programs, five days a week, for fifty-two weeks. I was very involved with the preparation of messages and the recording sessions. Pastor Dowdy was committed to lay the right foundation for the breakthrough of the Gospel being declared over the airwaves. I watched and listened as she would finalize a message for a broadcast. She would scrutinize her words and phrasing, so the Gospel message would be received by all who heard each broadcast.

I discovered that words are more than a means of communication; they can shape our beliefs, behaviors, feelings and ultimately our actions. When it comes to language and communication, the rule is "It's not what you say, but what people hear." Words are one of the most powerful tools that we possess; they can ignite revolutions, defuse tension and transform lives.

Having a part in producing some 270 broadcasts helped me discover that Rev Dr Naomi Dowdy is a great orator. Oratory is the art of speaking eloquently, fluently, forcible with appropriate expression. Oratory relates to the moving of one's passions. Oratory is designed to persuade, to provoke action and reaction.

The effect of successful oratory is literally to change the minds of the listener, to change the neural pattern of the hearers. The words used by an orator create images in the minds of the hearers and implant patterns of action. They can do this because words are not empty symbols.

We read throughout the New Testament the many stories that Jesus told the disciples and to all who would hear the words that He spoke. To those who had ears to hear, their lives were forever changed.

Now, as I teach and minister, I find myself very conscious of the words I speak and the phrasing that I use. There are times when I will start a sentence over or restate a phrase, just so I say the right words at the right time, to bring the desired result.

Throughout the years, I have witnessed thousands of lives healed, restored and transformed by the right words both written and spoken, at the right time, through my mentor and friend Naomi Dowdy.

Naomi, thank you for being obedient to the Spirit of God and being willing to go where He directs, to do what He asks you to do, and to speak what He asks you to say. I pray that I too will be a carrier of the Light that displaces darkness, sets the captives free, and brings hope to those who have lost their way. That I might speak words of Life and introduce them to Jesus Christ, the Word which became flesh.

I will continue to follow you, as you follow Christ!

Rev Dr Laurie Vervaecke
Vice-President, Global Leadership Network USA
Vice-President, ChildHelp (Wasatch Front Chapter)
Salt Lake City, Utah

Naomi Dowdy: A Present-day Hero of Faith

LES BOWLING

It is hard to describe, in just a few lines, the life of Apostle Naomi Dowdy and what she means to me, my wife Sheila and so many others. She has made an impact on all of our lives!

During our journey through life, God gives us special gifts of grace. I am so thankful that I have had the honor of meeting Apostle Naomi over twenty years ago. She is one of those carriers of grace whom God sent into my life at just the right time. Her wisdom has instructed me, her love and compassion have encouraged me, and her strength has helped me to keep going.

I love to read about church history and about the different key figures in church history who lived extraordinary, sold-out lives. I have often wondered where those history makers in my generation were – until I met Apostle Naomi. Not long after our introduction, it was evident that she was one of our present-day heroes of faith.

Apostle Naomi has modeled a life of exemplary Christian devotion. She possesses a unique blend of spiritual authority, maturity and next-level perspective with a spiritual passion and zeal. Not only has she focused on mentoring top-level leaders in the Body of Christ, but she has also encouraged the leaders and congregants of the local church.

Apostle Naomi has become an esteemed mentor whom I appreciate and honor very much. Because she has loved me enough to correct my mistakes – though it may have stung on occasion – it has propelled me higher. She has also become a very special friend of our family. She truly cares for us and never fails to inquire about how the family is doing. During the times she visited us, she would always take the time to visit with my aging mother, which always brought much joy to her.

Apostle Naomi's stamina has always been a great inspiration to me. I realize that it is made possible only by God's supernatural touch as well as a life of discipline.

I don't fully know the price she has paid, and what it has cost her to be her, but I do know the price has been high. Thank you Apostle Dowdy for being willing to pay the price, for your lifetime of dedication and sacrifice, and not being afraid of passing the baton to many sons and daughters of the faith.

If, for the rest of my life, I follow the apostolic ministry that you have modeled, and take the baton that you are passing and keep on running, I will be able to run with confidence and say, "*I have run well.*"

With love and grace,

Rev Les Bowling
Founder, Eagle Rock Ministries
Overseer, Eagle Rock Covenant Network
Originating President, Gospel and the Preacher Bible College
Columbus, Ohio

Reflections on Naomi Dowdy

MARGARET COURT

I want to encourage Naomi Dowdy because around twenty years ago when God called me to start a church, I didn't know of any senior women who led a church. Someone told me of a lady in Singapore who had a church of 5,000 people. Well, that was good enough for me! This encouraged me to pastor Victory Life Church.

I got to know Naomi ten years ago when she brought the apostolic teaching to Victory Life Church at a conference with Pastor Ong Sek Leang and a group of ministers. This was wonderful for me because I already had been operating in the apostolic in a small capacity, and didn't know it.

Naomi encouraged me as a woman in a 'man's' world, that what I was doing was a gift and call of God on my life as an Apostle.

Naomi is a very bold, courageous and focused lady and a wonderful ambassador for the Body of Christ. I am honoured to know her as a friend.

Congratulations Naomi on 50 years of International Ministry and enjoy your birthday celebrations with family and friends.

The best is yet to come!

Rev Dr Margaret Court
Senior Pastor, Victory Life Centre
Perth, Western Australia

Naomi Dowdy: An Extraordinary Role Model of Love, Honor & Excellence

ONG SEK LEANG

The name Rev Naomi Dowdy was well-known among the churches when l first started ministry in Malaysia more than 30 years ago. I heard how God was using her in many churches and nations through her conferences at Trinity Christian Centre, Singapore.

I was introduced to her when Rev Dominic Yeo invited me to speak at their Youth Camp. My first impression of her was that of an approachable pastor who believed God could use anyone who was willing and available. Over time, through the invitation of Pastor Dominic, I got to know her better and became well acquainted with her, the leaders and congregation at Trinity.

My ministry was greatly impacted after l attended my first conference with her, when she expounded from Scriptures and demonstrated through practical examples that anyone can change. "I must change; I can change; I will change!" was her rallying cry.

She herself has exemplified this willingness to change and to make the changes needed to fulfill the call of God upon her life. Although she began her ministry from a Christian denominational tradition, she shifted and embraced the apostolic call of God. She has great boldness and a deep determination to complete the assignment that God has given to her.

Over the years, I have had the privilege to observe Pastor Dowdy at close range. Time and again, I have seen how she takes a personal interest in a younger minister and invests her time in mentoring them, broadening their horizons, and connecting them to resources, relationships and possibilities they never thought existed. Apostle Naomi Dowdy has opened doors, created opportunities and affirmed my prophetic ministry as I ministered with her in different parts of the world.

Her apostolic ministry is not only marked by exploits for God but also by a genuine concern for those who are connected to her. God has used her pastoral heart, wisdom and background to help bridge the other offices of the fivefold ministries to that of the apostle and the apostolic call. She has taken great interest in my personal and family life, leadership and ministry. I often receive calls from her from different parts of the world, just to speak with me and to pray for me on the phone.

In recent years, I witnessed how she took deliberate steps to plan her succession to hand the church over to Rev Dominic Yeo. Although she has an international apostolic stature and influence, her love for the local church and submission to the leadership of the Senior Pastor truly raised the bar and exemplified for me what it means to be a servant and a part of a local church.

Apostle Dowdy, I am truly privileged to have known you and been mentored by you. Thank you for raising the bar and for being an extraordinary role model of love, honor and excellence. I salute you for embracing fully the high calling of God on your life through every season, and for paying the price to be you. We have been blessed indeed.

Rev Ong Sek Leang
Senior Pastor, Metro Tabernacle
General Superintendent, Assemblies of God
Kuala Lumpur, Malaysia

Naomi Dowdy, the Gentle General

PAMELA ANDERSON

I consider my relationship with Naomi Dowdy to be one of the great gifts that God has given me. I have told her again and again how I treasure her and thank the Lord for bringing her into my life.

I had heard of Dr Naomi Dowdy and her church in Singapore for several years before meeting her. Then in February of 2000, I was part of a ministry team led by Chuck Pierce on an around the world tour. Our final stop was Singapore and I was thrilled with excitement to finally meet Dr Dowdy whom I had heard so much about, and to see Trinity Christian Centre.

I will never forget the first time I heard her voice – so distinct, so confident, and so full of God. Pastor Beatrice Kang was there and I will always remember her laughter and the way she interacted with Pastor Dowdy. I found that interesting and not quite like the usual pastoral staff that I had encountered.

What I remember the most about that visit was that they were in the original building and had just purchased the property for the new church. We went over to see it and prayed over it, and then our team gave an offering for the building. It wasn't huge. We were just giving out of our traveling cash to a pastor who had an amazing vision for her church.

Through the next few years, I had occasion to hear Dr. Dowdy speak at the annual International Coalition of Apostles gathering and other such events. Always impressed, I respected her highly and held the memory of being with her and her church as a special highlight of my life. I never dreamed that God would divinely connect me to this general of God.

My ministry grew and passion for leaders and for other nations grew stronger in me. I traveled regularly and worked with another minister to build an apostolic network. I enjoyed speaking and ministering prophetically to individuals, pastors, leaders and nations. Building a network of ministers became a passion and brought such fulfillment.

On a personal level, our lives began to change. My husband had been a very successful businessman and the top salesman in Texas for his company for years. This allowed me the freedom to travel and minister without the burden of needing to supplement our income. But things began to change in his industry. Globalization impacted his industry, with parts and products being produced in other parts of the world. His company was sold to someone else. As his salary was totally commissions-based, he began to see his income decline for the first time in 20 years.

We moved to another house which we bought as we were fully assured that our home would sell quickly. So we bought a new house while still owning our old home, and soon found ourselves saddled with two mortgages, two property tax bills, and double the utilities and insurance bills. For some unknown reason, our lovely home on the golf course sat empty for two very long years as we struggled to own and pay for two prime properties on a declining income.

During the summer of 2004, the first Apostolic Women Arising Conference was held in Ann Arbor, Michigan at Shekinah Christian Church. It was a new thrust designed to release women into places of leadership and authority and to remove the glass ceiling many had lived under. Dr. Dowdy led the conference and the vision, with other women leaders among the speakers. A lovely Indonesian pastor with a six-month-old thriving church was there. It was there that I became friends with Pastor Indri Guatama. Little did I know how strategic that conference would prove to be in my life.

The atmosphere was charged with expectancy and enthusiasm. Dr. Dowdy preached with a powerful anointing. Prophecies were released. Women were set free. Something new and fresh was on the horizon. At a lunch meeting with Dr. Dowdy and some of the other speakers, I shared with her a strategic plan for branding "Apostolic Women Arising" and for multiplying it into groups around the world. As I handed her my written plan with a brief explanation, she amazed me by stopping what she was doing at that moment to read my plan and to talk with me about it.

I was shocked at the personal attention she gave me and that she took what I had to say seriously. This was a new experience for me, to see a leader who lived in the moment and took time to listen to someone whom she did not know very well. She really listened. She really processed it. She gave me time to talk. I walked away from that lunch quite amazed at my first personal encounter with the well-known Dr. Naomi Dowdy. Her humility caught me off guard.

Months went by and the financial frustration we lived with continued. The day after Thanksgiving Day in 2004, I went to the house that had sat empty for two years just to be alone. This was the house I loved. This was the neighborhood I loved. It was comforting just to be there looking onto our beautiful back yard and the golf course. I took my Bible and my notebook and was determined to pray and hear from God. God is faithful and He spoke some things to me that day.

One of the things He said was, "I am going to bring some new people into your life. I am going to give you favor with people of influence and authority, and this will open up a new season for you." I found these words to be comforting. It gave me hope for something new, hope that my future would not be devastating like the past year had been.

Because of being involved with the "Apostolic Women Arising" conference, I received an invitation to the Women in Strategic Leadership Roundtable held in December of 2004. This is a small group of 30 women leaders being given the opportunity to receive mentoring and personal coaching from Dr. Dowdy and to dialogue about subjects related to leadership and our various roles. I was honored by the invitation and had no idea what to expect as we all walked into the Embassy Suites in Grapevine, Texas that cold December day.

The format was inviting with encouragement, instruction and wisdom flowing from Dr. Dowdy. I quietly sat in the room, with the pain of the last two years eating away at my soul and yet feeling thrilled to be with such a powerful group of women. The sessions flowed with food breaks and prayer breaks and lively conversations. During one of the prayer times, we paired up in twos to pray. Laurie Vervaecke was my prayer partner and I only knew her as an acquaintance at that time. After we prayed, I asked Laurie if it would be okay if I asked Dr. Dowdy to pray for me. I had come from a ministry culture that created an unapproachable atmosphere around a prominent speaker, so I was shocked when Laurie said in her kind voice, "Sure."

As I approached Naomi and asked her to pray, something supernatural happened. When she prayed and embraced me with a hug that was full of warmth and genuine care, God touched a place in my heart. I knew then that our lives were divinely connected, and I didn't even know what that meant.

After the roundtable, she shocked me when she wanted to exchange contact information and gave me some tips on texting (texting wasn't common in the United States). She has been instructing me ever since!

Our house mortgage situation was resolved within one month of this divine connection in the most marvelous way. On Christmas Eve, our realtor brought us an offer for the house. It was a miracle. In the United States, the Christmas season is the most unlikely time for a property to sell.

God had indeed given me favor with someone of influence and He was about to open a new season in my life – all because of a gentle general named Naomi Dowdy.

Before December 2004 I never dreamed that I could be mentored via text messages from around the world. Between texting (or SMS as she would say) and Skype, my life and my thinking were challenged and changed.

In the ministry circles I had been involved in, bashing the role of pastors and the local church were common. Even though I had grown up in church and had always been part of a local church, I began to develop an 'attitude' and pretty much adopted the philosophy that God was moving outside the local church because He was finished with church as usual. The roles of apostle and prophet were highlighted while the role of pastor was mocked and ridiculed. Much of this controversy revolved around the issue of the tithe and who should receive it. There was a tug of war going on for loyalties and I found myself drifting towards a paradigm that was anti-church.

Dr. Dowdy very calmly and strategically challenged my thinking about event-driven ministry, about being prophetically driven, and about what it meant to really build something in the Kingdom of God. Then she invited me to travel to Singapore to Trinity Christian Centre's annual International Cell Conference and sit in her training called 'Seven Steps to Transforming Your Church.' The year was 2005 and it was a very eventful year for Dr. Dowdy and for the church.

At the close of that conference, a historic event took place. Dr. Naomi Dowdy passed the leadership of Trinity Christian Centre to Pastor Dominic Yeo in one of the most beautiful ceremonies I have witnessed in my church life. There was celebration. There was honor. Things transpired in the spiritual realm.

I watched as my mentor went into an event that had to have been so emotional for her. I have never seen anyone of such greatness and accomplishment move in such humility. It impacted me deeply. On her evening of all evenings, she chose to dress simply so that all the attention would go to Pastor Dominic and not to her. She charged him to take the work forward and to do more than she had ever done. She expressed the heart of a true apostle and a true mentor that night, and I am forever changed because of it. My esteem and respect for her grew even more.

As I sat with her in her office one day on that trip, my eyes were drawn to a frame on the wall that had money attached to a mat inside the frame. The money was in the form of several U.S. dollar bills. Curious, I asked her about it. She explained that it was an offering that had been given in 2000 by a team traveling with Chuck Pierce towards their new building. It must have been one of the first offerings and really meant something to her. I walked over to the frame and to my amazement realized that the $20 bill I gave as part of a small offering in the year 2000 brought so much encouragement to this pastor that she framed it and kept it on her wall. I find that amazing to this day.

The Seven Steps conference and the exposure to Trinity Christian Centre shifted my paradigm in the most dramatic way. It was as if God brought me to Singapore to give me a spiritual chiropractic adjustment that jerked me out of the error of anti-church philosophy, and back to my beliefs in a much stronger and intentional way. God's Word to me came to pass quickly and a new season had begun.

She opened doors for me by introducing me to pastors and leaders from various nations. Many of the pastors in Trinity became my friends. I traveled with her to many nations and watched her in full apostolic mode as she trained pastors in apostolic and prophetic leadership. I watched with awe as God's general challenged and trained and loved and led in nations of the world.

She encouraged me in my decision to attend graduate school and to go for my Masters' degree in leadership. My pace of learning accelerated as I read, studied, wrote and traveled on 15 international trips in two years. I was able to take one of my courses in Singapore and to interview Pastor Dominic Yeo and the other leaders in the organization to learn about a successful cell church. It was because of Naomi's influence and favor that I was able to walk through those doors and feel like Trinity was now my home.

Through her influence, doors opened to me in Indonesia with Pastor Indri Gautama and Apostolic Generation Church. God gave me a relationship with Pastor Ong Sek Leang and his church in Kuala Lumpur. He and his family became my friends and we traveled and spoke together in Australia, Colombia, Indonesia and Malaysia. I could name many others whom I have been privileged to get to know and to work with because my mentor and apostle, Naomi Dowdy, believed in me.

To know her is one of the greatest gifts God has given me. Her belief in me through some very discouraging times helped to sustain me and is a treasure that she has offered me freely.

Ten years have passed quickly since that awesome day in 2004 when the Lord divinely connected me to Dr. Naomi Dowdy. We have had very serious talks; we have laughed; we have traveled the world; we have cried. We have worshipped our God in difficult times and in good times. I have watched her work herself to exhaustion on so many occasions because she was determined to give God and the people she was serving her very best.

She has remained faithful to me through many serious challenges. I know that I have frustrated her and disappointed her on many occasions. Yet her love for me and her belief in me have always been steady. We don't allow very many weeks to pass without talking and catching up, both as friends and always with her as my mentor and my apostle.

Among the most precious moments of our relationship is when she concludes our conversations by saying, "Let me pray for you." I treasure the prayers of this powerful woman of God and the dear friend God has given me in the most surprising way. I honor her and regularly thank her for being so patient with me. I cannot thank God enough for bringing this gentle General of the Kingdom into my life. She is a gift to me and to thousands like me. We are different people because of her.

I couldn't have been happier to see the twinkle in her eye and the smile on her face when I recently became an associate pastor. I knew that she loved me no matter what I did, but that her prayers were answered on that day. I am so very thankful to be able to express the honor and love I have for this powerful woman of God. Happy birthday to the gentle General, Naomi Dowdy!

Rev Pamela Anderson
Associate Pastor (Relational Care), Gateway Church
Southlake, Texas

Naomi Dowdy: To God be the Glory

PANG EK KWAN

We give praise and thanks to the Holy Spirit for speaking and prompting His choice servant, Rev Naomi Dowdy to obey the Lord's call to come to Singapore to serve as a missionary and to bring the gospel message to the masses of people in this small nation.

We have known Sister Dowdy since the mid 1970s, and have found her to be a very humble, caring, down-to-earth, Spirit-anointed, and adventurous servant of her Lord Jesus.

It was in her first year in Singapore and she stayed in a bungalow house in Rosyth Avenue, near where Bethel Assembly of God was situated, in the Upper Serangoon area. The house in which she lived was actually rented from Fred and Margaret Seaward who were pastors of Bethel Church. At that time the Seawards were away ministering in Penang.

It was the Chinese Lunar New Year, and my wife knew that it would be difficult for Sister Dowdy, staying alone in the bungalow, to buy food in the first two days of the holiday period, as all the shops would be closed. So she felt led to cook a few dishes and some rice, and deliver the food to her place at Rosyth Road.

Imagine Sister Dowdy's pleasant surprise and joy in meeting us and receiving from my wife the cooked food, since we only met her once or twice after her arrival in Singapore. Sister Dowdy enjoyed the food very much, especially the delicious 'kiam chai ah' (in Teochew dialect) which is duck cooked in preserved salted vegetable. Sister Dowdy even learned to pronounce the dish 'kiam chai ah', so much so that whenever she met my wife on several occasions after that, she would hold her hands and repeatedly say, "Thank you so much for the 'kiam chai ah'" that you cooked for me during my first Chinese Lunar New Year in Singapore!"

We have known Pastor Naomi Dowdy for many years. From the depths of our hearts, we want to say that she is truly one who has been specially chosen by the Lord for such a time as this, to touch, impact and encourage many thousands whose lives have been so transformed by the power of the Holy Spirit!

We thank our Lord Jesus for using Rev Dr Dowdy to lead Trinity Christian Centre, which is the largest Assembly of God Church in Singapore. She has indeed been an apostle chosen by the Lord to be of such impact and encouragement to thousands of His servants in Singapore and many countries in the world.

We give praise and thanks to our Lord Jesus Christ for having chosen a handmaiden of such exemplary character, trustworthiness, integrity and anointing to serve Him in this part of the world! To God be all the glory.

Rev and Sister Pang Ek Kwan
Honorary Pastor/Itinerant Minister, Bethel Assembly of God
Singapore

Naomi Dowdy: Anointed To Be A Builder

PETER LOO

I got to know Apostle Dowdy through my predecessor Rev Chua Wee Hian who wanted her to be his apostle and to help our church to grow in the cell-based model after Trinity Christian Centre. Our church board, of which I was the chairman, asked if she should also become the apostle of our church.

My first impression of her was that she was a no-nonsense lady, passionate about the Lord's work, with great insight in people's motives, who was fairly direct and yet spoke with grace and carefully chosen words. I was initially wary of people just coming in to become apostles, but in a short time I realized she could be trusted. There was no form of pride and her heart was there to serve rather than to get. I am so glad to find Apostle Dowdy who is anointed and whose heart is sold out for the Lord and His people.

She was instrumental in arranging for me and my wife to understudy at Trinity Christian Centre for a year with Pastor Dominic and his pastors, before I became the Senior Pastor of Emmanuel Church in Westminster London. She told me to 'catch the spirit' and learn as much as possible in how Trinity Christian Centre exercises faith and a spirit of excellence.

Over the last seven years since I became senior pastor, Apostle Dowdy is always there for me, just a Skype call away. She always gives me her time and enquires about my family. She is a woman of vision and faith, and keeps encouraging and stretching me in my faith. She is also very down-to-earth with 'her gift of suspicion' of people whose motives which may not be entirely godly. I appreciate her prayers especially in times of crises and making major decisions.

My wife and I had the privilege to take her with us on a two-day holiday to visit William Shakespeare's birthplace and Oxford. After the two-day trip, she told me that she finally realized what people do when on holiday! We are privileged to take her on a holiday which she could experience! I suppose her 50 years of life and ministry has been a work holiday with the joy of the Lord.

Pastor Dowdy is full of energy and her passion is to see each person rise to his or her destiny. She believes that God wants to do with each person much more than where he/she is currently at. She uses encouragement and challenges to spur us on. She always uses faith-building words rather than discouraging words.

When I was on attachment with Trinity, she demonstrated her humility by inviting me to join in with Pastor Beatrice and a couple of other pastors in giving her feedback on her Sunday morning sermon so that it could be improved for the next service. I was bowled over that the "Queen of Altar Calls", as we affectionately call her, was so humble as to let me observe how feedback was done even for her preaching.

Some of her most memorable words are:
- Say to one another, "Wro..oo..nnngg thinking."
- What is your vision?

- Keep praying and inviting non-Christians to the cells.
- We must never use people. Don't just be interested in the person's ministry but also in their families.
- The thing that governs our decision should be what is best for the church.
- Don't keep saying it works in Singapore and not in the UK!
- You are doing well, brother. Keep going.
- Make sure my room is well heated up. If necessary, get me a portable heater (even in summer).
- I prophesy that I am not a prophet but I am anointed to be a builder.
- The key to a powerful ministry is to be able to wed the Word of God and the anointing of the Holy Spirit.
- When dealing with conflicts, she would quote Isaiah 1:18 – "Come, let us reason together..."

Apostle Dowdy is anointed to be a builder. She has great faith and vision to see potential in people as well as to know how to challenge their faith level without any manipulation, to give of their lives and resources into the kingdom of God. It is relying on the Holy Spirit to bring conviction and grace into the person's life, motivated by God's love.

Pastor Dowdy enjoys a hearty meal. She likes lobsters, steak, calves' liver and is not so keen on fish and on spicy stuff. She also has an amazing memory for people's names even though she sees some of them only once a year.

I was surprised to discover that she had Cherokee blood in her. I sometimes wonder if that's where her boldness comes from!

I think her legacy will be, "Have a strong faith in God. There is more in you that God wants to transform and use for His Kingdom."

Thank you Apostle Dowdy for sowing into the life of Emmanuel Church, our staff members, leaders and church members. Thank you for the privilege of knowing you and receiving from you an impartation of boldness, faith and genuine love for people. Thank you for being an example of what it means to be a servant of the Lord. We are grateful.

Pastor Peter Loo
Senior Pastor, Emmanuel Evangelical Church
London, United Kingdom

Classic Naomi Dowdy

PHILIP LYN

I first met Naomi Dowdy at a dinner function in Singapore a few years back. My wife was a fan of hers and had been listening to her messages, so I went over to tell her so. I said that I too, was an unwitting fan of hers, by virtue of having to share the same car with my wife periodically. (I didn't mention I had been initially, a reluctant fan). She smiled, more at my tongue-in-cheek remark, I think, than at my watered-down impudence. Our spirits knitted. And so one thing led to another, and she agreed to speak at our leaders' retreat later that year.

Our church is embedded in a five-star hotel in the city and surrounded by a 27-hole golf course. Before she came, the grapevine had leaked that she was a formidable golfer and so I mentioned that to her in a text message. She summarily dismissed it by saying she talked more golf than played it and told me not to listen to inflated rumors. But I wasn't so easily palmed off. Deep down inside, I was struck with the angst of a more senior woman outdriving me on the course so I took some pains to hone my rusty, weekend hacking skills into something more proficient before she came. She never did, that year, at any rate. An illness set her back a week before she was due and she had to cancel. God had given me the grace of more time! But it made no difference. I still lost to her when she came the following year.

People tell me she's an iron lady. She brooks no nonsense for sure, but I have never found her domineering or intimidating. On the contrary, she has continued to maintain a posture of softness before the Lord which, when mingled with her gigantic faith and God-given wisdom, have made her such a wonderful person to know and a friend to treasure. I have always appreciated the graciousness in her manner, gracefulness in her countenance and grace in her ministry.

I have been a bi-vocational pastor for many years, which not a few full-time ministers have subtly hinted is an unsustainable anomaly or an ongoing muddle of spiritual ministry. Not Naomi Dowdy. She's never ever urged me to drop the doctor-pastor label. On the contrary it is rare indeed to see a senior Pentecostal minister like her, urging the body of Christ as a whole to raise a complementary genre of believers and pastors to engage, influence and transform our cities and the marketplace for God. In this she is ahead of many of her peers in seeing, among other things, that the largest unreached mission field today is still the 9-5 window.

Partnering with her in marketplace ministries has been an honour and privilege. Her relaxed posture and leadership among business people speaks volumes about her heart's calling in this season of her life. I saw her in action when both of us shared at Asian Marketplace Conference last year. She is rarely 'religious' when it comes to relating to marketplace folks. On the contrary, there is this rare combination of mountain-moving faith with an earthy business approach and sensible practical prescription which business people can understand and then set out to do. Her track record in the arena of leadership succession has also been a great personal tutorial for me as I look towards plans for my own succession in the future.

And so what else can she do? She can dance! It happened two years ago after she had spoken at our church's Anniversary Gift Day event. There had been an amazing overflow of joy towards the end of the service after I had announced that we had reached our faith-giving target. People cheered and clapped. I glanced down from on stage, saw the gleam of excitement in her eyes and mischievously pulled her up to dance with me before the Lord. Here was no dusty, musty, cobwebbed armchair apostle! She was flesh and blood, full of life and zest and filled with the Spirit of the Lord as we danced with joy! The people loved her.

Last year, just a week after having undergone hip surgery, she came in a wheelchair to preside over an international apostolic roundtable for women, held at our church. As a doctor, I was stunned by her hardiness. There she sat for hours with a sore hip while convening endless meetings that lesser mortals would have foregone.

But she had a surprise in store. During one break, with a twinkle in her eye, she invited the group to a durian party by the poolside of the posh hotel! The ladies were stunned. Firstly she had somehow managed to overcome the hotel's strict no-durian law! Secondly, a durian-loving white apostle? You've got to be kidding!

But perhaps that's what makes her so special among us in Asia. Anyone who loves durians has got to be "one of us"!

Pastor Dr Philip Lyn
Senior Pastor, Skyline SIB Church
Kota Kinabalu, Sabah, Malaysia

Naomi Dowdy: An Apostle, But Still My Pastor
RAYMOND CHOUDHURY

I first met Pastor Dowdy sometime in the late 1970s through my parents who joined Trinity in 1978. I saw her in action as the senior pastor during the time when Trinity was worshipping at the American School in King's Road.

My first impression of her was a pastor who wore many hats, except leading worship. She was resourceful, innovative, creative in resolving problems, personal and caring.

I began to get more acquainted with her when I finally joined Trinity in 1986. I took an immediate liking to her. With her, I could speak freely and also accept her input and wisdom on many issues. She has always encouraged me and has never given me negative advice. We shared common interests in food and travel.

I guess my relationship with Pastor developed when I started getting involved in mission trips in the 90s to India and thereafter in community transformation programs through business. I had the privilege to travel with her to Indonesia, United States and Colombia.

Over the years, our relationship grew closer and I consider her as my 'spiritual mum.' She has never failed to make time for me, whether it's for coffee, dinner or just a phone call. She is someone whom I can trust and depend on in good and bad times.

Traveling with Pastor is a great experience. She is a multi-cultural person who can easily adapt to the environment and to the culture of the country. She is a people person and was always surrounded by people at all times, whether it's for prayer or counsel. She can easily adapt to the ordinary person on the street or to the level of a prime minister of a country. I have worked alongside her and always found it a pleasure watching her in action.

She is also a charismatic leader. During one of the crusades in Chennai, India, I overheard a local pastor saying that Pastor Dowdy carried herself like Indira Gandhi.

Pastor Dowdy can take a context from the Bible and make it so clear and challenging for us as business people. I remember one sermon where she challenged the business people to use their business to bring a change in the community. She gave an example how Peter allowed Jesus to use his fishing boat to preach to the masses on the shores in Galilee.

Sometime in the mid-nineties, my sister Ranee met with a fatal accident in Australia. Her family had migrated to Brisbane, Australia and so the funeral would be held there. Despite Pastor's heavy work schedule, she travelled to Brisbane on her own account to conduct my sister's funeral service. Another incident was when I had to undergo heart surgery. She took time to be with me before the surgery and visited me again in the evening to make sure I was okay. She is an Apostle but to me, she is still my Pastor.

Pastor Dowdy only expects the very best when it comes to serving the Lord, and her expectations are high. It's natural to expect the best service when we serve an awesome God. She always tells me to "believe and have faith." Her legacy is that "Nothing is Impossible with God."

What keeps Pastor on the move is her love for God. But I do hope to see more of her in Singapore, and less traveling for her. We still have a tango date that has been on hold for quite some time now.

Pastor Dowdy is warm, personal and wise. She is the first 'ang moh' (Caucasian) pastor I know who loves eating durians. She does not like French food, especially escargots, and prefers popiah anytime.

Pastor, it has been an honor and a privilege to know you for the past thirty years. You have made an impact in my life. Thank you for being my Pastor.

Lots of love,
Ray

Raymond Choudhury
CEO, Antioch Singapore Group
Singapore

A Christ-Honoring Visionary

RAY AND JUDY RACHELS

Dear Naomi

Judy and I wish for you the happiest and best of birthdays!

It was Florence Beck, one of your many faithful and loyal staff members in Singapore, who first created the bridge for our friendship. While we were pastors in Long Beach, California, you invited us for a weekend of Marriage Retreat, in which we taught the most wonderful people, people whom you had spiritually led and pastored, and who received us with such endearing hospitality.

And, you invited us back again. You loved us then, introduced us to your congregation and friends, accepted us with grace, and have, through the years, been the same great friend and leader.

Thank you for being 'more than enough' in so many ways, and terrific at the task of leader and partner in your role as a Christ-honoring visionary!

You are loved and highly esteemed as a friend and fellow Christ-follower!

Rev T. Ray Rachels
General Council Executive Presbyter, Assemblies of God

Rev Judy Rachels
National Chair, Network for Women in Ministry, General Council, Assemblies of God

Huntington Beach, California

Tribute to Apostle Naomi Dowdy

REINALDO CASTELLANOS TRUJILLO

My reflections on Rev Naomi Dowdy and her life:

- The Holy Spirit has given much love and wisdom.
  The task God has given to her, she has assumed with love, dedication and sacrifice.

- The anointing of the Holy Spirit is on her, to impact both the natural and the spiritual realm.
  The Holy Spirit has placed in her gifts and talents that make her a blessing for the people of God and even those who do not know her.

- She is a woman of holiness; a servant to impact nations for eternity with the message of God's Word.
  Every time she appears in any auditorium, she is a blessing from God, with the right word for the circumstance. She is a leading example in the knowledge of God's Word. She arrests people's attention with the words of wisdom.

- She is a passionate leader with passion whom everyone can see and follow.

  She is a secure leader who knows how to delegate tasks to other leaders and evangelization and support other Christian leaders. She has trained other leaders in the field with compassion for the lost.

- She reflects the presence of Christ our Savior in her apostolic assignment.

  She has been a leader and a blessing to the nations. Her leadership and the word of God she carries, shakes people and nations to the core of their being.

General Reinaldo Castellanos Trujillo
Ex-Commander, National Military of the Republic of Colombia

Lessons from the School of Naomi Dowdy
STEVEN TAY

I first got to know Pastor Dowdy in 1986 when I became a member of Trinity Christian Centre. The more frequent interactions started when I joined Trinity as a full-time minister in 1987.

Over the years, she provided me many ministry platforms. I also had opportunities to travel with her to India, Ghana, Colombia, Australia and Denmark. Of the many incidents that I remember, here are two that I would like to share.

A Lesson on Honor

In 1995, the Assemblies of God in Andhra Pradesh, India, invited Pastor Dowdy and the team from Trinity to conduct the Local Church Breakthrough Seminar for their district. The venue was in the city of Anantapur, 220 km north of Bangalore.

We travelled for four hours by a non-air-conditioned rented car on a bumpy road from Bangalore to Anantapur with the day temperature being about 35 degrees Celsius (95 degrees Fahrenheit). The three-day conference had more than a hundred pastors and leaders from various churches. It was conducted in a non-air-conditioned hall with a zinc roof.

There were many occasions when the electricity was cut during that week so that the city could manage the demand for electrical power. While it was 35 °C (95 °F) outside, the actual temperature in the hall was closer to 40 °C (104 °F). At the end of each session, the sari that Pastor Dowdy was wearing would be drenched with perspiration. When we returned to Singapore, some friends commented that I had a sun tan. My reply was, "It was no suntan. I was microwaved".

Our hosts had placed us in the best hotel there was in the city at that time. Intermittent air conditioning and hot water were available only during certain times of each day. Throughout the entire week, I did not hear any complaint from Pastor Dowdy. She was focused on doing her best to serve the pastors and churches.

Her only personal request to me during the stay was, "Steven, please help me get rid of the cockroach in the bathroom."

This incident reinforced my perspective that Pastor Dowdy always puts God's honor and the ministry above personal preferences and comfort. As I observed how my then sixty-year-old senior pastor handled the physical conditions in Anantapur, it caused my respect for her to go up another notch.

Lesson: No matter how long I may have been in the ministry, I should not have any sense of entitlement. It should always be about God's honor and what God wants to accomplish through the ministry.

A Lesson on Humility

In 2013, Pastor Dowdy was preaching at the Saturday 5pm service at Trinity@Paya Lebar. She had just returned from a seven-week ministry trip to USA and Colombia.

The sermon she preached was probably a new sermon prepared on her way back to Singapore. Although powerful in content, I felt it could be better organized.

During that season of time, I had the privilege of hosting her whenever she preached in Trinity. To my surprise, after the service, she asked for my feedback.

Essentially, I suggested that she combine the first and second points, make the third point her second point, and use her content in her introduction as the concluding point. She took my advice and went home to adjust her sermon for the Sunday morning service.

Pastor Dowdy was my Homiletics lecturer when I took the course in TCA College, way back in August 1987. Yet she remained humble enough to ask for feedback on her preaching, and made changes based on that feedback.

Lesson: No matter how experienced I may be in any given area, I should always be humble to learn from others.

Rev Steven Tay
Trinity Christian Centre
Singapore

Naomi Dowdy: A Vision for the Nations

WAYNE AND JUDY CAGLE

We first met Naomi Dowdy in the early 1960s at First Assembly of God in San Diego where she attended the church pastored by Judy's father, Emil Balliet. God saved her, filled her with the Holy Spirit and called her into missions. She went to the Marshall Islands in 1965, working with Sam and Florence Sasser in founding Calvary Bible Institute (CBI). She was among the first faculty of the school.

The young people who attended CBI were young people saved and filled with the Spirit during the first outpouring of the Holy Spirit in the Marshalls under the ministry of the Sassers, Naomi Dowdy and others. Many future pastors and leaders were trained in this school which at one time had as many as 325 resident students. CBI was located on Majuro, the main island of the Majuro atoll. Other missionaries and Marshallese leaders joined the faculty and work force in the maintenance and establishment of the developing ministries.

We visited the Marshall Islands in the summer of 1968 participating in a youth camp along with Paul and Leta Bruton, leaders from the Southern California Assemblies of God Youth Department. We saw hundreds of young people commit their lives to Christ and be filled with the Spirit during the camp, giving vibrant testimonies of God's work in their lives. We discovered the need for qualified teachers to join the CBI faculty. Both of us had California Teacher Credentials and had felt God's call for missions for several years. We felt God's urge to pursue this opportunity for missions and immediately applied to the Foreign Missions Department of the Assemblies of God for missionary appointment. Naomi Dowdy applied for official missions' appointment as well and we all were among the new appointees at the same time in June 1969. Wayne & Judy arrived as a young couple in January 1970 to begin our missions' career.

Naomi moved to the island of Ebeye in the Kwajalein atoll of the Marshall Islands, but continued to serve on the Board of Directors of Calvary Bible Institute. Ebeye was considered to be the most populous island in the Kwajalein atoll. Today it has a population of 15,000 people crowded on 80 acres of land, possibly the most densely populated island in the Pacific. Children comprise half the population. With the American Ballistic Missile Defense Test Site located there, over 1300 Marshallese laborers work on Kwajalein island.

From Kwajalein, Naomi undertook boat evangelism to many of the 32 atolls in the Marshall Islands, developing evangelism and discipleship materials. She developed radio evangelism as well. Naomi trained local co-workers who assisted her in the rigorous boat evangelism ministry. She was an outstanding evangelist and was fluent in speaking Marshallese. Naomi played an important role in the developing national church of the Marshall Islands, instituting Missionettes and other discipleship ministries alongside Marshallese leaders. She was a mentor and role model for many of the young pastors and leaders. Naomi was culturally sensitive and well acquainted with Marshallese customs and protocol. She worked closely with the local leaders in this pioneer work.

Naomi was not only a missionary colleague and part of the leadership in our Missionary Field Fellowship, but she was also a friend. Her location on Ebeye and Kwajalein proved to be very important to Wayne & Judy personally. Kwajalein had a Foodland grocery store that provided Stateside groceries at a good price and available to the military personnel and to Americans who lived on Ebeye. Travel between Ebeye and the main island, Kwajalein, required a 20-minute boat ride using old WWII landing crafts called 'water taxis'. Naomi blessed the Majuro missionaries by often sending a styrofoam cooler with hamburger meat, cheese, taco shells, lettuce, tomatoes and Dr. Pepper colas via Air Micronesia planes! The Majuro missionaries, including us, were always thrilled to receive these packages! We spent Christmas holidays several times with Naomi and her co-workers at her house in Ebeye. These were very happy times and a chance to get a break from our duties on Majuro.

However, Naomi's hospitality was especially important to us at the time of the birth of our first child. Judy was pregnant in 1972 and scheduled to give birth on Majuro the end of July. The American doctor on Majuro explained to Judy a month before giving birth that his contract would expire and he would be leaving the island. The doctor had made arrangements for Judy to give birth in Ebeye, Kwajalein with a Peace Corps doctor instead. The doctor determined that Naomi Dowdy's house would be the best place for the birth to take place instead of the local clinic. So, unexpectedly, Wayne and Judy flew to Kwajalein and rode on the 'water taxi' to Ebeye to take up temporary residence and wait for the baby's birth.

Naomi graciously opened her home. She was on a boat evangelism trip when we arrived, but we made ourselves at home along with some family members and other missionaries there. We were later joined by Judy's parents. Wayne set up his camera for pictures of the newborn and a tape recorder for the baby's first cries and taped signs on the doors. It was a jovial atmosphere as we all settled down to wait. However, the waiting period turned out to be more than 36 hours. The Peace Corps doctor recommended that Judy be transported by boat to the Kwajalein Army Hospital on emergency basis where several hours later Judy gave birth to Catherine Sue Cagle. God miraculously orchestrated these events as after birth, Judy began hemorrhaging and it was necessary for the doctor to find blood donors for her AB+ blood type and stop the bleeding. When Judy and baby were finally released from the hospital, Naomi hosted a 'welcome home' gathering with the Peace Corp doctor and family, the missionaries and others.

From the Marshall Islands, Naomi moved to Singapore and became the pastor of Trinity Christian Centre (TCC) in 1976. It became a major center for evangelism and the discipling of thousands of Singaporeans – Chinese, Indians, and other Asian ethnic groups – during the outpouring of the Holy Spirit in Singapore in the 1970s and 80s. People from many Asian ethnic groups as well as church leaders received the baptism of the Holy Spirit in a sweeping spiritual renewal. Again, Naomi Dowdy became a mentor of young men and women who were raised up in ministry through TCC and the training school that she founded. She was a key figure in the discipling and conservation of the tremendous harvest in Singapore. Naomi eventually set her sights on surrounding nations as well, encouraging younger leaders to help pastor the church in Singapore as she evangelized in India, Sri Lanka, Indonesia and many other countries.

Wayne and Judy moved to Indonesia in 1974 and had opportunity to travel to Singapore and visit TCC. Judy's parents, Emil & Gladys Balliet traveled to Singapore to minister at TCC and enjoyed great fellowship with Pastor Dowdy and the growing, dynamic work in Singapore. They continued their journey to Bali, Indonesia to speak at the Indonesia missionary retreat in 1977 and had the chance to see their children and granddaughters. Naomi and her missionary friend, Barbara (Liddle) Cavaness Parks from Malang, attended the Bali retreat as well and had fellowship with the other Indonesian missionary families. Our daughters loved getting to know Aunt Naomi and Aunt Barbara. Six months later, August 1977, in San Jose, California, Pastor Emil Balliet died. Judy will always remember the Scripture that Naomi shared with her to comfort her grieving heart from Psalm 84:5-8.

It was a joy to sit under Pastor Dowdy's ministry as we traveled on occasion to Singapore. She is a woman of faith and teaches the Word of God with great anointing. Her vision for the nations and her commitment to reaching the unreached and preaching deliverance to those in spiritual bondage has been the defining call on her life. She has faithfully served the Lord Jesus these 50 years and has left a legacy of outstanding leadership abilities, excellence in ministry, fulfilled vision and compassion for the next generation. She has lived her life well, filled with faith and the power of the Holy Spirit enabling her to accomplish wonderful feats for the Lord Jesus Christ, her Savior. We count it a privilege to have served with Dr. Naomi Dowdy and congratulate her on this great milestone of ministry.

Rev Dr Wayne Cagle
Former Director for Training and Leadership Development, Asia Pacific Assemblies of God World Missions
Former Chancellor, Asia-Pacific Theological Seminary

Rev Dr Judy Cagle
Former Faculty Member, Asia-Pacific Theological Seminary

Springfield, Missouri

My Tribute to Naomi Dowdy

YANG TUCK YOONG

My first recollection of Pastor Dowdy was in the early 1990s. We had just moved into the World Trade Center Conference Hall and Trinity Christian Center, the church that Pastor Dowdy was shepherding, was beside us.

One Sunday, we had a traumatic experience when a young man went berserk and manifested demonically. I remember the demons were so fierce and brazen that we lost a whole bunch of people, who were freaked out by the explosive manifestation. We had to bring the young man out and we tried to cast out the demons.

I vividly remember Pastor Dowdy passing by, and instead of going over to her service, she stopped and helped us battle this demonic entity, which we finally did manage to cast out. The good news is, that man is still in church today, and faithfully serving where he can. But that was my first recollection of Pastor Dowdy – her willingness to help us, even at the expense of her own service, and it left an indelible mark upon me as a young pastor. I was deeply impressed, to say the least.

The next time we met was a lunch between Pastor Dowdy and myself. This was in the early 2000s and I can still remember where we had lunch – Pete's Place at the Grand Hyatt, and what she had for lunch. That I won't say. But I bring this up because it was such a defining moment for me, to be able to be mentored by someone of her stature. I will never forget that. She made time and was concerned for a young fledgling pastor who was trying to make sense of ministry.

Our next personal lunch meeting was several years later. Again I remember vividly where we met and what the focus of the lunch was. She was taking me to task about someone I had invited to my church. She asked why the prophetic statements made by this particular preacher were not tested and challenged.

Pastor Dowdy basically instilled in me the responsibility for the preachers I brought into the city, and that's just the apostolic anointing over her life. Apostles generally tend to be concerned about such things, and rightly so. A foreign seed or a false prophecy can overthrow the faith of many. She was teaching me accountability for prophetic statements and the need to correct them when they are false or erroneous.

Recently, in August 2014, we met again. This time, she came with a prophetic word over my life. We were sitting around in my boardroom and just chatting about ministry when she said, "I have come to give you a prophetic word."

I won't tell you what that word is, but it was one of the most significant prophetic utterances over my life and it put steel in my backbone. I couldn't help my tears from falling. It was a precious and truly defining moment in my life.

Pastor Dowdy has made an incredible investment in my life and – I do not say this to flatter – her encouragement and ministry has raised me to where I stand today. For this, I am so grateful. I want to thank you, Pastor Dowdy, for your life and I salute you as one of the great generals whom God has raised in this generation. I will gladly follow you into battle.

Rev Yang Tuck Yoong
Senior Pastor, Cornerstone Community Church
Singapore

Is God calling you to move up to the next level?
These books will help you get there!

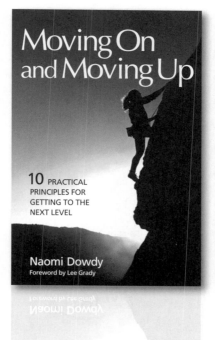

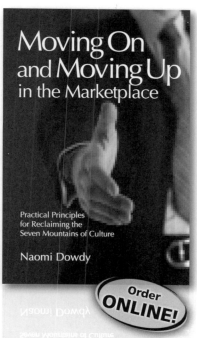

How I wish there were more Naomi Dowdys in the world!
If anyone is qualified to speak on the subject of moving to a higher
level in God, she is a prime candidate. This important book
will equip you in many practical ways to move to the next level
and to become the leader you were called to be.

— J. Lee Grady, former editor, Charisma magazine

How you transit determines
whether you finish well.
Reinvent yourself, define your legacy
and move up into significance!

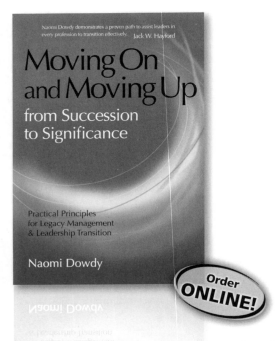

Among the greatest challenges leaders face today is the wise
management of transitions, and generational succession is
the most demanding. Naomi Dowdy demonstrates her experience,
wisdom, and character in providing a practical, spiritually proven
path to assist leaders in every profession transition effectively.

— Jack W. Hayford, Chancellor, The King's University

Also by Naomi Dowdy

Books
Commissioning
Moving On & Moving Up*
Moving On & Moving Up In the Marketplace*
Moving On & Moving Up from Succession to Significance*
Strength To Stand

* Also available in Chinese and Spanish

Audio Teachings
Aligning Two Worlds
Alignment That Secures Your Future
Alignment – The Key to Authority
Becoming a New Wineskin Church
Declaration for Transformation
Divine Alignment for Divine Assignment
Healing
Kingdom Giving
Kingdom Growth*
Living & Leading in Turbulent Times*
Lost Identity, Discovered Destiny
Paralyzed or Powerful?
Priesthood of the Believer
Refresh Your Anointing*
Return to Pentecost
Revelation Knowledge
Taking Hold of God's Promises
The Cross – Rediscovering Its Power for Today
What Can I Do For You?*

* Also available online as instant downloads

Order online now   **www.naomidowdy.com**